Lenuta Hellen Nadolu was born in Cluj, Romania. At the age of four she and her parents moved to Bucharest. As a little girl she learned that overcoming hardship could foster resilience. The struggle for her personal freedom began in Romania, a male dominated society. She married against all odds and her path took her to Ghana, Africa, in the 1970s where not only was the society dominated by men but polygamy was accepted and encouraged by tradition. Her struggle reached its peak the day she smuggled her children out of Ghana to return to Romania. In 1984, she fled to Australia and claimed political asylum. Hellen now lives in Sydney with her three children and her grandchildren.

I dedicate this book to the European lady
I saw lying in the gutter at Makola Market, Accra, in 1982
I never knew your name
But you could have been me
When I saw your plight, my pain turned to strength
and my tears changed to courage

Contents

Prologue

The Monk

My father, a truck driver, is called Gheorghe. 'You know, Lenuta,' he tells me, 'I once picked up a hitch-hiker on this road who told me about a Catholic monk who lives in those mountains over there.' He points through the window. 'He tells fortunes. Shall we go and see him? I'd like to know if you'll get into university or not.'

My father believes that some people can foretell the future. Long ago a gypsy told him that he would marry a poor woman—and he did.

The track to the top of the mountain where the monk lives is narrow and rocky, not built for trucks. When they hear the roar of the engine, people come out of their houses and gardens to watch us struggle up the road. They use only horses and carts. We keep stopping and asking them for directions. Everyone knows this Transylvanian monk.

My father's face is set in concentration. He does not speak. I realise that he is conquering this road and I see what an excellent driver he is. For once in my life I feel proud of him.

We climb for a long time and finally reach a ramshackle building right at the top of the mountain. Lush green valleys fall away below us and the air is fresh and clean. I feel I can almost reach out and touch the sky that shines pearl white and the palest blue.

The monk's house is a heap of scrap metal and wooden boards tacked together. In front of it a young boy is stacking hay with a pitchfork. He doesn't look surprised to see our truck pull up. Without pausing in his work, he calls over to ask what we want and we tell him that we have come to see the monk.

The boy rests the handle of his fork on the ground and leans his arm across the prongs. I wonder why they don't hurt him. 'Do you have two candles?' he says. 'I can light them for you.' We didn't know that we needed candles.

He asks us to follow him around to the back of the house and into a tumbledown shed. Inside, people are sitting on a wooden bench holding lighted candles. I hesitate, but my father squeezes my hand and we enter. The boy hands each of us a candle and asks us to sit down and wait. I perch on the hard wooden bench and look around at the others. I am the only young person, seventeen.

My father turns to the man next to him. 'Where have you come from?'

'Brasov.'

Brasov is a long way off. We are travelling from Bucharest, also far away. This monk is very famous.

'Have you been here before?'

'Many times. He only ever asks for a lighted candle. The Militia used to arrest him and accuse him of exploiting people. But they couldn't make the charge stick. He never asks for money.'

'We have to help him,' says a woman at the far end of the bench. 'We give him something in return for what he tells us.'

'When he was held in the cells he told the Militia men's

fortunes,' the man continues. 'That scared them so badly they stopped arresting him. Now they leave him in peace up here on his mountaintop.'

After a while the boy reappears and asks us to follow him. We enter a one-room shack with a rough-hewn table in the middle and a bed in the corner. A black habit hangs on the wall. The bed is just a wooden box and its mattress is a big sack stuffed with straw.

The monk is tall with a long grey beard and wears a threadbare robe. He seems different from the monks I have seen in the monastery. They have an air of remoteness separating them from ordinary people. This one looks as if he is his own man. Without his robe you would never know he was a monk.

'Gheorghe, sit down.'

My father turns pale. How does the monk know his name?

My father sits down on the bed and, because he is a big man, his weight makes him sink into the straw mattress with his legs dangling as though he were sitting inside a giant tea-cup. He looks small and scared.

The monk tells him, 'You have three children. One will be lucky in marriage: your son.' Pointing to me, he says, 'She will be the one to disappoint you most.'

He pauses and I feel my heart thump in my chest.

'You have two houses on the same land, one old and one new.' True: my father built another house next door to the one in which we live. 'In front of the window of the new one there's a cherry tree. Soon it will die.'

He looks at me with eyes that seem to see right into me. 'You, young woman, are going to deeply disappoint your parents. You will marry a man in uniform. Your first child will be a girl. I see she is very dark.'

If he knows about the cherry tree, can he also predict what will happen to me? No, surely not. I know exactly the type of man with whom I will fall in love. My own skin is olive but I am attracted to boys with blue or green eyes and fair skin.

The monk is talking nonsense.

He turns to my father and says, 'She will get into the school where she wants to go but she will drop out. At work she will be dressed in white. She will sit down and do something with her hands to earn her daily bread. She will be lucky with money. She will never lack that.'

He looks at me again and says, 'You will travel a long way, over the seas. Before you are twenty-nine years old you will be left alone with many children. Afterwards you will travel even further over the seas, to the end of the world.'

With that he is finished. How ridiculous, I think. My father struggles to get up out of the mattress. He puts some money on the table, the monk blows out the candles and we leave. Outside, we thank the boy who is still forking the hay.

On the way down the mountain track my father is silent. He concentrates on the road, his face still pale. He does not want to look at me.

The monk's words resonate in my head. How could I possibly disappoint my parents? I always try to be so good, to make them happy. I believe that one day I can bring happiness to our entire family. Now this unknown monk tells me that I will disappoint them.

None of this can be true. What's more, the cherry tree looks set to flourish for many seasons.

Afterwards, my father and I never speak about the monk's words. We would not even consider telling my mother. She thinks all fortune telling is rubbish.

After Christmas, as the snow melts and the new year starts, I watch the cherry tree closely. I'm sure buds will appear as usual. Every morning I look up at the leaves, seeking the first signs of blossoms. I keep telling myself that the monk knows nothing about us.

I

My Rock

All of us are climbing the same mountain
but we each carry a different cross.
Mama Draga

Mama Draga, which means my dearest grandmother, had six daughters but only one son who died of pneumonia the year after I was born. She lost three other children, too. There is something regal about Mama Draga, something calm and quiet and beautiful. I see a little woman, her apron tied high, just beneath her breasts, who is all warmth and hugging and loving softness. You wouldn't think her capable of so much love. She fills me up with it. Her love pours into all the empty places inside me, enough for a lifetime of loving.

My grandmother's loss of her son remains part of her everyday life. From that day forth she wears black and dark grey clothes to show she is in mourning. She prays for his soul each afternoon in Auntie Ileana's bedroom. I often find her kneeling at the edge of the bed, looking up at an image of Mother Mary. Next to this is Jesus Christ on the Cross:

one image of love and compassion and the other of pain. I kneel next to my grandmother, bringing my little hands to my heart. I watch the way she prays and try to follow her. She recites 'Thee, Our Father' three times, loudly. Tears flood her face. I don't know the whole prayer but I repeat as many words as I can. I hear her asking Jesus to forgive her son's sins and her own. I don't understand what a sin is but I repeat the words after her and feel her pain.

I'm not sure of Mama Draga's heritage. She was born into a family of servants who have always lived in Transylvania, a central region of Romania that was once a part of the Austro-Hungarian Empire. Although Romanian is the official language, many people speak Hungarian in public. Ethnic Hungarians do not want to learn Romanian. Mama Draga speaks perfect Hungarian and Romanian. In Transylvania, Romanians and Hungarians, like many neighbours, have a history of mutual recognition but silent antagonism.

Mama Draga grew up in the city of Cluj, once the Transylvanian jewel of the Austro-Hungarian Empire. Cluj, now the second largest city in Romania, is also my birthplace. It is a graceful town of narrow cobbled streets and churches with tall spires and steeples, modestly brown and white, set among hills, farms and quiet fields. A river, the Somesul Mic, flows through its centre and bridge after bridge, all stone, connect both banks.

The main square is watched over by St Michael's church, built in the fifteenth century, and a statue of Matthias Corvinus who was King of Hungary over 500 years ago. The Banffy Palace is vast and majestic in the Baroque way. Three-storey Hungarian-style houses built of stone and wood stand beside grand old buildings like the Palace of Justice.

In Romania before World War II, everyone knew their

place in a rigid class system built on tradition and history. When the Communists came to power, they attempted to destroy this system. For the first time, through education, people could escape the class into which they were born. By that time Mama Draga was too old for school—but she appreciates the pension and free health care the Communists brought.

We live on Plopilor Street, meaning the street of poplar trees. The branches reach high over our heads and drape in graceful arcs. Every day Mama Draga cleans the enormous house of a judge who lives across the road. In the evenings she is a mother to her children. The Communist government has not managed to eliminate the upper classes from the cities as they have in the countryside by confiscating their land. The city elite is educated and professional with strong roots.

I love crossing the road to the second house on the left where Mrs Giurgiu lives. She is always happy to see me. There is a walnut tree in her garden which I like to stand beneath and look up to see if the walnuts are ready to be picked. At first, they are covered in green but then their shells turn brown and hard. I always feel safe and happy under this big old tree. It makes me feel as if I'm being hugged.

I try on hats for Mrs Giurgiu and parade up and down. 'How beautiful your hat is!' she tells me. 'How beautiful you are!' She gives me an apron-full of walnuts.

I carry the walnuts home to Mama Draga. From the wardrobe in the room where Auntie Ileana sleeps, I take another hat and race back to Mrs Giurgiu to parade for her again and collect more walnuts. Eventually my grandmother puts a stop to this.

'Lenuta, the woman has other things to do,' she tells me.

I look forward to breakfast every morning. Each day, the

milkman delivers our fresh milk and yoghurt, both in glass bottles. Mama Draga places the bottles on the verandah under the bench in order to keep them cool. In summer, she boils the milk so that it will last longer.

Mama Draga walks to the corner store which sells everything from salami to soap. Big round loaves of thick bread are delivered there hot every morning. Although she never complains, I see that Mama Draga tires easily. She limps from severe burns on her hip and leg as a young woman.

I want to help her. I hop, skip and run around her, impatient to reach the shop so that we can get back home for breakfast.

'Can I help buy the bread?' I ask her when I'm old enough.

'Lenuta, you must speak Hungarian,' she tells me. The lady in the shop is Hungarian and if we do not speak to her in her own language, she won't serve us.'

'I will. Please, please teach me.'

Mama Draga teaches me the words 'please' and 'thank you'. Once she is happy that I will remember them, I set off clutching the coins tightly in my hand, whispering the words over and over under my breath so as not to make a mistake. I'm so excited. The faster I go, the sooner breakfast will come. How I look forward to a thick slice of bread with yoghurt or milk!

Every day after that I run to the little shop on my young legs. The bread arrives between nine and ten. Sometimes I am there too early and must wait outside. When they hand me the half-loaf of heavy bread, I am so proud. I carry it home in my arms like a baby.

Mama Draga cuts a big slice and gives it to me with my yoghurt. No breakfast since has ever tasted so good.

2

My Palace

The house where I was born, Mama Draga's house, is made from mud and straw and has a corrugated iron roof. Inside, the floor is pressed earth. Our toilet out the back is a hole in the ground and it feels very fragile. When I sit over the hole, I feel that the wooden seat is moving under me and I worry I'm going to fall in. I never look forward to going there.

'Put your shoes on. Only chickens go without shoes,' Mama Draga tells me as I run around the house barefoot.

There is no fridge, so we keep food on the wooden verandah where the cool air can circulate around it, on a long wooden bench out of the sun. We hang our clothes to dry here and they flap above our heads in the breeze. Auntie Ana sleeps with Mama Draga in the living area and Auntie Ileana sleeps with my mother in the second room. Their beds are plain and made of wood; their mattresses are filled with straw.

There is a gas stove for cooking and a long table with a bench seat where we all sit and eat. Off to one side of this area is a small room like a shed, full of pieces of wood and other things we don't use. I've been told this is where my maternal grandfather passed away. It seems a dark and heavy place to me. Sometimes I peek through the window or the door, never daring to set foot inside.

There is no running water in our house so I often help Mama Draga fetch water from the taps at the end of our street and carry it home in buckets. In summer, my grandmother puts a big enamel pan in the garden. I get in and she pours warm water over me, soaps me and rinses me clean. As I get older, I take a bath closer to the house so the neighbours won't see me.

I like to spend time with Mama Draga in her garden. There she is relaxed and happy as she tends her tomatoes, cucumbers and lettuce. She treats the tomatoes as if they are living things, patting and stroking them. When I walk in her garden I tiptoe so as not to step on any plants.

In that garden, everything has its own place. Everything is in order. Everything is green and cared for. Everything is as it should be.

Mama Draga takes me out into the street to help pick up horse dung which we put in a bag and carry home to fertilise the vegetables. Although I hate its smell, I forget all about it when I sit down to a plate of those huge shiny tomatoes. My desire to eat them is overwhelming.

Mama Draga keeps chickens in the garden. When their eggs hatch, she pets the fluffy yellow chicks, stroking and cooing at them. For some reason, I hate the helpless little things. Their pecking and strutting irritates me. I crouch on my hands and knees and watch them as they shelter under the bench. One day, I tip it on top of them and manage to kill some. I don't bother to hide the little bodies from Mama Draga. In fact, I leave them there for her to find.

On warm late afternoons, I help my grandmother carry the garden bench through the gate and out to the pavement.

We sit there together, Mama Draga and I, the little olive-skinned girl wearing a solemn expression, hair tied with a bow over a straight dark fringe.

Sometimes we sit with Mama Draga's sisters as they talk about women's things and greet the neighbours as they pass. I love to share their afternoon ritual. The youngest sister is the bossiest and I have no warm feelings towards her, but the oldest sister is kind and well balanced. Her Catholic faith is strong and sometimes she goes to church twice a day.

Beyond the concrete wall of Mama Draga's house is a green lawn, a bank full of trees and then the Somesul Mic River. I remember the green of the grass and its sweet smell, and the sun filtering through the leaves. Beyond the trees the river is ten metres wide, clear and fast flowing. When we do our washing, my grandmother and I carry the clothes in baskets through the gate in the wall, cross the grass and reach the bank where there are wooden steps on which the women squat to scrub their clothes. Below the steps, the river is deep. It bubbles over the stones of the riverbed as if it is boiling.

Washing days are always sunny. One day, when I am almost four, I take my doll and climb down the steps holding her tight. I bend down to wash her but she slips away from my little hands and is taken by the current. I follow her into the river and it takes me too. The water churns around me. My feet are nowhere near the rocky bottom.

As I am swept away I hear Mama Draga screaming along with the other women. The water swamps my ears until I cannot hear them any more. I try to come up and breathe, fighting for air, wanting to live, struggling against the current. But there is no air for me. My head slips under the water. I open my eyes and see green water all around me. Then suddenly the current pushes me to the surface. I take a breath but get pushed under again. Water floods into my mouth. I see nothing but black.

Our neighbour, Mrs Giurgiu, crossing the little bridge over the river, sees my head with its mass of long black hair rising and falling in the water. She jumps in and pulls me out. On the bank she presses hard on my stomach, expelling the water.

When I open my eyes, I am in my grandmother's arms and feel her warm tears on my cold face. Mama Draga is crying and covering my face with kisses.

'Mrs Giurgiu, you have saved my Lenuta. Thank you! I'll be grateful forever.'

Mama Draga never forgets. She reminds me often that I must be grateful to our neighbour for turning me away from death. I am happy to do this. Gratitude feels good.

Afterwards when I go to the river, I keep my distance. I sit on the grass and play with my new doll. Ever since that day, water scares me. When I shower, my throat tightens and my chest constricts.

★

From my grandmother's garden I can hear bells ring out every hour from the church where I was baptised. It stands above us on a hill, inside a ring of fir trees. The Calvaria Church of Cluj is an impressive stone building thought to be one of the oldest churches in Romania. I love its tall, thin arched windows and its red roof leading to a double-pointed spire. As I enter, I gaze up to the sculpted Virgin who looks down on me.

Every afternoon, Mama Draga attends Mass. Around four o'clock she calls, 'Lenuta, put on your nice dress and let's go to church.'

She walks slowly as we climb the hill. I run to the church entrance before her to see how many of her friends are there and then I run back down to let her know. I can do this once, twice, even three times while my grandmother is climbing to the top.

Inside we sit together and listen to the priest speak of Heaven. Its promise is intriguing to me. As she listens, Mama Draga starts to cry. Is she thinking of her dead son?

One day, as we are leaving the church, I see tears in my grandmother's eyes. Why is she crying? I ask myself. Is Heaven as bad as all that?

I look up at her and ask, 'Mama Draga, are you scared of Heaven?'

'Oh no,' she says. 'I'm looking forward to it. It's death that frightens me.'

'Where is Heaven?' I ask her.

She looks up and points to the wide blue sky. 'There.'

When we return home we sit outside and greet her friends. The branches of the poplars lining the street bow down. I watch as rays of sunlight dance in patterns on the asphalt. I think to myself that life will be like this forever.

Mama Draga's house is all I know. It is a palace to me and I am happy there.

3

Love

Nobody quite knows how long it has been since I arrived inside my mother's womb. My father shouts at her, 'Rosalia, I told you it was just an affair! And how do I know it's mine?'

My mother, soft and in love, starts crying. 'I didn't know. I didn't know,' she keeps repeating. My father is doing his two years of compulsory military service and has built himself a house down south in Bucharest. Afterwards his parents want him to come back to their village, marry a local girl they have chosen and run the family farm. But lives have a habit of going astray.

My mother Rosalia is small and fair, like a doll. Her hair frames her small-boned face. She works in a factory that makes vodka and tuica, liquor from fermented plums. She is always pensive, always waiting. She does not make decisions on her own and she does not ask for anything.

'Gheorghe wants me to have an abortion,' she whispers to Auntie Ana. My mother will do anything for my father. His wishes are law.

Auntie Ana takes her hand and squeezes it. 'If that's what you want, I'll help you,' she promises, although her own sorrow rises to the surface. She has had her own love tragedy. 'I'll keep your secret, Rosalia.'

Mama Draga, fiercely Catholic, must not find out.

Gheorghe has organised an abortion for my mother at the military hospital. The night before, my grandmother finds her weeping into her pillow. 'I know what you're going to do,' she tells my mother, stroking the back of her neck. 'You mustn't. I will look after the child.'

But her love for my father is too strong. The next day Gheorghe picks her up and drives her to the hospital while my grandmother kneels on her kitchen floor and prays.

Although abortions are illegal, they are performed far and wide. They are part of the black market even here, at the military hospital. If my father thinks he has taken care of everything, it is my mother who feels the shame. As her heart beats hard in her chest, she lies on the table while the doctor's fingers knead her belly. 'It's too late,' she hears him say. 'The foetus is four months along. There's nothing we can do.'

He turns away and scribbles a note. My mother sits up and adjusts her clothes. She feels numb.

'He wouldn't do it! I swear I didn't know,' she vows to my father in the car.

He doesn't believe her and part of him will never forgive her.

When my mother arrives home, Mama Draga finally stops praying and gets to her feet. 'Is it done?' she asks.

My mother shakes her head.

Mama Draga almost weeps with happiness. 'God answered my prayer!'

*

The day of my birth, 21 September 1953, is a beautiful one,

with sunshine and bright skies. My Auntie Ana calls my father. 'You have a little daughter, the very image of you,' she tells him.

He comes to visit my mother and me in hospital. He leans low over my crib and stares into my eyes with his own hazel ones. 'She's mine,' he says.

My father chooses my name. Later my mother finds out Lenuta is the name of his first love.

After my birth, my father confesses to his parents, the wealthiest people in their village, in the southern Romanian region of Oltenia. They are the only family to live in a two-storey house. The Nadolus are horrified. They forbid my father to marry my mother, a girl from a family 'in service'. They offer to take me in and look after me so that he is free to marry the good Oltenian girl they have chosen for his bride.

My father asks my mother to hand me over to his family. 'Not without me,' she replies. 'It's both of us or neither one.'

In Oltenia, marriage is taken very seriously and involves complicated rituals. When a couple choose to be partners, the man gives the woman a ring, and a dowry is negotiated with her parents. The groom's father must pay for the wedding celebrations. Godparents buy presents for the couple, the bride's veil, the flowers and the candles.

The bride embroiders a shirt for her future husband and a kerchief that will be used during the ceremony. She will assemble her dowry in a decorated chest. It contains embroidered linen, clothes and quilts, carpets and a bottle of wine, two glasses and two earthenware plates. The chest will be carried from the bride's house to the new home she will share with the groom.

At the beginning of the wedding week, other young

people move through the village carrying hipflasks of plum wine or brandy. Whoever joins them to drink must come to the wedding.

On the wedding day the bride, dressed by her godmother and friends, stays at home waiting for her groom. He arrives with his godparents as the wedding guests are gathering. The groom must pay to enter the house to look for his bride. She circles a table with her future father-in-law, then they spill a glass of wine and discover money beneath a napkin. They go outside together and visit three wells. At the third, three buckets of water are spilled on the ground. Then everyone dances the hora, a traditional Romanian folk dance. Before the wedding party goes to the church, bread is broken over the head of the bride and the couple eat it together.

After the church ceremony, the feasting begins. The couple sit together, apart from the guests, and share a bowl of food, eating with a single wooden spoon while they drink wine from the same bottle. This shows that their lives are now united. The guests dip bread in wine, and eat eggs, chicken soup, cabbage, meat jellies, pickles, steaks and pastries. Plum brandy is drunk in enormous quantities.

Finally the culmination of the ceremony is reached: the uncovering of the bride. She is invited by her godmother to sit on a pillow, and the godmother tries to remove her veil and tie a kerchief over her head. Three times, the bride resists but finally she accepts. Now she is truly a wife. She stands before her groom and all the wedding guests to dance a special hora to show she has entered the world of married women. Everyone joins in, dancing with the bride and giving her money which will be hers alone. There are also many other gifts. Whatever people can afford, they bring: animals, rugs, crops and even sheets.

All night there is dancing, joy, food and drink, in a huge celebration across the generations that unites the villagers and sends everyone home with warm hearts. Weddings bring the community together.

Every wedding in Oltenia poses a huge question: is the bride a virgin? On the day after the ceremony, her nightgown will be inspected for the tell-tale stain. The godfather visits her parents carrying a cask of brandy tied up with ribbons. Others join him and fiddlers serenade them all. If the bride is proved to have been a virgin, the brandy will be sweetened with sugar and dyed red. Her purity will be celebrated with more dancing and drinking. But if not, the brandy will be mixed with ash and chilli peppers, the groom's mother will laugh at the mother of the bride and the girl's father must offer his new son-in-law compensation: money or land. That is the debt he must pay for the loss of his daughter's honour.

*

My father strongly believed in these traditional wedding customs. By marrying my mother, he was denied the birthright of every young Oltenian man. He will always resent her for that.

4

Mama Draga's Daughters

During the Ceausescu regime from the 1960s until the fall of Communism in 1989, the economy, so the official statistics tell us, grows between six and nine per cent each year, and investment is strong. Despite this display of wealth and development, people starve while our food is exported overseas. We endure constant power cuts and run out of basic food, medicines and other goods. Rationing is introduced. So determined is he to pay off Romania's foreign debt brought on by rapid industrialisation, Ceausescu ignores the welfare of his own people.

Auntie Maria marries a man who has a wooden leg from the knee down. Mama Draga tries to stop the marriage but her daughter will not be discouraged. Her husband beats her, often with his wooden leg. Like Mama Draga, her eldest daughter gives birth to seven children, six boys and a girl. Of the seven, she loses four after they become adults. The first son dies of lymphoma, the second, a welder, is burned when faulty equipment explodes and the third son commits suicide. The daughter dies of stomach cancer.

Auntie Maria is trampled to death while queuing to buy a chicken during the hunger years when the Romanian government is selling off our resources.

Mama Draga's fourth daughter, Auntie Ileana, is caught in a bomb blast during World War II while playing outside. This affects her brain and she remains child-like, always laughing and acting in a silly way. But she is the one member of our family who is always happy. She works as a cleaner in a shoe factory six days a week and lives with Mama Draga and my Auntie Ana, enjoying a bottle of beer with Sunday lunch.

I like to spend time with Auntie Ana at home with Mama Draga and Auntie Ileana. Auntie Ana is closer to me than my own mother. She has dark curly hair and loving eyes. She mourns the loss of her only brother and her heart was broken years ago and she weeps at night.

I hear my grandmother and great-aunts whisper about what happened as we sit on the bench beneath the trees. Auntie Ana, they say, fell in love with an army officer, another handsome man like my father. A real charmer. He asked her time after time to come with him to another city and be his wife. But she refused because her father was close to death, sick with asthma. Ana loved her father and besides, everyone in the family depended on her help.

Her boyfriend thought that her love for him should be enough for her to leave. 'It's now or never,' he told her. But she felt she couldn't follow him.

A few weeks after my grandfather died, she searched for her boyfriend's new address, packed her bags and followed him. When she arrived in the town where he was stationed and knocked at his door, another woman answered it.

'Can I help you?' she asked.

'I'm looking for my Ion,' said Ana.

'I'm his wife,' the unknown woman answered, and shut the door in her face.

Auntie Ana returned home heartbroken. She was even more devastated when she found she was pregnant.

Whispered stories. Family myths.

'He didn't wait for me,' weeps Auntie Ana, burying her face in my grandmother's shoulder. Mama Draga caresses her daughter's pretty hair and sighs to herself that once again happiness seems beyond her children's reach. She leads Ana to bed and holds her hand until she falls asleep.

Ana has an abortion. She regrets this all her life. She returns to work at the cigarette factory but loves the army officer forever. When he dies, she visits his grave and places flowers on it.

As a child, I watch as every night she listens to romantic music on the radio while rubbing night cream onto her lovely face. In her heart, I think Ana is someone who knows that living can be a celebration. But she finds this hard to express in her own life.

5

In Oltenia

Oltenia is where my father's parents live. I don't like to visit these grandparents. I am not comfortable with their strange customs, their odd way of speaking or their strict way of life. They live on a big farm. When I visit them, my grandmother Fataluta takes me out to work every morning. She and my grandfather Petre work the fields together, their backs bent over their hoes as they till the fields. Just two people—and their fields are so big. Since the Communists took over, their life has become harder and harder. There are no more servants and almost all the young people have left the village for better jobs in the cities.

We carry our lunch in a cotton bag: cold cooked polenta called mamaliga, some slices of onion or leek, a few tomatoes and only one egg which we share. In my grandparents' house my stomach is always rumbling. The work is hard and I am not used to the beating sun which makes me feel dizzy.

When it is mealtime, my grandfather goes down to the cellar with the bunch of keys that are always tied around his waist. He unlocks the lid of the coffin he has made for himself and scoops out some polenta which he stores there. He carries this upstairs, careful to spill not even a grain, and gives it to my grandmother. She boils it up in the traditional way.

My grandfather is a cold and arrogant man. I watch him going off to the fields in his cart. It is very fine and he is proud of it. Mama Draga doesn't have a cart nor a beautiful white horse with a bridle connected to reins.

My paternal grandmother shows me a picture of her husband dressed in traditional Oltenian costume. He is young, handsome and proud and wears an embroidered waistcoat over his white shirt and in his hands he holds a small book. With his straight back and square shoulders, he is a man who knows what he wants.

When he visits us in Bucharest, he takes me with him to the market, striding along and stopping only to sample watermelon after watermelon. He uses his walking stick to fend off the children who follow us.

Only when he has tasted every melon will he return to the stall he likes most. 'Yours is the sweetest watermelon,' he says to the seller. My grandfather knows, because he grows them himself. But when he is told the price, he exclaims how expensive it is. He will only hand over money after extensive bargaining.

If he weren't a farmer he would have made a wonderful businessman. I am embarrassed to be with him while he is negotiating in the market. I creep away, trying to pretend he is not related to me. But he raises his voice to call me, 'Lenuta, come here. Stay close to me.'

I know he only brings me to the market because he wants me to carry home the heavy melon in its bag. I struggle along behind him feeling as if my arms are being pulled from their sockets. He strides ahead, turning now and again to make sure the melon doesn't fall out of the bag. This makes me feel as if I am a servant.

Fataluta is tough too, but she has a soft spot for me because I look just like her eldest son, my father Gheorghe, her pride and joy. Like lots of people in Oltenia, she is religious and superstitious. People here believe in bad spirits and ugly vampires or ghosts. In spring and also in times of drought, they dance to the traditional paparuda, calling for rain. My grandmother joins in enthusiastically.

After only a week staying with my grandparents, I am eager to leave. My grandmother understands even though my grandfather does not. I think she knows that although we share the same blood, I am not cut out for peasant life. Nor am I part of their culture and traditions. I look like them but inside I am a Transylvanian girl. I am Mama Draga's granddaughter, not theirs.

6

Favoured Sons

In our culture, little boys learn that they are very important people.

When I am only a few weeks old, my mother sits in the garden under the fruit trees with my father, Gheorghe, who is visiting her at our house in Cluj. It is late autumn. The grass is damp and covered with golden-brown leaves.

Inside the house, Mama Draga has calmed me. 'Tell Rosalia to come in and feed her daughter,' she tells Auntie Ana who stands in the doorway looking down at my tiny angry face. 'And you can tell that man to go back to his rich parents and leave us alone.'

Mama Draga cannot stand being near Gheorghe. It is hard for her to forgive her daughter for loving him.

'Shh, Mama,' says Auntie Ana, wrapping her shawl around herself as she steps outside.

My grandmother never pauses in her work, washing sheets and towels and nappies, eager to get them spread on the rocks near the river before the afternoon clouds roll across the sky. There will be plenty of time for crying later when everyone is asleep. But by then, Mama Draga will also have the next day to plan.

Auntie Ana buys my clothes. She dresses me up and pinches my cheeks to make me smile. Along with Mama Draga, she is the centre of my world. When I think back I can see Ana's soft curls and my grandmother's craggy, loving face. Try as I might, I cannot remember my mother's.

After what happened to Ana, Mama Draga does not trust handsome men with her daughters. With his slicked-back hair, his firm brow and broad shoulders, my father turns women's heads in the street.

But Rosalia is soft and needs someone gentle to take care of her. Mama Draga prays silently that Gheorghe will go away.

My father was introduced to my mother in 1952 by one of her best friends who worked in the same factory. He had come for my mother's friend, hoping to ask her out.

'I already have a boyfriend, so don't waste your time,' the girl had said, tossing her head. 'But Rosalia is single.'

When she pointed to her, my father looked her over. She was blonde and pretty, but her eyes glanced away in terror.

'The army trained me to drive trucks. But I can drive anything,' my father boasted.

Truck driving would suit him as a job, he had decided. The open road. Time away. There would be space for other women but he would still be able to come home to a family, to the comforts of an adoring wife.

My father transports everything in his truck: barrels of oil, sweets, bags of wheat, wood, equipment for building factories, cylinders for generators. Everything. Sometimes he drives slowly, no more than five kilometres an hour, so the goods won't get damaged on the dreadful roads. Sometimes there is a police car in front of him and another with an engineer on board. Sometimes the machines he carries are so tall that electric wires must be cut to let him pass.

My father is proud of what he does. He knows that not many men are trusted to do such work.

'You're a wonderful driver,' my mother would later agree. He will never find another who loves him more than she does.

Gheorghe marries my mother on 6 May 1954, not long after he finishes his military service. I am seven months old. He comes to live with us in Mama Draga's house. Is it because of me, because of my mother, or maybe to have a household of women looking after him?

On a cold winter's day in December 1955, my younger brother is born. He is given the same name as my father. 'Hold our son,' my mother says, and is overjoyed at how pleased her husband looks.

On the way home from hospital, we pause for a photograph. Tata, my father, lifts me up on top of the huge front tyres of his truck and holds me there. I see joy in his eyes and I feel strong and confident. I know I am the big sister. My mother's eyes are fixed on the newborn bundle in her arms.

My brother Gheorghe will become the prince of the household. Ours is not the only culture where boys are favoured and girls told to stand back. But if my brother hits me, I hit him back—and take the consequences.

As he grows up, my brother is quiet and shy. He seems to have more of our mother in him, while I am more like my father.

7

The Other Woman

Forgiveness is the fragrance the violet sheds
on the heel that has crushed it.
Mark Twain

will bring Lenuta every year,' my father swears. 'From June
till September, she will be yours.' Sad and scared, Mama
Draga wrings her hands. My parents pack. I try to remember
what I felt upon leaving Cluj. There is nothing, just a void.

All I remember is waking up one morning to find myself
in a different house. Mama Draga isn't anywhere to be seen. I
step out of bed and search for her. I run from room to room.

I find my father in the kitchen. 'Lenuta,' he says. 'My Lenuta.'
He lifts me up and gives me a big hug. I feel comforted but
know that something has changed forever.

My father sits me down and looks straight into my eyes.
'Lenuta, now we are going to live here.' He means Ferentari,
on the outskirts of Bucharest. There are no trees or flowers,
just potholes in the streets and lots of stray dogs.

'Your Mama Draga will stay in Cluj, far away, but I will
take you to see her.'

'When?' I ask at once.

'Next year.'

At four years old, I am too young to understand what *next year* means but already I miss my Mama Draga. Somehow I know that it will be a long time until *next year.*

But I also know my father loves me. Here in Bucharest he will be the focus of my life.

My father has built our house from mud and thatch. It's much bigger than I'm used to, with four rooms and a storage area like a shed at the back. Inside there is a small kitchen and beyond that, another smaller room which is used as the kitchen in winter, when everything outside is covered in snow and ice.

On either side of the second kitchen are bedrooms, one for my parents with a big wardrobe, a table and chairs. There is a nice Persian carpet on the wall and another on the floor, but the room is unheated and always cold. The other bedroom is heated for my brother and me. We share a big warm bed.

Our new house is kept spotless. My mother cleans it relentlessly.

The best part is our garden. There are flowers and fruit trees: the cherry tree, an apricot tree and a grape vine. My mother plants tomatoes and onions, a whole bed of vegetables.

One day I realise my father has not come back from work. Days pass. It gradually becomes clear to me that he doesn't live with us any more. I don't know where he is. I feel anger at the edges of my life, like a fire closing in.

Spring is almost upon us and I am playing with my brother outside. I hide the ball from him and he stumbles forward to find it, groping and laughing. My mother has gone shopping. Almost every morning she goes out to buy the milk, meat and cheese we will eat during the day.

I am wearing my favourite red sweater because there is still a chill in the air. Suddenly, I look up and my father is standing close to us. His eyes are bright and his cheeks are flushed.

'Tata!' I cry, but he doesn't throw his arms around me as he usually does.

'Inside, Lenuta,' he orders. He picks up my brother, who is frightened and begins to cry. My father hurries us inside. 'Pack the things you'll need,' he tells me.

I stand not knowing what to do while he searches through drawers for my brother's clothes. 'A jumper. Socks,' he is muttering to himself. When he notices me standing there, not moving, he is angry. 'What do you need? Where are your things?'

Finally, when he has squashed Gheorghe's things into a bag, he rushes towards the door, urging me to hurry up.

'Where are we going?' I ask. My eyes look around this room that holds all the things I have and treasure. What has my father packed for me? I don't know. I do know I don't want to leave my home.

My father takes us on a long drive to another house. The woman who lives here is from his village. She is dark and mean, with a look that freezes me. She has a daughter who is just as dark as she is, and about my age. I stare at the girl and think that she looks like a peasant. Her hair is cut in a bob, her skin is olive and she is skinny where my flesh is round and soft. I don't think she is pretty.

Her mother screams at her, 'Step back! Let the little ones in.'

I take my brother's hand and stand without moving. The woman comes up so close that I fear she will strike me. My father steps past me into the house and drops our little bundle of clothes onto the floor. He scoops water from a green bucket and splashes it on his face.

'It's fine,' he is saying. 'She wasn't there. I just went straight in, picked them up and left.'

The woman peers inside the bag looking at the socks and underwear and Gheorghe's winter coat and mittens. 'Is that all you've got?' she asks him.

My feet are shifting over the doormat. My father has told me nothing. He hasn't introduced me or even invited me into this house which may or may not be his.

Beside me, little Gheorghe trips and wails. I know he is as scared as I am.

My father picks up my brother again. He pats him on the back and jiggles him up and down.

The woman's back is turned as she boils water to make coffee for my father and herself. It's as if we are not there. I feel like crying. I think of my mother left alone at home, my sensitive, gentle mother.

Before long, my father says he must return to work. When he goes, I am still standing awkwardly in the strange room. The woman tells me to sit, and I do sit where I'm told. She dumps Gheorghe down on a bundle of cloth in the corner and he is so exhausted that he falls asleep.

Then she tells me to clean and so I do. Afterwards she gives me a corner of bread which I chew despite my pride. All the while, her own child floats about the place with arms spread, eyes rolling back in her head, chanting a mad song of her own devising. She and her mother do not speak to one another.

At meal time three bowls of food are plonked down on the table. The girl grabs a spoon and the deepest bowl and shovels the stew into her mouth. I am not used to eating like this. At home, we have a system, a routine. My mother asks us to lay the table and then we sit together and pray before we begin to eat. Here, before I have even managed to sit Gheorghe beside me and put a spoon into his hand, the girl is finished and is shouting around the room.

There is barely a scoop of food in the bottom of my bowl. It is a soft lump of mamaliga with half a boiled egg on top. My brother's bowl is the same but his portion is even smaller. We eat in silence. I feed myself and help Gheorghe with his spoon. He mushes the mamaliga between his lips and lets it fall down his chin.

'Eat!' I urge my brother. 'There's nothing else!' When we're finished, my hunger feels even sharper than it was.

The woman has placed cups of dark, smelly well water in front of us. I do my best to swallow it. I hold Gheorghe's cup up for him to drink. He tastes and then spits it out. One of his hands knocks the water away.

The woman swears and threatens to strike him. 'If he's going to waste water, he'll have to learn to fill his cup himself.'

Night comes. I sleep with Gheorghe on blankets by the door. I wrap my arms around him and keep him close.

My father does not return for many days.

'Where is our father?' I ask the woman one morning. She has still not fed us properly.

'Driving! Where do you think?'

I rise to go outside so at least I'll be able to feel the morning breeze on my skin. As I step across the threshold, I see my brother bent over the dog's bowl. His hand is up to his mouth and I realise with horror that he is eating the dog's food, yesterday's leftovers. His lips are stretching, closing, stretching, closing and his tongue is moving about, licking the flecks of food from his lips. His eyes are dull.

33

Only then do I realise how hungry I am.

'No!' I cry and slap the dog's bowl out of his hand. I reach out and try to wipe the food from his mouth, but he is still chewing and swallowing.

I storm back inside to the woman and tell her what he's been doing. She puffs her cigarette and laughs. 'What kind of boy eats a poor dog's food?' she asks. Then she shrugs as if such a question can never be answered.

'Give him bread!' I shout. Again she shrugs and then points in the direction of her cooking pots and bowls. 'If you can find it, he can have it.'

Later I see the woman's daughter chewing a bun spread with jam. I know there is a pot of jam on the top shelf. I watch the girl eat, then look away.

The next day as I am playing in the sand outside the back door, the woman comes up to me, unbuttons my red cardigan and wrenches it off. She is rough with me. I don't know what she is doing but she is an adult and I have been taught to respect adults.

When she has removed my cardigan, she holds it up in her right hand. 'Daughter!' she calls to her child. The girl runs over and the woman holds my red cardigan up against her. She puts it on her and buttons it up.

I realise what has happened and so I retaliate. 'It's mine!' I shout and try to pull the jumper off her.

'What are you doing?' the woman screams. 'Are you crazy? Who taught you to be so rude?'

I don't know what's happening. We are far from home. My brother has stooped to eating dog food. And now this: the warm cardigan which Mama Draga sent me for Christmas, my one and only treasured possession, has been stolen. My tears flow. I want my mother and my home.

Then the woman hits me and I back off, still crying and rubbing my face. 'Look at my girl,' she is saying. 'How beautiful she looks in that cardigan.'

I am crying and crying but there is nothing to be done.

At the end of the day, the girl comes up to me and tosses the red cardigan into my lap.

'You can have it,' she says. 'I hate it.'

I pull the cardigan on once more. It means so much to me.

Then I hear the rumble of a truck outside and my father walks through the door. Suddenly his mistress is all smiles. She gives him a plate of specially prepared food.

'Lenuta, what's wrong with you?' he asks as he shovels in large mouthfuls.

I am crouching in the corner, my face streaked with dirt and tears. 'They stole it. They stole my red cardigan,' I say, wrapping my arms around myself. 'And she hit me.' I point at the woman and burst into tears again.

'Is that true?' my father asks.

The woman scoffs and shrugs her shoulders. 'Of course not. I wouldn't lay a hand on your girl. She didn't like it when my daughter wanted to try on her cardigan. She went crazy, screaming and kicking. She went mad.'

'That's not true!' I shout, jumping to my feet.

'See? She's out of control,' says the woman, shrugging her shoulders. 'You should be paying me to keep her in my house.'

My father turns to me and wipes his mouth. He pushes his plate from him and sits back in his chair. 'Why are you lying to me?'

I cannot speak. My father, the man I have until this moment loved so dearly, who has lavished hugs and kisses on me and who has always trusted me, believes this woman, this stranger, instead of me. In that moment, even though I am only five, I feel my heart shatter and I know it will never be repaired.

I learn that this is what love does to you. You betray yourself. You are cruel. What was precious loses its value. You drop it, tread on it, forget it is even there.

8

Easter

My mother arrives at the door to take us home. Goodness knows how she has found us. The woman folds her arms across her chest and looks bemused. Despite her own rough state, she looks my mother up and down with a critical eye. It's as if she feels sorry for her for loving my father so much.

'You can take them,' she says. 'I didn't want them here at all.'

I notice tears running down my mother's face, tears of joy. She has found her children. We hurry to the station without a word. It is a long trip home. On the train, she holds Gheorghe tight on her lap and I sit close beside her. She tells us things about daily life. There is a bird in the roof. The fruit trees have finished flowering and the buds are growing into apples and cherries.

At every new station, my mother is growing tense because we travel without tickets and a guard could climb aboard anytime and get us into trouble.

Finally we arrive back in Bucharest. As I walk through our gates my dog, Red, runs to greet me. I wrestle with him in the sandpit behind our house. He has a beautiful red coat. He is my constant friend. I bury my face in his neck.

In Bucharest, my mother needs financial and emotional help. When she left Cluj, she turned away from Mama Draga's Catholicism and joined the Greek Orthodox Church, my father's religion. My grandmother was horrified. She couldn't believe that her daughter would turn her back on her religion just to please her husband.

Gina, one of our neighbours on the next street, comes from the same region as my mother, Transylvania. Kind and gentle, Gina never involves herself in arguments with the other neighbours, she keeps to herself. Her husband is gentle too. They have no children. 'Rosalia, come to our Church and bring the children. We will help you,' Gina tells Mama.

I look at mama and I hope she says no…no more black robes, no more rough cleansing of sin when the Orthodox priest comes to our house before Easter and Christmas. He almost suffocates us as he covers my brother and me with his cloak and mutters the Lord's Prayer. He stinks of alcohol, since at each house he visits, people give him a glass of wine or schnapps.

Under his thick black robe, I start sweating. I cannot breathe. I feel as if water is entering my mouth and I am back down under the churning water of the river. I hear its deafening roar. Once released from the robe, I breathe deeply as my mother pours the priest a drink and he prepares to move on to the next house.

Easter for my mother means a time of rebirth, a new beginning. In the weeks before Easter Sunday, ritual cleaning begins. My mother paints all the walls and washes, scrubs and polishes as she prepares for when the priest will come to bless our house and drive away any evil spirits. I never feel that he has driven the bad spirits out of our house.

On Good Friday I stand on our garden fence to see what is happening in the street but at the same time I remain apart. I feel safe and calm because my mother is baking cozonac, a sweet bread, and the smell of it fills the house. She also colours eggs, red, green, yellow and blue. She hides them under the bed so they're out of sight and we're not tempted to eat them before Easter Sunday.

From the garden fence, I see a man approaching our house. I can see that he has a beard and is wearing a long black coat. My chest tightens. It's the priest, I think to myself, returning to torture me some more! I jump from the fence and run inside to my mother, crying, 'The priest is here again.'

'But he came last week,' says my mother, laying down her work.

'He's coming, he's coming. Come and look!'

We go outside, open the gate and step into the street. My mother is silent. When she looks at me, there is disbelief in her face. 'That's your father,' she says.

My father. As I look at him all I remember is the pain he caused me when he wouldn't believe what I said about my red jumper: when he believed his mistress instead of me. I don't want to see him again, ever. I run into the bedroom and hide behind the stove.

As I crouch there, I think how peaceful our life has been without him. My mother has been happier, calmer. I think she has accepted that this is her life: two children and kind neighbours. Now he has returned, I know the anger and arguments will start again. My mother will certainly take him back. She will not have the strength to say she doesn't want him.

'Why are you here?' she asks him tightly.

'I'm sorry, Rosalia. I've come back,' he says.

From my hiding place I peep out at my father. His hair is

long and wild and his new beard is untrimmed. From the smell, he has barely even washed. I've never seen my father in this state. I wonder if the other woman is treating him badly, too.

I hear him step across to where my brother Gheorghe lies napping.

'Where is Lenuta?' he asks.

Perhaps my mother gestures to my hiding place because I feel my father's arm reaching in and pulling me out. He tries to hug me. I can't run away because he's holding me tight—but I'm scared of him. I'm scared he will take me away again and leave me with his mistress. As soon as he lets me go, I run to my room. I hide in bed and won't come out again. I don't trust him.

On Easter Sunday we all go to church looking immaculate, well-dressed and happy. My brother and I have new clothes and new shoes. My shoes are black patent leather with a shiny buckle on the side. I also have new white socks and a beautiful new red dress. My mother has bought them with the money she has saved by washing and selling dirty bottles, and with the money Mama Draga and Auntie Ana have sent her.

A few days before Easter, my mother irons my dress and hangs it over the back of the chair in her room. I tiptoe in, take my shoes from the wardrobe, put my new socks inside them and position them under my new dress. I keep returning to admire my lovely outfit, impatiently waiting for Sunday, the day I can wear it.

Outside the big iron gates, my mother puts on a smile and pretends that all is right in her world. I wonder if anyone has heard my parents' arguments, heard all those times my father has lost his temper. For the moment, we pretend all is well. Such things never happen at Easter.

My mother cooks us the Transylvanian dishes she knows, those that my father likes. They are less expensive which is just as well because he only gives her a small housekeeping allowance. She has learned how to make Oltenian mamaliga, in which polenta is cooked slowly in salted water in the bottom of a cast-iron pot. Sometimes she adds sour cream or milk and we eat it with spoons. At other times we roll it into balls with a little cheese inside. But nothing disguises the fact that it is stodgy and almost tasteless. It is a poor man's food.

When she can afford chicken, my mother makes goulash and I love the smell that fills the house when it cooks. Sometimes we have chivtele, rissoles made from pork or beef, or mutton if there is not enough money. My mother tries to hide the smell of the mutton with parsley, but she cannot fool me. When she uses mutton, I refuse to eat.

In spring she makes spinach puree with milk, flour, garlic and oil. I love this because it tastes of gardens. I love my mother's eggplant dip too, although it makes my tongue break out in painful sores.

'Why do you eat it then?' my father laughs.

'Because I like it,' I say stubbornly.

One morning I wake to a silent house. There are only the three of us, my brother, my mother and I.

'Come here, Lenuta,' my mother says when she sees me. She sits on a chair and I stand between her knees while she ties a ribbon around my hair. 'Your father left us again.' But this time she does not cry. A huge weight has been lifted. I am glad he is not with us any more. I think how peaceful our life will be.

Gina's church is different, more cheerful than my father's Orthodox church. Here I don't shrink from the cold drops of water that fall when the priest waves the bunch of basil soaked in holy water above me. I am surprised to see people's faces turned up instead of bowed down. Their hands are open as if what they are receiving is solid and heavy. Each Sunday morning Mama gets up early, bathes us and dresses us in our best clothes.

First we walk to Gina's house and then we all walk to the tram station together. They always pay the tram fares for all of us. It is a long tram ride. I am excited and I love it! It's the longest one I have ever been on. The church is a large hall with long, shiny wooden benches in neat rows. All is clean and in perfect order. Inside I see no church ornaments, no pictures of saints on the walls, just a tall wooden table placed in front of the seats. I wonder who stands at that table?

Everyone arriving seems joyful like Gina and her husband, their faces shining with happiness. I sense peace and comfort. Everyone is welcoming us, I have never seen so many kind people in one big room. They belong to Pocait, which means repentant in English. During the mass a basket is passed around the room for donations. We have no money to put in the basket. We pass it to the next person.

At the end of mass, we all gather outside in the garden for refreshments. There are biscuits and tea and a cake. Gina asks Mama to follow her. I hold my brother's hand and I follow Mama. We enter a small room around the corner from the big hall.

'Rosalia, please take the money from today's mass collection,' the man who stood and spoke at the tall wooden table in the church tells her.

I look at Mama. She is shy and her face turns red. She takes the money with tears in her eyes. From the church collections, money is given to help poor people like us. We are grateful. We have had a wonderful day.

One hot summer afternoon, I hear the noise of my father's roaring truck engine. I am not scared, Mama is home. He cannot take me away! I avoid him but my brother adores him. His stays are getting longer and longer and sometimes he sleeps in our house.

As my mother combs my hair one morning, I lean back and feel a lump in her stomach pressing against me. I look up and see a half-smile on her face.

My father smiles broadly as if he's been waiting for this moment. He comes over and lifts me up.

'You'll have another little brother or sister, Lenuta. Aren't you happy?' I smile so that he will put me down. No matter what he does, things can never be the same between us.

The day my sister is born, before she emerges, my mother walks around and around the room, striking her forehead and cursing my father. He is away driving the truck interstate. 'Go and fetch Adela. Tell her to come quickly.'

Everyone knows Adela, the dressmaker. She wears fashionable floral gowns that are gathered under the bust and make her look even larger than she is. The skin of her big round face is soft as a peach. She is very kind.

I run all the way to her little house and arrive out of breath. She jumps up from her sewing machine and runs out after me. I speed ahead to tell my mother that Adela is on her way. She puffs along after me.

My mother is holding onto the bed frame and howling as sweat slides down her face. I run back to escort Adela to the right room, although she will surely find it for herself with all the noise. Adela enters and tells my mother to lie down. She shoos me out. 'There are some things little girls aren't supposed to see.'

This is not fair. They have used me as a go-between and

now they want to push me out. This is the first time I have not been allowed to be next to my mother. Usually when she cries I go and sit next to her.

Separation makes me feel helpless. I need to look after her, to be in charge. But she'll be all right in Adela's hands, I decide. We all love Adela because she makes pretty dresses for us. If I hear anything go wrong, I will dash inside again.

I run out into the street calling to my friends. 'Quickly, quickly—come to our house!' I round up five girls and boys. My throat is tight, I am almost suffocating, and I don't want to be alone. We stand in our yard under my parents' bedroom window and peer in. I jostle for the best position so that I can see the bed side-on.

My mother's legs are wide open and Adela is doing something with her hands there, something I can't fathom. I'm terrified.

Beside me, my friends are peeking in, eyes wide, mouths open. Then I hear the cry of a baby. My mother has stopped screaming and cursing. There is dead silence. Adela is cutting something with scissors. She holds up a slimy little body. I am amazed that babies come out so dirty and ugly.

My friends and I look at one another, speechless.

We watch as Adela goes to a neighbour's house. The neighbour runs out and sets off down the street towards the public phone. When the ambulance arrives, we children disappear so as not to be caught peeping. Later I am in trouble because they tell their parents, who then complain to my mother.

My father returns from his trip and we go to collect my mother from the hospital. He has bought a smart wooden pram, hand-made. We have to walk to the hospital, an hour away, because the conductor won't let us on the tram with the pram. We are annoyed yet at the same time proud because all the way to the hospital everyone admires our pram. Then we walk all the way back with my mother beside us, even though she is just out of hospital.

I love my baby sister because she is white and her hair is as pale and wispy as sweet corn silk. Cornelia is our little doll. I love her tiny clothes and boots, her good nature. Her birth has made me feel I am responsible for someone. Sometimes I forget I am her sister and think of myself as her mother.

My parents love her too. They treat her differently from me. I feel they love her more, perhaps because I am the cause of their pain.

9

Pig

It is nearly Christmas and so it is time to slaughter the pig, a brutal Romanian tradition. In spring my father bought a piglet which he has kept in the garden, feeding him choice scraps and comparing his growth against piglets our neighbours have bought. Now in every home the pigs are held down while their throats are slashed with knives. I saw it done once, saw the bright blood streaming out over the white snow.

This year I run to the wardrobe and hide myself deep inside. I press my fingers into my ears but nothing can drown out the sound of the pig's agonised squealing.

My father tells the neighbours he has some business to attend to so that they will kill his pig for him. I know it is because he cannot bear the slaughter either. I am too young to understand the stranglehold of tradition.

When the pig lies dead, the men strip off the skin, pull out the intestine and cut it into pieces. They give my mother a bucket full of the long bloody tubes which she will clean over and over again with cold water in the kitchen.

My mother prepares sausages, filling the long tubes with finely chopped pork mixed with spices. The smell makes me feel nauseated. My mother fries the rest of the meat with the sausages so they can be preserved in lard over the winter in big glass jars. One leg of pork and the ribs are smoked in a smoke-room at the back of the house. The lard will be used for cooking or my mother will spread it on bread and sprinkle it with salt for us to eat.

Afterwards my mother cleans everything, rubbing each surface with vinegar to remove the odour of pig. Even then, I can still smell it and I feel as though my nausea will never pass.

I am distracted a week later when Christmas parcels arrive from Mama Draga and my aunties. The first package contains walnuts and poppyseed rolls baked by Auntie Ana. The second parcel is full of beautiful clothes.

Christmas Eve is magical for me. All the children dress in heavy winter coats, boots and gloves. Around our necks, we hang a square bag which juts out from our chests.

'Come on! Come on!' I cry, running outside, eager to join my friends.

It is a freezing night and snow is falling all around. We knock on our neighbours' gates and sing carols for them. When we finish, they fill our bags with dry pretzels, apples, sweets and biscuits. The heavier my bag gets, the more joyful I feel.

Christmas Day is meant to be a day like any other. The Communist government does not recognise Christianity. Behind closed doors we eat our smoked ham and fried pork. We eat stuffed cabbage rolls, sour pork soup, poppyseed rolls, and cozonac, the sweet bread with swirls of ground walnut paste inside. We drink hot cocoa. It is a feast.

For weeks after Christmas, we eat pork, pork and more pork.

10

School and Summer

I am almost eight when I start school. I want to go but I am also scared. Every day I cry when my mother leaves. My first teacher is an old lady with red hair, a round face sagging with age, and the biggest teeth I have ever seen. She is not very nice.

'Pay attention!' she screams at us, and slaps a cane down on the desks of the students who sit at the front.

I am not only scared, I am overwhelmed. I slide down from my chair and sit under the desk, quivering. I become terrified that this will earn me some dreadful punishment, so I force myself to sit back up again and keep my back straight.

It doesn't take long for me to adapt to school. I neatly form the letters I am taught. I speak up. I am clean and organised. Soon the teacher is saying, 'Well done, Lenuta.'

'Len-u-ta!' my friend Mia calls outside my house each morning. I stroll out to meet her as if I'm not in any hurry.

'We'll be late!' Mia urges, but I shrug my shoulders.

It takes half an hour to walk to school. Other children straggle along around us. After our first class, we have a break and all the children pile outside to eat snacks and play. This is the time I stay close to Mia because every day she brings a sandwich with butter and jam that her mother has packed. Luckily for me, she doesn't love jam sandwiches the way I do. She gives them to me.

Mia follows me everywhere. I know that she needs me more than I need her. She annoys me by asking the same questions over and over again. I refuse to repeat myself and this makes her angry. Sometimes we fight. She scratches my face with her long nails and I retaliate by pulling her curly hair, but by the next morning we are friends again. 'Len-u-ta!' I hear early each day. Another day, another fight and another jam sandwich.

I am bad at drawing and maths. My houses look like people. My people look like plants. But I'm good at Latin and Romanian literature and poetry. I excel at history and I like geography. Soon my parents are waiting enthusiastically for my school results. I realise that being a good student is a role I can play well. I know it pleases them.

'Did you top the class?' my father asks me and I nod, because only a boy got higher marks. Boys are boys, and I know they will always win.

'Lenuta is a clever one,' my mother proudly tells a neighbour.

In Bucharest, every day is a waiting game for summer. I think of Cluj as a sunny island in the middle of a storm and dream about the day in mid-June when I will go there.

Finally June arrives in a blur of sweet-smelling grass and exhaust fumes. It is almost 500 kilometres to my grandmother's house. My father drives me there in his truck and we usually stop halfway at his brother's house. My aunt does not welcome my father although she is kind to me. She worries that Gheorghe will have a bad influence on her husband. Sometimes my uncle turns up at our house with another woman and my father orders my mother to treat her like a sister-in-law. I can see that my mother doesn't like this, but she pretends she does just to please my father.

On our journeys to Mama Draga's house, my father and I stop at an ancient monastery by a mountain on the River Oltu. The gardens are well tended with plants bordering the paths. The monks have long beards, stern eyes and hold their backs very straight in their immaculate robes. I am deeply touched by their presence. It brings tears to my eyes. Everything looks too perfect to be true.

I had considered becoming a nun but gradually realised how isolating convent life is. You have to live far away in the mountains where life is hard. In our atheist country the nuns and monks are virtual outcasts who can barely feed themselves. Some people respect them for their strength and faith, while others believe the official government line that they are mad.

As soon as we arrive at Mama Draga's, I leap from the truck and run towards her house. It always seems so long since I've seen her. She appears in the doorway and doesn't speak, just wraps her thin arms around me.

'Wave to your father,' my grandmother says softly and we turn and raise our arms. There's still no love lost between Mama Draga and my Tata but I see by watching them that silence is a gift one can practise when there is no love. Saying nothing is dignified. I know my father wants me to be here and I know Mama Draga is grateful to him for bringing me. I am the most important person between them and they do not want to hurt me by hurting one another.

Soon my father is gone in a cloud of dust and three long happy months stretch before me.

I unpack my bag and hang my clothes in Auntie Ana's wardrobe. After a while, I hear my grandmother gently asking her to turn down the songs on her radio.

'Ana, I can't stand it any longer,' begs my grandmother, humour in her voice. 'Lenuta and I need to sleep.'

Ana sighs deeply and flicks off the radio. I kiss them both goodnight.

'Lenuta! It's not the same when you're not here,' Ana says, hugging me. My grandmother does the same. I have missed the peace and quiet of their house and the love that comes, not only in words, but in a soft cloud that envelops me.

I lie in bed next to Auntie Ana. I can smell the night cream she has rubbed onto her face. It's called Farmacia. It is expensive and must be prepared by the pharmacist. I snuggle close to her underarm and inhale her scent over and over again as I fall asleep. It fills me up and becomes part of me. I wonder if this is what the bond between a child and a mother feels like?

This is something only Auntie Ana can give me. I feel such love from her, love I never receive from my mother.

Every day I go to the river and lie in the sun on the grassy bank. Sometimes I wade into the water up to my knees. I also go to the market each day with my auntie. It's too far for Mama Draga with her hurt leg.

Some nights Auntie Ana takes me to a movie, often an Indian one. They're cheap and the Communist government likes the fact that they're not full of western propaganda. I lean against Ana and watch the love stories and the crazy dances without understanding much of what I see. I think none of us does.

Mama Draga likes it when I cook for her, food from the south, dishes from Oltenia. She doesn't like to admit it but I know she thinks my father's people eat well.

I cook mainly vegetable dishes prepared in earthenware

pots. Oltenia is famous for its leek dishes: leek soup or leek with olives. Sometimes leeks are eaten raw, sliced and added to salads, or sprinkled fresh on cooked dishes so they don't lose their aroma. Stinging nettles are cooked too, and sorrel and green onion. Soups are made sour with cabbage and tomato juice. Dishes are spiced with horseradish and chilli pepper. At Christmas, people in Oltenia eat steak cooked in fat, jellied meat, and thick sausages, and at Easter the delicious pasca, a sweet pastry made with cream cheese.

I make a vegetable stew and beef rissoles for Mama Draga and my aunties. We sit together, enjoying our meal. Here in Cluj, the influence of the Romanian Communists barely reaches us. The Hungarian way of life remains strong. Communism is still weak in Transylvania.

'I don't mind the Communists,' I sometimes hear Mama Draga say to Auntie Ana. 'Why would I? They give me a pension. They let me go to the hospital whenever I want.'

Auntie Ana shrugs her shoulders and mutters to herself. I like to try and follow their conversations, since my own parents never talk about such things. My mother would be too scared even to give an opinion.

The wonderful summer passes too quickly.

11

Outsiders

When I come home to Bucharest, my mother welcomes me with my favourite bread and jam. I feel alone. We live in Ferentari on the outskirts of the city. Nearby, the gypsies have set up their camp. After school I sneak out and run to see what they're doing. The gypsy children remember me from last year because I was the only Romanian child who would play with them. The others stay away because it's believed the gypsies steal children. Parents warn that if we go to the gypsy camp we will never come home. That seems fine to me.

In Cluj the gypsies are known as Gabor and have blue eyes and fair skin. Mama Draga shoos them away when they come around begging, children in tow, offering to tell her fortune. She calls them thieves and liars. The gypsies just laugh. Later I understand that they have been badly treated for so long that they simply shrug off insults.

The gypsies in Bucharest are called Ursari and are much darker. My skin has always been dark so I warm to them. They arrive in early spring, travelling in groups in canvas-roofed caravans that are pulled by two horses. The children run ahead shouting, 'Dirty bottles! Bring out your dirty bottles!' When

I hear these cries I feel as joyful as I do when I go to see my grandmother.

The dirty bottles the children call for were used for sunflower oil, thick, pungent and yellowish-brown. The gypsies clean them to sell. They wash the bottles in a big barrel of caustic soda and rinse them with clean water in another barrel. I love the sight of the bottles sparkling in the sunshine as they dry.

I also admire the gypsies' clothes which smell of old oil. The women wear traditional dress with full skirts in bright reds and oranges. Their arms jangle with bangles and they wind beads around their heads and necks.

I play with the children while the adults wash the bottles. I feel free since no one is keeping an eye on me. Then the men make a fire and the women prepare dinner. They heat up two pots, one with mamaliga. In the other they fry fatty pork with garlic. When the meal is ready everyone sits down together. The men sing about their love for the women and children, clapping their hands in time to the tune. Their soulful songs make me cry.

After dinner we play games. We gather around the big puddle that has formed in the middle of the camp during recent rain. Laughing together, we roll little mud balls in our hands and then spit inside them, covering this up with more mud. We stand back and shout and point and throw our mud balls to the ground. If they burst and make a noise, you win the game.

When we're tired of that, we jump into the big puddle and splash about like pigs in mud. I've never had so much fun in all my life. There's mud on my face and in my hair, in my ears and all over my arms and legs. We jump and jostle and splash.

I am having such a good time that I don't realise how late it has become. Suddenly I look up and see a woman approaching. Oh God, my mother!

She has obviously searched the neighbourhood and eliminated all the other places I might have gone. I decide that if I continue jumping in the mud she won't be able to tell me from the others. I am as short and dark as they are and we are all covered in mud.

She stands close to the puddle. 'Lenuta. Lenuta!'

I pretend not to hear her. I want to delay my punishment for as long as I can. Then some of the children say, 'That lady is calling you. Is she your mother?' Who else could she be, blue-eyed and blonde? Finally, I admit that she is and give myself up.

She pulls me out of the mud by my long hair and makes me walk home in front of her. When we get there she starts screaming. 'I've told you never to play with the gypsies!'

The next morning my scalp is itchy and I begin to scratch. My mother checks my hair and finds lice. She slaps me. 'Promise me now that you'll never, ever play with the gypsies again.'

I don't promise. I just let her continue slapping me.

12

Pain

My parents argue all the time about my father's affairs which he does little to conceal.

'Are you perfect?' he demands of my mother. 'Well—are you?'

As usual with their arguments, I am their audience. They do nothing to hide it all from me. Angry, my father takes jars of food and throws them out the window. I cringe at the sound of shattering glass. He never hurts my mother physically but he abuses her emotionally.

Always, whatever the argument, he repeats the dreadful mantra, 'What do you want me to say...that I married you because of Lenuta?' Every time I hear these words coming from my father, guilt and sadness fill me. His words seem to press down on me like the current that forced me to the bottom of the river.

I remind myself I am in Bucharest, not Cluj. I am not drowning. I go outside to be on my own.

One day they begin arguing while I stand in the kitchen between them. My father picks up a glass soda siphon and I hear it smashing to the floor, the noise exploding in my ears. Glass shards shoot up. One spears my leg.

'Mama?' I cry. 'Tata?'

I feel warm blood but even then my mother does not stop screaming at my father. I hold my breath fearing what might come next. I have to get help. I hobble outside and down the street, a hundred long metres, to the house of Florica, our neighbour.

She is friendly and warm, open and happy. I feel comfortable in her house and often go there. When I am with her, I wish I lived there. Her house is new and beautifully furnished so that she is the envy of the whole rough Ferentari area. Her husband works for the military secret service. He adores her and neighbours say he even helps her with the housework.

Florica's dark eyes smile in a way my mother's don't. This day she sees me coming, notices the blood, and opens her arms to me.

'Lenuta, what happened?' she asks. I can't speak. She rushes to her kitchen to fetch an enamel bowl and then to her bedroom to get an old sheet. She sits in a chair opposite me and I stretch out my leg and rest it on her knee.

She asks me to close my eyes while she pulls the shard of glass out of my leg. I pretend to close my eyes. I want to see what she does. I'm not scared. I feel safe in Florica's house, almost as safe as in Mama Draga's.

She grips the shard, squinting, almost closing her own eyes. Then in one quick movement she pulls it out.

'Oh God, what a big piece of glass!' she exclaims. It leaves behind a hole which becomes a scar I carry all my life. A reminder of my childhood. One among many.

Florica bends down and looks me in the eye. 'You don't belong in your family, do you?' she says. 'You're so different. I can't understand it at all.'

I realise how much I miss Mama Draga and Auntie Ana

as I sit on Florica's sofa and wait and wait. No one comes for me even though they must have seen my blood on the floor. Eventually when darkness starts to fall, I worry I'll be late for my curfew. I limp back home alone in the dark.

As I walk in the door, I see that no one has missed me.

Life is tough for everyone in Ferentari. Down the road from where we live, a man hangs himself. Before they can cut him down, word is out and all the children in the neighbourhood run to have a look. I see him hanging from a beam in the shed behind his house. His tongue is sticking out, all blue and dark. It scares me so much that for days I cannot sleep.

A few months later, a woman in our neighbourhood does the same thing. There is only so much love to go around.

We don't talk about it in my family. In our neighbourhood, people are happy enough to build a house from mud and straw or mud bricks, and that the government has given them jobs and looks after them if they become ill. Nobody dreams very much.

One day my father storms out to his truck. He has a big delivery to make in Oradea. As he slams the garden gate behind him, I hear my mother call out to him, 'I'm going to kill myself tonight. I'm going to poison myself.'

I'm sure he has heard, but he doesn't react. Perhaps he doesn't believe her. Perhaps he doesn't care.

When my mother threatens to kill herself, I understand what that means. After all, I have seen the man with the blue tongue. I stay close to her all day, not touching her but always watching. She does her work as usual but all the time she is crying and muttering to herself, 'That's it! Tonight I'm going to poison myself. I'm going to drink Verde de Paris.'

Verde de Paris is thick and green as a swamp. It's an insecticide and we kill rats with it, putting it on bread and then leaving it around the garden or outside the toilet. I know exactly where the bottle stands in our shed. I wonder if I should run and hide it. But then she'll be angry with me, so I do nothing. I vow to stay awake and, if my mother tries anything, I'll plead with her and pull her back to us from the brink of death.

That night, when she puts Gheorghe, Cornelia and me to bed, she is still lost in her own thoughts. 'Goodnight, Mama,' I say. 'Will you go to bed soon?'

She nods. I am very afraid. I try to stay awake, but after a long time waiting, my eyelids will not stop closing. Every time I hear a movement, I sit up straight and listen, trying to work out if it is my mother going outside. Eventually I fall asleep.

I wake to the sound of the back door creaking. I hear my mother's footsteps. I run to the window and peer out from behind the lace curtain. If I follow her, I will get in trouble. I should be in bed. The evening air is chilly and in the garden I can see the stalks of dead sunflowers shaking like skeletons in the darkness. Her steps are leading her to the outside toilet. She goes inside. I wait. Then she comes out, returns to the house and goes to bed.

I close my weary eyes. I listen to my heartbeat. It's midnight. My mother is still alive.

13

Good Student

My parents labour through the years and somehow stay together. Occasionally they go away for a week or more at a time, visiting his relatives or hers. They know that I can cope alone with my siblings. Everyone in the neighbourhood says how capable and efficient I am, old beyond my early teenage years.

I enjoy the peace of my parents' absence. They can go away as much as they like! I wake up every morning full of energy and optimism. I take Cornelia to kindergarten and then lead Gheorghe on to our school, where I take him to his classroom before going to mine. After school I bring them home. I cook and wash. I do my homework and put us all to bed.

When my parents return, they never ask me how things went.

My childhood has periods of blackness, periods when the days creep past and nothing happens that I want to remember. I am just surviving, avoiding punishment, and seeking joy where I can. School is my release. Because I excel at my lessons, it is the only place I can be proud of who I am.

At the end of primary school, students must sit the entrance exam for high school. Each school has its own exam. In the best schools, wealthy students are tutored privately for years in order to pass. I have already worked out that my future freedom depends on learning as much as I can. The high school I am aiming for is called Mihai Eminescu, after one of Romania's greatest poets. It's a privileged school and the parents of the children who go there are doctors, lawyers, judges and architects. I study and study in order to be admitted.

On my first attempt, I fail. My mother and father try to persuade me to go to our local high school—but I refuse. I stay home and study some more. All that year I study alone, day and night. This time when I take the exams, I'm successful.

It is September 1969 and I am almost sixteen. Mihai Eminescu is a long way from our house and I must walk for forty-five minutes, rain or shine, to the tram that will take me there.

I had thought that passing the entrance exam and keeping up with my studies would be the hardest thing I ever achieved. But it's nothing compared with enduring the teasing and taunts of my classmates. When they find out that my father is a truck driver and that I live in Ferentari, my life is not worth living. No one will be my friend. No one even wants to sit beside me in class. My only friend is a tiny girl with glasses thicker than any I've ever seen.

My heart is sad. I can't bring myself to study and soon I decide to return to my local school. My friend is sad to see me go and tries to persuade me to stay. For the moment, I know I have to go back to where I came from.

My local high school is called George Calinescu. My plan is to study here for three years and then go to university in Cluj, escaping Bucharest forever. I do well and my confidence grows. Here it doesn't matter that our family has no money, my father is a truck driver or my mother never embraces me with love.

My only true friend at school is Petronella. She is tall and intelligent and has the longest legs I've ever seen. Since she dislikes schoolwork and gets bored easily, she often asks for my notes. I also do her assignments for her. When we have exams, I spend the night studying while Petronella writes the answers on her thighs using tiny letters. She can store a lot of information that way because of her long legs. During exams, she makes me sit where I will block the teacher's view of her lifting her dress and looking down at her notes.

Although she's my friend and honesty is important to me, I pretend I don't see her cheating. I'm terrified she will get caught, but she never does. And she always passes the exams.

Boys stare at my hair which is long and dark and glossy. My face is round and they admire my olive skin and hazel eyes. My clothes are simple but I take care of them. People stare at me when I pass and I know they say I'm one of the most beautiful girls they've seen. I walk proudly until I enter the gate of my house and my confidence falls away.

'Come to my place,' one of the boys in my class says. 'We're having a tea party.'

Tea parties have nothing to do with tea or cake. There is food and soft drinks and music. For most of us, the music is the biggest attraction. The government doesn't allow much western culture to penetrate Romania, limiting radio and television broadcasts, which somehow trickle in anyway. The Beatles is one of our favourite bands. The more foreign music that can be played at a tea party, the more we enjoy it.

Our neighbour Florica has a son, Nicu, who often holds parties at their house. I never have to ask permission from my parents to go there because Florica's house is my second home in Bucharest. Nicu is talented at creating and repairing anything to do with electricity. For his tea party the room is strung with coloured bulbs to make it look like the discos we've only seen in movies.

Tea parties usually start at six o'clock and go on until ten. I'm invited to a party by a boy at school. I want to go but am told I must be home by eight at the latest, even though in summer the sun doesn't set until late. The boy says he will visit me at home and talk to my mother.

'She isn't allowed to go to parties,' my mother tells him. But the boy keeps begging her. Over and over again, my mother gives him the same answer. 'No. She is not allowed.'

My mother is obeying my father's rules. Beautiful girls are thought of as less intelligent and more likely to be led astray. It is easy for parents to marry off an attractive daughter. The risk is that she might fall prey to a devious suitor and lose her virginity before she meets the man she will marry. I must be kept away from any situation that may endanger my virginity. I have heard my father say that tea parties are where girls lose it.

For people from Oltenia, tradition is sacred and is based on customs that have endured for generations. To Oltenians, a bride's purity is essential. Ever since childhood my father has impressed upon me that I must still be a virgin when I marry. 'If you lose your virginity before you marry, I will cut your flesh and put salt on it,' he tells me.

I believe him. Violence is never far away from our lives. A strong man was killed in his own house not far from ours, in front of his wife and child, by members of a gang. When we woke, there were knives abandoned in the street and a pool of blood in their doorway.

My father plans a traditional wedding for me: the wedding

he never had. The morning after the first night, he wants the elders to show everyone the bloodstain on my nightdress.

My father is so obsessed with my purity that when I am seventeen he sues one of the boys in our neighbourhood for defamation. This boy has called me a whore because I refuse to talk to him. To prove he was slandering me, I am taken to a gynaecologist to obtain a virginity certificate, quite a common practice in Romania at the time. The boy is sentenced to a year in prison which he is spared only after his parents approach my father to apologise for their son's behaviour and beg for forgiveness.

14

A Woman's Duty

I t is a woman's duty to raise children for her country,' we are told by Elena Ceausescu, the President's wife and chair of the National Women's Council. Our ruling family wants more Romanian babies so they can create a new generation whom they can mould. Women should have at least four children, they say. If mothers can't look after them all, the children can be placed in a state-run orphanage and brought up with the state and the President as their 'parents'. Deprived of love and often hungry, they will be conditioned to be obedient. They will wake up praising Ceausescu and in the evening they will fall asleep praising him. It is from such children that the President's armies and the secret police of the Securitate will be recruited.

Contraception is banned and so abortion has become the only form of birth control. In 1966 abortions were criminalised but they persist as illegal, often dangerous, procedures. If these abortions are discovered by the authorities, the women can be sent to prison. Some women prefer to take their own lives first.

Agents of the Securitate keep an eye on women in gynaecological wards and it's their duty to report any who request abortions. If a woman or her family offer a bribe, sometimes the police will look the other way.

Over the years this policy of increasing the number of births in fact leads to the deaths of thousands of women and the creation of many orphans.

I hear constant talk about all this, but my worries are different. I wait and wait but my period never comes. Around me at school all the girls are whispering self-importantly and comparing their suffering.

My mother decides to take me to the doctor to find out why I'm different from my friends. The waiting room is crowded with older women. Blood tests are done and we are asked to come back for the results. I wait anxiously to find out what's wrong with me.

The doctor is in his mid-fifties and wears a long white coat. As he starts reading my results I watch his eyes through his thick glasses. 'Polycystic Ovary Syndrome,' he says, looking straight into my own eyes. He reads aloud: 'PCOS is one of the most common female endocrine disorders. Both genes and the environment contribute to it.'

With growing horror I learn that it affects the reproductive, endocrine and metabolic functions of the body. It produces menstrual disorders and infertility, interferes with ovulation and causes acne and excess hair. It can affect the insulin production often associated with obesity and Type 2 diabetes.

He pauses and says gently, 'You may never have children.'

I feel as if a knife has stabbed my heart. Terrible pain strikes me dumb. Surely my life will not be worth living?

I stammer, 'What do you…mean?'

'You may never have children,' he repeats in a louder voice.

I start sobbing. As we leave the surgery, my mother takes my hand.

All the way back home neither of us speaks. My mother never really wanted children and my birth was never planned. She must know, deep in her heart, that she was born to be a wife rather than a mother.

I know that I want children. Surely this dream can't be cruelly snatched away from me?

To comfort myself I repeat over and over what the monk predicted just a few months ago, that I will have many children. Please God, let him be right!

I keep turning over in my mind the symptoms the doctor noted. It's true that since I was twelve I have battled with my weight. In Cluj during the summer holiday of my sixteenth year, I followed a strict diet, taking a few spoonfuls of apple cider vinegar every morning on an empty stomach, followed by a glass of boiling water. I shed many kilos but the diet left me with an acid reflux condition from which I still suffer.

And what about excess hair? On a tram a boy says to me, 'You'd be more beautiful if you didn't have a moustache!' I feel like crying but my pride won't let me.

After we return from the surgery I tell my mother that I need to see my friend Petronella. I know she will understand my pain. She will hold me and tell me that the tests are wrong. Perhaps they are not my results? Her mother is the head of nursing in a hospital. I hope she will tell me that mistakes are often made.

I walk into Petronella's room sobbing. 'What's wrong? What's wrong?' she asks.

When I tell her, she says I shouldn't worry. 'You may never have children—but I'm sure you'll have a happy marriage.'

'I want children,' I sob.

The pain wraps itself round my heart.

15

No Brother

By February 1973 there are only four months until I finish school. Before my father leaves on another trip in his truck, he takes me aside to talk.

'Look after your mother. She's not feeling well.'

This is not welcome news. I'm studying as hard as I can to pass the entrance exams to the university in Cluj. My father pays for my private tutoring. University is my only hope of escaping Ferentari.

Late that evening while I'm studying in my room, my reading is suddenly interrupted by my mother's voice, sobbing and cursing. She's clearly in pain. I rush to her bedroom. 'What's the matter?'

'Look under the bed-clothes.' There, in a pool of blood, lies a tiny foetus. I know she has just aborted what would have been a baby boy.

Among our neighbours there have been many similar episodes. The local midwife charges 500 lei, the average monthly wage. She puts a tube into the uterus and with a syringe injects alcohol and water, or soap and water mixed with geranium leaves. Later the woman aborts in agony.

The midwife earns an ordinary wage from her job at the

hospital, yet she lives in one of the finest houses in the district. Everyone knows where the money comes from, although this is supposed to be secret. If she avoids prison it is probably because policemen's wives need abortions too.

I pull the sheets right back and look at the baby. It has hands, feet, legs. It is fully formed and its skin glistens with blood. The tiny boy is dead. 'What do you want me to do?' I ask my mother.

'Put it down the toilet.'

I cannot do what my mother asks. I cannot throw a baby into that stinking cesspit. I pick him up, wrap him in newspaper and go out to the garden, not even stopping to put on a coat.

I am holding a human being, a small creature about eight inches long—and he terrifies me. The foetus looks more like an alien than a human. His head is huge compared with the rest of his body. His eyes are closed but his face is a perfect miniature. He has obviously been dead for a while and his skin already has the bluish-black colour of dead flesh.

I have never held any dead creature, and here is my dead brother. I shake with cold and fear, my heart racing, my mouth dry. The wind whips around my head and legs as whirling snowflakes choke my mouth and blind my eyes.

I set down the little body wrapped in its paper shroud. My feet are cold since I am barefoot and I shiver. In the dark I look for a spade in the shed. I can hear rats scuttling.

I find the spade and hold it firmly. Thrusting it at the hard ground, I manage to dig a shallow grave in the shelter of the outside toilet. This is where I lay my brother to rest. I cover him over with the earth I have dug. By morning the snow will have covered the tiny grave and no one will ever know what has happened.

But perhaps someone already suspects? I pray that my mother will not be arrested. When I re-enter her room she's still groaning in pain.

'Shall I call the ambulance?'

She looks up wildly. 'No—no, you can't do that.'

'Shall I get Angela?' Angela is a neighbour from two houses along.

'Don't you dare!'

She screams and sobs and moans all through the night. I can't sleep either. In the morning I find her semi-conscious. She mumbles something.

'Do you want any food? Water?'

She shakes her head and waves her hand. I understand she wants all of us to go to school. I dress and feed my brother and sister and we leave.

Usually after school I stay back in the library to study, but that afternoon I hurry home. I've been worrying about my mother all day. When I arrive, she isn't in her room although the bed is a bloody mess.

I run to Angela's. 'Thank God,' she says. 'I had to call the ambulance because I was afraid your mother was going to die. She's at Brancovenesc Hospital.'

I gaze at her in horror. 'Don't worry,' she says. 'I went with her and we were lucky. We were seen by a very kind black doctor, Dr Victor. He could see how urgent it was, how close to dying she was, so he admitted her straightaway without any confession. He did a D & C on her. If he hadn't, she would have got septicaemia and died.'

Once a patient is diagnosed with septicaemia, the hospital staff make her confess to having induced an abortion. If she doesn't tell them what happened, treatment is supposed to be withheld. That means she dies. After a 'confession', women are picked up from the hospital and taken to prison.

I am amazed that my mother has managed to negotiate all this without being punished.

'I'm going to the hospital now,' I say to Angela. 'Can you please lend me money for the tram?'

'There's no point. You can only visit on Thursdays and Sundays between two and four. It's Tuesday—so they won't let you in.'

'I don't care. I'm going. I'll get in to see my mother somehow.'

She lends me some money and I set off in the middle of a snowstorm. On my head I wear my Russian squirrel-fur hat, but my fashionable black coat has a deep slit at the back which lets in the cold wind.

The main entrance to the hospital is closed to visitors so I go around to the side gate where there is an office.

'Can I help you?' the attendant asks as I approach.

'My mother is sick and my father is away. I'm the eldest child and I have to see her.'

'You'll have to wait until Thursday.'

'It's serious. I have to see her now.'

We argue for a while as I stand in the freezing wind. I refuse to be turned away. While we're talking I notice a dark man coming towards us across the hospital grounds. Instantly I somehow know that he is the doctor who has operated on my mother. There are other foreign doctors training at the hospital, but I have no doubt that this is Dr Victor.

As he approaches I feel a surge of relief. I'm sure he'll help me.

Dr Victor looks exhausted. His eyes are flecked with red. He is a solid, well-built man and the sleeves of his brown check coat are too short, with the buttons straining across his stomach.

I guess that he's at the end of his shift. The attendant jumps up from his chair as a sign of respect to the doctor.

'What's wrong? Can I help?' the doctor asks me.

I gaze right into his face. 'I hope you can. This morning my mother was brought to the hospital and you did a D & C on her. I must see her.'

'What's your mother's name?'

'Rosalia Nadolu.'

'How do you know I treated her?'

'Our neighbour brought her in. I have to see her. My father is away and she has no other relatives except me. She's alone.'

Dr Victor exchanges some quiet words with the attendant. Somehow he convinces him that mine is a special case and we walk together towards the hospital entrance. 'I'll take you to your mother's ward. But before that, we must go to my room. You need to put on a white coat and pretend you're a student doctor. Then we won't get into trouble.'

We go to his little room which has a bed for resting during his thirty-two-hour shifts. He takes a white coat from a hanger and puts it around my shoulders. As he does so, a jolt of electricity shoots through me, making me tremble from head to toe. Dr Victor hadn't touched me. He had just gently draped the coat around my shoulders, yet my reaction was intense.

My mother lies recovering in a ward, attached to an antibiotic drip. Dr Victor asks how she feels.

'Better, thank you, Doctor.' Her voice is sweet and low.

'The doctor very kindly let me in to see you,' I tell her. Beside me, I can sense his discomfort. He knows that my mother, like most other Romanians, appreciates what he does for them as a doctor, but sees a clear boundary between that and a social visit. His dark skin is the obstacle.

As he excuses himself before leaving, I turn and thank him. He has certainly saved my mother's life and deep in my heart I know that he has also saved her from prison.

When my father returns from his trip, he sends me back to the hospital with some money for Dr Victor. When I present it to him, he says, 'Please tell your father that I don't take tips.'

'He'll insist.'

'No thank you. I don't need it.'

I give him a very big smile instead. 'Thank you from both of us for saving my mother.'

'It's a pleasure,' he says, and gives me an equally big smile in return.

16

Victor

I now have a boyfriend. Doru is one of the country's top Roman wrestlers, with a fine physique, a square face, short blond hair and blue eyes. His job is with the secret police.

Every couple of months, when he isn't training or competing in a tournament, he picks me up in his car and takes me to the movies. We sit through the film without kissing or even holding hands. At 7.30pm, as instructed, he takes me back home.

I'm afraid that being in Doru's company is dull, dull, dull. His only topic of conversation is wrestling. At this stage of my life, however, I want to make my parents proud of me, so I go along with what appears an enviable relationship. Doru and his parents like me. We're not formally engaged, but my father expects that after I get my degree I'll make Doru a good traditional wife.

Everyone hopes this except me.

I am studying hard. It is May 1973, only a few weeks to my final high school Baccalaureate examination. One morning the classroom begins to spin before my eyes. The next thing I know I'm in hospital. A nurse leads me to the gynaecological examination room and tells me to undress. 'The doctor needs to have a look at you.'

I am alarmed. What exactly are they going to check? When the doctor comes in, I see the first female gynaecologist I have ever encountered.

'I'm a virgin,' I tell her nervously.

'Get up on the bed and we'll see how pure you are.'

Hot with embarrassment, I obey. She examines me. 'Right.' She says nothing more, but simply leaves the room. I can hear her saying outside, 'Dr Victor, if you haven't seen a virgin before, we have one here.'

A calm voice I recognise replies, 'No thank you. I don't need to see her.' Somehow I know he has remembered me.

The female doctor comes back in. 'Have you been playing around?'

'What do you mean?' I begin to cry. 'I've never been touched by a man. I don't know what you're talking about.'

'I'm going to admit you to hospital today,' she says. 'We'll do some more tests on you tomorrow.'

They tie a skimpy gown around me and put me in a bed near the entrance to the ward. I sob with fear, shame and humiliation. Another patient asks me what the matter is.

'That lady doctor. She's so horrible,' I answer.

'Oh don't worry about her. She's like that with everyone. You're actually lucky. This is Dr Victor's ward. He's one of the kindest doctors in the hospital.'

I say nothing but am pleased and relieved. Next morning I have some blood tests and later the doctors do their rounds. When he comes in, Dr Victor smiles at me but passes my bed and begins with a patient on the other side of the ward. I am the last to be examined. Finally he stands by my bed, holding my file against his chest.

'We've met before, haven't we?'

I nod.

'How is your mother?'

'She's very well, thank you. And thank you too for not intruding yesterday. I was so embarrassed.'

He tells me not to worry. 'We'll see what has to be done, from the tests.'

We start to chat. He tells me that he has been in Romania for eight years. He and some other students from his country, Ghana, have been awarded scholarships to study and train here with others from the rest of Africa and the Arab world.

'It's a wonderful opportunity—but life isn't easy for us here.' Each student is monitored by the Securitate, with special interest being taken in their friendships. For a Romanian to befriend a foreign student is risky. The Securitate's files are constantly updated by its network of spies and informers. The secret police are especially interested in Romanian citizens who become close to foreigners. They can expect to be watched, tailed, detained, questioned without warning and investigated. Many people fear being arrested or even vanishing forever.

This adds to the anxiety and fear for our lives. We know the secret police are above the law.

All the foreign students first study our language for a year. After that they attend university classes with Romanian students. I can hear that Dr Victor speaks Romanian very well.

'Are you at university?' he asks.

I shake my head and tell him I am still in high school. 'I hope to go on to do philosophy and law.'

'Here in Bucharest?'

'My father would like me to, but I want to go to Cluj, my

76

home town. My grandmother still lives there. Do you know it?'

I tell the doctor I want to go to university there so that I can fulfil my childhood dream of living with Mama Draga again. The last fifteen years with my parents have been very difficult, with only the prospect of my three months of summer holiday sustaining me for the rest of the time.

After we have chatted for a while, Dr Victor suggests that we sit outside in the corridor. He talks more about his home in Ghana and tells me about his work in Germany during his holidays. I am fascinated by his stories of these faraway places. He seems very knowledgeable and sophisticated.

We talk for a long time, two or three hours, until it's nearly time for dinner. Unless they are confined to bed, patients are expected to use the dining room. I sit down at a table with some other women from my ward. One of them turns to me and says, 'Be very careful.'

She means, with the doctor with whom I've just spent so much time chatting. I dismiss her words immediately. I was simply enjoying his company. Occasionally I think about the electric jolt I felt when Dr Victor put his white coat around my shoulders. That was completely new to me. But now, I tell myself, I am just enjoying some interesting conversation. I feel a connection with him and he makes me feel comfortable.

My test results confirm that I am not pregnant. 'You have a serious hormonal imbalance,' Dr Victor says. I say that I already know this. 'We need to perform a D & C—but there is, of course, the matter of your virginity.'

'Oh no! I don't think my father will agree to that,' I cry. My father's threat resonates in my head. I can almost feel the salt on my flesh. For a moment I go blank.

'Are you OK?' the doctor asks.

I reassure him, 'Yes, I'm OK.'

He asks my parents to come to the hospital so he can explain the seriousness of my condition and the necessity of the procedure. My father behaves exactly as I predicted. My virginity is sacred. Dr Victor is clearly astonished that a father would risk his child's health in order to maintain his family's reputation.

He suggests an alternative. He has a friend who works in Germany who might be able to send medication so that I can avoid having the procedure.

When the medicine arrives I am treated. Finally at the age of nineteen, I have my first period.

I am also discharged from hospital. With the discharge notice comes an invitation from Dr Victor. 'Would you like to see *The Sound of Music* with me?'

The following day I skip tutoring, my only free time outside school hours. Dr Victor is so exhausted after a double shift that he falls asleep and snores throughout the film. I try to wake him but he continues snoring. I hear laughter and bad jokes from the other members of the audience. 'Listen to that black man snore!' This is my first exposure to such casual racism. I feel sad for Dr Victor and am ashamed of the vulgarity and cruelty of my own people. This is also how they treat gypsies.

After the movie, Dr Victor, who now asks me to call him just Victor, suggests we meet again. He gives me his phone number and says I can ring whenever I like. I make no promises. It is only a few weeks to my exams and I am studying day and night on my own as well as with my tutors.

Victor and I meet a few times for walks in the park near the hospital before or after my tutoring sessions. He is practical, not romantic. There is no hand-holding or kissing. He never crosses the boundaries and I always feel safe. He's a friend, someone older I can trust. He listens to my dreams of becoming a lawyer and of having a perfect marriage based on respect and love.

Sometimes we sit on a bench under a big old tree. Victor is a good storyteller and he has a wonderful sense of humour. He tells me about the world outside Romania, the struggles of foreign students in my country, and the cruelty of our Communist state in its treatment of women.

There is a warmth about Victor. There is something in him that appeals to people. He's known for his big heart. He has a beautiful smile and a slow, relaxed manner. He's a bit taller than I am and on the chubby side. He has a little goatee that he likes to stroke. When he isn't stressed through overwork, he exudes compassion and love. His big laugh is infectious and his conversation is exhilarating. His stories are full of images of exotic people, places and experiences.

I think the fact that he is an obstetrician is attractive to most women. They can see that he really cares about his patients.

Victor went to boarding school in Accra, Ghana. He did well and then worked in an office there before applying for an overseas scholarship. He could have studied in Russia, Romania or Yugoslavia. He chose Romania. After learning Romanian and beginning his medical studies, he needed to spend summers in Germany working, since his parents sent him no money. He laboured on building sites or in the country, loading and unloading freight.

I'm amazed. I have never heard of a medical student earning money like this. We Romanians are supported by our families until we can earn a salary. I assumed that foreign students were looked after in the same way.

After he became a doctor, he tried to help a girl of sixteen who was brought to the hospital after an abortion. Her friends had inserted a tube into her uterus and injected pencil lead dissolved in water. Although the girl had septicaemia and was on the point of death, she refused to 'confess'.

Victor was the most junior of the three doctors on duty that day. Normally he was left to do the reports and would write that the abortion had been spontaneous. He would ask questions in such a way that neither he nor the patient could be incriminated. Unfortunately one of the other doctors was with him that time and began to ask the girl pointed questions about what had been done and by whom. Victor stopped him. It was clear that the girl would die without intervention; she was already turning blue. He wanted to dash to the sterilisation room to fetch the necessary equipment for surgery but for that he needed the approval of all three doctors. Victor had his signature and one other. He asked the third doctor to sign. He refused. The girl died.

Victor says he was sickened by such cruelty and injustice. He believes this is not something a doctor should inflict on anyone. He works to save a lot of women from death and prison. 'I hope I get the black doctor,' many women in trouble pray when they arrive at the hospital with complications caused by abortions.

I am amazed at the stories he tells me about the outside world, especially the western world. Raised in a Communist country and with an entirely Communist education, many things are beyond my understanding. I don't even know what happened in my own country before the Communist era. All that history has been wiped out. I know a few stories from my paternal grandmother about the land they used to own and the servants they once had, but everything else is a mystery.

'You Communists, you don't know anything about the rest of the world!' Victor likes to exclaim.

Of course he's right.

'You bring people like me here from Africa, but sometimes you don't know how to treat us.'

Right again. There are many people like my mother who are frightened of foreigners, even if they don't know why. Life for students with dark skin in Romania means that every day they face racism. Most Romanians have little contact with foreign students lest the Securitate think they might be involved in anti-Communist activity.

'I'm certainly grateful for the opportunity to study here,' Victor tells me. 'Most of the time. Outside the hospital, I ran into another woman whose life I saved. She saw me and for a moment her face lit up. But then she crossed to the other side of the road without speaking. I followed her across and greeted her. Do you know what she said to me? "Sorry, Doctor—you know I'm not supposed to talk to you because you're black." Inside the hospital walls, I'm a good doctor. Outside, I'm only black.'

I feel sad for him but also respect the way he handles himself and retains his dignity.

When I come home, my mother is waiting for me, her hands on her hips. 'Tell me the truth,' she demands.

When I say nothing, she grabs a wooden spoon and hits me on the head and body.

'Promise me you won't see him again!'

She is afraid of my father finding out. He'll blame her if he does.

'Promise me! Promise me!' She hits me again.

Just as when she forbade me from seeing the gypsies, I promise nothing.

17

Bird in a Cage

Although I am almost twenty, I feel isolated like a bird in a cage. My father controls my life.

I arrange to meet Victor in a park near the hospital. I need to tell him that I must stop seeing him before my father finds out. I fear what he will do. My mother's blows were bad enough but my father will punish me much more. I will probably be locked up. I can't risk this since I need to work with my tutor to help me achieve the very best marks for my university entrance exam.

I have resolved that going to Cluj and studying at the university are at the top of my list of priorities. But something lingers within me, like smoke after fire: that strange charged feeling when Victor draped the white coat over my shoulders. I felt so alive! The harder I try to put it out of my mind, the more it overwhelms me. It's like the current in the river in Cluj that lifted me up and pulled me under again. I'm scared and I wonder if this time I really will drown.

No, I won't drown, I tell myself. *I can control my life*, I say over and over.

We meet. Victor looks deep into my eyes. So many women are attracted to him but I feel that I am the most special of all.

I tell him that I will not see him again. He nods silently and I walk away.

My intellect is the gift I treasure most. But it isn't the only one I possess. In a country that boasts of having the most beautiful women in Europe, I am considered a prize, with my fine-featured face, hazel eyes and long jet-black hair that turn heads on the streets of Bucharest. If I have one complaint, it is that my skin has the noticeably olive tint from the Mediterranean side of my father's lineage.

I treasure my good brain more than my beauty. I realised very early that my intelligence was going to be the key to a better life for me, better than my parents have, especially my mother. Romanian women are only good for childbearing, cooking, washing and cleaning. That is a view ingrained in our culture. I want to rise so high above this Romanian prejudice, that I can see the horizon in any direction.

So I set out to make the most of my intellect. The result is that in 1973 I pass my high school exam with a mark of 9.33 out of 10. It is the highest mark achieved by any girl in my year. Oh, yes. I am proud of myself!

It is the night of my final-year ball. I'm wearing a low-cut, tight black dress. There is a yellow choker around my neck and my hair is swept into a French roll. When I enter the hall, everyone turns to look, all the teachers and students.

There is a beauty prize and I win it. Everyone tells me how lovely I am: my black hair, my hazel eyes, my olive skin. But I'm not interested. All I want to do is prove my worth as an intelligent woman.

Next the train carries me to Cluj where I will sit my university entrance exam in the main building of Universitatea Babes-Bolyai. I love this building. I am drawn to it as one is drawn to old books and wise women who, over the years, have seen everything. The room is heavy with Hungarian history. Classes here were once given in the Hungarian language and I love the connection it has with a past I yearn to explore. Communism and leaders like Ceausescu have tried to reduce the Hungarian influence in our country but have not succeeded in erasing it.

The room where I sit the exam is like a stone cavern with high ceilings. Even though it's summer, I am cold inside these ancient walls. But they feel familiar and I have a sense of belonging. I am where I am meant to be.

On a beautiful crisp morning in September 1973 I arrive back in Bucharest by train to collect my clothes before moving to Cluj. My mother is waiting on the platform. She gives me a radiant smile. Her daughter has passed the university entrance exams. She tells me that when she was a girl she would stand in front of the big gates of Babes–Bolyai University, that huge enticing campus near Mama Draga's house, watching students coming and going. Now her daughter has earned a place there, the first in my grandmother's family to reach so far. My free education as well as my hard work have made this possible and I feel grateful to the government.

Everyone in the neighbourhood has heard my wonderful news. It is rare for a working-class girl like me from a poor area such as Ferentari to pass the university entrance examination. I am my family's pride and joy.

When I move to Cluj, I will miss my little sister. I have always looked out for Cornelia. I ran to fetch the midwife to help my mother deliver her safely. I led her to school, her hand in mine. We have shared a bed all these years. Cornelia loves to fall asleep holding me around the waist, her leg across my stomach. She insists on this. At night she needs my comfort and warmth. All these years I have been her little mother.

She is still only fourteen but she is smart and much more streetwise than I was. 'Lenuta,' she says, 'some doctors from Brancovenesc came looking for you.'

'What doctors?'

'Romanian doctors.'

I conclude that Victor has sent some of his Romanian colleagues to my house to find out where I am.

Every day I wake up a little happier than the day before. Every day I move closer to the moment of release. One morning I wake feeling the sun's energy flooding into my room through the lace curtains. It spreads through my whole body, warming me physically and filling me with profound joy. I have a plan which will at last set me free. The past fifteen years in Bucharest have been hard and full of work and pain. But now I can glimpse the light at the end of the long tunnel through which I've been crawling. The way before me is clear. I know exactly where I'm heading. I can't wait to start university.

I get up, pull back the curtains and open the window. The fresh autumn scent is the strongest I've ever known. I inhale it deeply, letting it penetrate every part of my being. It fills me with tranquillity and leads to a trance-like state that later I come to associate with meditation. As I breathe in, a thought enters my head. I must ring Victor. It will be kinder to tell him in person that I'm leaving Bucharest and am unlikely ever to see him again. I know I can make that call. My turbulent past has given me strength, determination and resilience.

I set myself a deadline. I'll do it before lunch. I go to the nearest phone box and ring Victor at the hospital.

'Hellen! Where have you been?' Hellen is the name he has chosen to call me. I'm surprised to hear such happiness in his voice.

'Hellen!' His tone surprises me. It's as if he's found a long-lost friend. I understand immediately how strong his feelings are.

'Dr Victor, I wanted to tell you that I passed my final exams. Now I'll be moving to Cluj to go to university.'

He's silent for a moment, clearly surprised that my tone is so formal. 'Can I see you just once before you go? Maybe you could come to my house?'

'I don't know if I can get away.' Thoughts are rushing through my mind. Perhaps it will be all right to see him one more time.

I ask when he'll be home. 'Around six,' he tells me. 'Go and tell your little sister. Maybe she can come with you.'

Secretly, I ask Cornelia if she'd like to accompany me. She's a daredevil. She tells my parents that we're both going to the cinema and will be back right after the movie. She convinces my father and mother because she can look straight into their eyes and they never guess her true intentions. They are completely fooled. Little Cornelia can do no wrong.

We leave and I phone Victor again from the phone box. When he knows we're coming, there's relief in his voice—and delight. He gives me his address.

His home is in a large residential area built by the Communist government called Berceni. Victor throws open the door and greets us with a huge smile. Inside is the warm heavy smell of soup made from peanuts.

He has only just arrived home and hasn't changed out of his hospital clothes. 'You must be Cornelia,' he booms and my sister grins. She has never been as close as this to an African man. 'Would you like a Coke?' he asks her and her eyes move to the brown bottle as if it's something she's craved for years.

Victor's cramped one-bedroom apartment is brightly lit.

We sit on his little sofa and he turns on the television. From the kitchen, as he cooks, he calls out questions. He brings us an African meal, peanut soup with rice.

As we eat, I tell him about Cluj and how excited I am. 'It will be wonderful. I'll be living where I've always dreamed. I'll be studying so that I can have my own career.'

I look up into his eyes and feel, for a moment, the same tingle I felt when he draped his doctor's coat around my shoulders. I've been pushing my food around my plate, not really eating it. He finishes his own meal and sits back, hands folded on his stomach. As she sits between us, Cornelia stares at the television.

'Can I have another Coke?' she asks, without moving her eyes.

He brings her another bottle and a tin of peanuts. Such things are rare in Romania so my sister even stops looking at the screen for a moment in order to fully appreciate her luck.

'I want to talk to you,' Victor says to me quietly.

I get up and follow him into his bedroom.

There on the bed I am a tingling compliant body, nothing more.

I stare straight ahead, my mind blank. There is not a single conscious thought in my head. I seem to quiver with pure emotion. I don't look at Victor sitting beside me but his presence sends that electric current flowing through me.

As I sit there, a message that is trying to reach me from far, far away tells me that something is about to happen. I try to think, but nothing comes into my head.

On this September evening a few weeks before I turn twenty, the Universe has already plotted a very different path from the one I've mapped out for myself. Fate is about to intervene in my life.

It begins with a gentle hand caressing my shoulder. Fingers sweep aside my hair and begin to stroke my neck.

I only realise that I am no longer a virgin when I look down and see the blood. My vision is blurred. I feel pain and heat and the extraordinary closeness of another human being.

Victor did not force me, I tell myself. I chose.

18

Consequences

After it happens I know I've stepped through a door into another world, one where everything is utterly unfamiliar and where there is no future that I've planned.

I see my father's face. I hear him saying, 'If you lose your virginity before you marry, I will cut your flesh and put salt on it.'

Victor has known all along what this means for me. I have repeated my father's exact words to him. At the hospital he heard my father insist that I remain intact.

Only minutes ago Victor sat with me, listening to me talk excitedly about my future. He knows that without my virginity, I will forfeit my freedom.

Somehow, I walk out of his bedroom and join Cornelia who still sits in front of the television, eating peanuts and drinking Coke. I have no idea what to say to her.

What is relentlessly passing through my mind is that I have lost control of my own life.

'Cornelia, let's go.'

'No—it's too early. We don't have to leave yet.' She doesn't take her eyes from the screen.

'It's getting late. It's dark and past eight o'clock, our curfew. Mama and Tata will be waiting for us.'

I manage to convince her. Victor doesn't try to stop us. He must realise that I need to be alone.

All that night I lie awake, wondering how this has happened, worrying. I've only met Victor a few times. How can such a short-lived friendship turn my whole world upside down?

Then I remember the cherry tree. It died this spring. The words of the monk rush back to me. Is it fate or some greater force? Did the monk see deep inside me to my true nature?

At sunrise, I hear my father leave for work and finally I manage to get out of bed.

'There are black circles under your eyes,' my mother says as I sit uncomfortably on the edge of the chair and drink the tea she has prepared. 'Why are you sitting like that?'

I sit up straight in spite of the discomfort and don't answer her.

All day I remain in shock. I barely speak a word. I catch her watching me and when my father arrives home, she takes him aside and whispers. I'm in the garden when he comes to look for me.

'What's happened?' he asks.

'I don't know what you mean.'

Perhaps I'm not a convincing liar. Perhaps he can read it in my face.

My father's eyes narrow. 'Are you still a good girl, Lenuta?'

I nod though I don't feel I'm convincing him.

'Perhaps it's time to take you to a doctor at the polyclinic, just to check you're still a virgin. Your mother can take you tomorrow.'

I nod again. Issuing virginity certificates keeps doctors busy. At the breath of a rumour or hint of suspicion, parents rush their daughters to the clinic for a check-up. Certificates of virginity are then waved like prizes above 'good girls'' heads.

The sky is turning peach as the sun sets, but the beauty of nature is lost on me. I feel only panic and fear. As soon as I think I can, I tell my mother that I'm going to visit a friend. I ring Victor from the phone booth.

'Are you all right?' he asks.

'I'm scared to death,' I tell him about being taken to the clinic.

'Which clinic?'

I give him its name.

'Don't worry. The gynaecologist there is a colleague of mine. We were in final year at uni together. I'll have a word with her, Hellen. Everything will be fine.'

I breathe more easily. After I hang up, it occurs to me that he didn't say he's sorry.

When we arrive at the clinic, the gynaecologist calls me in alone, despite my mother's objections. 'If you wanted to see, why didn't you check her at home?' she says, shutting the door on my mother.

I burst into tears.

'This is a stupid process,' says the doctor, and hands me a certificate that is already completed. Her smile is gentle. 'Dr Victor rang me.'

I take the certificate gratefully. I cannot bear to meet her eyes. This is the end of it, I think, with huge relief. I'm safe.

My mother is satisfied with the certificate. My father is not convinced.

'I'll take her myself to another place. Tomorrow. A private clinic. It's always good to have a second opinion,' he tells my mother.

As soon as I can, I ring Victor again from a phone booth. 'My father is going to kill me when he finds out. He vowed he'd cut my flesh!' I cry.

Victor should be the target of my anger but now I feel helpless. I'm numb. I've lost everything, much more than my virginity.

'Just come to the hospital,' Victor tells me. 'Then you can live with me.'

I feel as if I am walking into a dark alley from which there will be no escape, no turning back. I imagine I begin to walk faster and soon I'm running. Things are flying past me, out of my grasp.

I hang up the phone and walk back home. Despite my growing fear, I'm not ready to run away. Not yet. I sit with my family and eat dinner, the five of us silently swallowing my mother's soup, breaking our bread and chewing it.

I need to find strength inside myself to bear this.

The following morning, I'm sick with anxiety as I stand with my father at the tram stop. We left early and there is an hour to spare before my appointment.

'Let's get something to eat,' he says. We walk into the restaurant and are taken to our table. 'What are you going to have?'

'I'm not hungry,' I say. 'I have a headache. Can you please give me money to buy some aspirin.'

For some reason, my father is feeling sociable and he seems to be enjoying my company. It's almost as if he's forgotten the purpose of our trip. He hands me money from his wallet.

'I'll wait here,' he says.

I hurry out the door in the direction of a pharmacy. I know, however, that soon a tram will be leaving for the hospital. I keep glancing behind me in case my father is following. By the time I pay the conductor, my tears are starting to fall. I never imagined that I would leave my family in such a way.

When I arrive at the hospital, Victor hugs me. 'Don't worry,' he says. 'We'll get married and everything will be all right.'

Is that what I want? I do not know. In the days since it happened, my life has changed completely.

I fall asleep in his hospital room.

Later that day, sitting with him on the sofa in his apartment, I hear what has happened with my family. 'I asked Dr Frank to come with me to see your parents,' Victor tells me, excitedly squeezing my hand. I nod, nervous about what will come next.

Dr Frank is Victor's close friend. He's Ghanaian too and arrived in Romania around the same time as Victor. Dr Frank specialises in sports medicine. Like Victor, he has a generous nature, but unlike Victor, he is slim. He drives a fancy sports car. Although he says he will only ever marry a Ghanaian girl, this doesn't stop him having lots of Romanian girlfriends. They are mainly blondes and he treats them to such luxurious gifts as Kent cigarettes, Colombian coffee, Lux soap and Fa deodorant. Romanian girls love such special presents.

'So we drove the Beetle to your house,' continues Victor. 'When we knocked at your gate, your mother came running out. I took her by surprise. "Where is Lenuta?" she kept saying. "She's fine," I said. But she fainted.' Victor chuckles to himself. 'Your father didn't know whether to go to her and revive her, or come out and shake his fist in my face. So in the end he just stood there, shouting, and it was left to me to go to your mother and help her up. The first thing she said when she opened her eyes was, "You, black man!" I said to her, "Yes, Mrs Nadolu, I am a black man. It's me, Dr Victor, and I've come to your rescue."'

Victor says that he and Dr Frank then helped her to bed.

'Your mother started shouting at me, saying that I had spoiled you, destroyed the family. I tried to defend myself but she just wouldn't listen. And in the meantime, your father had gone to Dr Frank's car, opened the rear engine compartment and was wrenching out all the wiring. Then he drove off in his truck to report me to the police.'

Victor tells me what happened at the police station.

'Your father yelled, "That man drugged my daughter so he could have sex with her!" Then the police asked, "How old is your daughter, Comrade Nadolu?" Your father told them, "Nineteen." And they said, "Then your daughter is an adult and free to do whatever she wants."'

Dr Frank and Victor investigated the damage my father did to the car, reconnected the wires and drove away.

By this point in the story, my head is in my hands. I don't want to hear any more. I can't imagine ever seeing my mother or father again.

Of course, lots of women would be happy to be me. Marriage to a foreigner has many rewards. For a start, it entitles you to a passport, the dream of many Romanians. Some girls who date foreigners are also informers for the Securitate, but others are so desperate to leave our Communist paradise that they aim to fall pregnant to make the men marry them. This tactic often fails and the children end up in orphanages along with the other unwanted Romanian boys and girls.

Others live with a foreigner while waiting for their marriage to be approved by the government. I realise I have now joined them. We are labelled sluts and whores, insults we will bear as long as we live in Romania.

I reflect that I never dreamed of leaving my country. A passport is not something I ever wanted. All I really want is to return to my hometown, Cluj, where my heart belongs, and study to pass my university exams. Now it's too late. If I leave Victor, I'll always be known as a woman who has been abandoned by a foreign man. I'll be abused by my father who will also call me a slut and a whore.

I see family and friends disappearing from my life. My friend Petronella, now dating an army officer, has already broken off with me.

'Lenuta, I know this will hurt you,' she says, crying down the phone, 'and it hurts me too. But I really can't see you any more.'

I tell her I understand. The Romanian government prohibits army officers having any contact with foreigners. Petronella and I have made our choices. It is these that now separate us.

Soon, Victor will be all I have.

19

Speaking to My Heart

Now my life has no purpose but housework. I cook, wash, iron and polish Victor's shoes. My sister comes to visit. She watches me polishing and the look on her face shows that this causes her pain. In her eyes, this is humiliating. She sees me paying a high price to become Dr Victor's wife.

I often dream about the life I had planned, studying at the university. I imagine myself among the carefree students pouring out of its big iron gates. I see my grandmother waiting for me on a bench. I imagine the rich smell of her delicious goulash. Then I wake from my daydream to the terrible reality.

'You should study medicine,' Victor tells me.

Maybe he's right. That would be a practical option, but I've never wanted to become a doctor. It isn't easy to go against your heart's desires. Philosophy and law were what I wanted to study.

I feel lost.

One morning I wake up beside Victor and examine his peacefully sleeping face. I ask myself, 'Is this the man with whom I'll spend the rest of my life?' A voice within me whispers, 'No.'

I feel drained. Will he leave me for another woman? I don't know.

The monk's predictions keep coming to my mind. He told me that the cherry tree would die. He said I would not complete my studies and that by the age of twenty-nine I would be left alone with many children. That I would travel across the seas. That I would reach the end of the world. I think back to the time just a year ago when the cherry tree died. I met a man in a doctor's uniform, it's true. Will all the rest follow? Being left alone is not an option; there are no divorces in our family. No—the monk can't be right. These are just coincidences, I tell myself. I leave the bedroom.

My father goes to see Victor at the hospital.

'Son-in-law!' he jokes.

When Victor comes home he tells me, 'They want to make peace. Your Uncle Mitru wants to talk to you.'

'Don't trust my father,' I say.

I respect my uncle. He has an open mind and a kind and gentle heart. His own marriage seems made in Heaven. He adjusted very well to city life after the Communist takeover, unlike so many others. Mitru and my father both come from the same family, comfortably off and well known. But how differently each of them has turned out! Mitru was fortunate; he was able to receive higher education just before the takeover. My father was denied education. The Communists didn't want children from wealthy families like his to succeed.

My father knows that I will agree to go and see Mitru. He is the hook to catch me. I'm scared but I agree to do it.

My father picks me up in a car. He has grown a beard. I remember when he returned to our house after having left his mistress: he wears the same mad look. My mother sits quietly in the back seat.

No sooner am I sitting beside him than my father starts calling me a whore and a slut. 'You have shamed our family!' He is weeping, pounding the steering wheel as he drives.

'Where are we going?' I ask, trying to stay calm. I turn around to my mother and see that there is a bag packed on the seat beside her.

'You are going to Cluj,' my father says. 'You are going to university.'

We arrive at the station.

I think of Victor's warmth and how he has looked after me. I don't know what I want any more.

My father buys two one-way tickets to Cluj and my mother and I board the train. He stands and watches us go so I would not jump out as the train begins to move.

As we travel, I cry the whole night while my mother sits beside me, upright and pale, keeping watch.

'Your father beat me because of you,' is all she says.

This time, arriving in Cluj doesn't bring me the usual peace and joy. My Auntie Ana looks at me sadly. 'How could you have slept in the same bed with a black man?' she asks.

Only Mama Draga hugs me.

I go to bed and hear them whispering together.

The next day they sit me at the table and introduce me to the local Catholic priest.

'He will drive away the evil spirits that have clouded your mind,' my grandmother tells me.

The priest is a handsome young man with blond hair and wide blue eyes. I smile to myself and wonder if this is part of Mama Draga's plan. But of course a Catholic priest cannot marry.

'Do you love this doctor in Bucharest?' the young priest asks me.

'Father, I think I do.'

How do I know? I have nothing with which to compare my feelings for Victor. Perhaps love is the jolt of electricity that passes through my body when Victor touches me. Perhaps it is how flattered I feel being wanted by a man so well respected and compassionate. Or perhaps I am just trying to convince myself that I am in love, so I can explain my situation.

And I am terrified of my father. He is capable of crushing me. I feel my world closing in.

The priest prays with me. Then he says, 'You should go to university and take your degree.'

He's right. But it's too late now. The university year has already started. I will have to wait another year.

'She should stay here,' my mother whispers down the phone to my father. 'She's fine away from him.'

But my father wants me home and so Rosalia does as she is told. We pack our bags and book the train for Bucharest.

'I'm coming home,' I tell Victor on the phone. I've been calling him whenever I have a chance to be on my own. Of course he loves to hear from me.

'I'm so happy, Hellen. You must come back to me.'

His words speak to my heart.

20

My Two Worlds

At Bucharest's central train station, my mother and I are met by my father. As he comes towards us, I catch sight of Victor's face in the distance behind him. Victor! He is half-hidden behind a stack of luggage, waving and smiling. I fight to keep a straight face. My father orders me to live at home, work in an office at his company and re-sit my university entrance exam next year.

In my parents' house, he continues to abuse me, calling me a slut who has brought shame on my family. 'You have disgraced yourself. You should be ashamed.'

What I feel continually is humiliation.

I lie in bed watching snowflakes falling from a white sky. The sight of them carries me back to the joyful Christmas Eves when I was a little girl singing carols in the streets with a white cotton bag around my neck to collect treats. That was such a simple time. I close my eyes and breathe deeply, remembering. Such innocent moments help me cope.

My childhood home is too small for me now. From the kitchen, I can hear my mother and a neighbour whispering about me. I enter the room and silence them with a stare.

'I'm hungry,' I say to my mother, 'but there's no bread.

Gheorghe's hungry too.'

My mother rises, hugging her arms across her body. I can see that she doesn't know how to respond.

'It's freezing outside,' says the neighbour. 'Don't go, Rosalia—not with your cough.'

'I'll go,' I say.

My mother looks at me suspiciously but in the end she gives me money and a bag for the bread. As I step outside, I'm wearing only slippers. I hang the bag with the money on the fence and walk away. It is a long way to the Brancovenesc Hospital and the ground is covered with snow. Instantly my slippers are soaking wet and I regret that I didn't change into boots. Now there is no turning back. I close the iron gate behind me and hope it is for the last time.

Back with Victor in Berceni we submit our marriage application to the Communist Party. The government must give its permission before we can do anything further. There is also another hurdle. My parents' signatures are required. They know they have that power over us. I hear that my father is telling anyone who dares ask, 'I would rather bring flowers to her grave than see her marry Victor.'

I feel sadness in my heart, for my father and for me as his daughter. The old ways are more sacred to him than the love a father should have for his child.

★

Victor loves cooking. 'I'll teach you how to make Ghanaian dishes,' he says. He makes deep-fried fish, soup, fufu and kenkey. In Ghana fufu is made from yam or cassava but in Romania these are not available so instead he uses potato flakes and cornstarch. Kenkey is fermented maize meal mixed with raw maize dough and rolled in corn husk.

I tell him that I'd love to learn Ghanaian cooking but that I still enjoy Romanian food.

I lean over to serve him before taking my own seat.

'Your top is too low,' he suddenly snaps. 'And your skirt is too short. One day they'll meet in the middle and you won't be wearing anything at all.'

'It's the fashion,' I say. I'm beginning to realise that I've escaped one web of rules only to find myself enmeshed in another.

Cornelia comes to visit. There is sadness in her eyes. 'Dad beat me for being here when it happened,' she tells me. Once again, I am the cause of violence in the family. I don't know what to say. Instead, I ask her about school.

There are days when I don't see Victor at all because he's working and studying for his specialisation in obstetrics and gynaecology. When he comes home at night, my sister watches the way he talks to me and how he criticises the food I have made him. She notices that he doesn't ask what I've been doing all day. I know she wants to speak up but she doesn't. Such helplessness infuriates her.

After she's gone, Victor asks why she keeps coming to see me. 'Because she's my sister. I love her. And because she wants to escape my parents too.'

21

Homecoming

I had thought it couldn't happen—but it has. I'm pregnant.

Victor greets the news with simple joy. For me it is different. When I find out, I'm overwhelmed with excitement. I know now that this is what I want more than anything. I want to be a mother. But I know my future with Victor is anything but certain. What if he abandons me?

'What's wrong?' he asks.

'Do you love me?'

My face, covered in tears, must be red and blotched. He looks at me as if I'm mad.

'Don't be like this, Hellen. What's wrong with you?'

His reaction makes me weep harder. I cry and cry.

For a man who has been close to so many female patients, who shows so much compassion for them, he seems not to see what I'm going through. I feel emotionally fragile, always on the verge of tears. Is it like this for all mothers-to-be? I don't know. This is all new to me. Why doesn't he say something?

I dream I'm buying flowers. The seller, a gypsy woman, has a stall in the street next to the hospital. She wraps up a bunch of pretty blue flowers for me. When I get home and unwrap them, I see that they are dead and rotten.

This is not a good dream. I trust the meaning of my dreams and this time I try my hardest to dismiss it.

Victor and his professor, Dr Onicescu, believe I will be safer in hospital under medication. I want a child so much that whatever is asked of me I will do. I pack my bag and Victor drives me to his hospital. Because he works there as a highly respected gynaecologist and obstetrician, I receive special treatment. I have my own room and can wear my own nightie and robe instead of the straight white hospital gown everyone else is wearing.

Victor helps me unpack and get settled. He kisses me goodbye and tells me that he will come every day. As he shuts the door behind him, I start crying again. Why did he say he would come each day to see me? He makes me sound like a patient on his hospital rounds, visiting me just another duty.

That afternoon Dr Onicescu comes to see me and tells me how he intends to treat me. I am to be given Gestanon, intended for pregnant women in cases where there is a threat to the health of both mother and child. Some foetuses, he says, give up in the first trimester, some in the second and others in the third and final one. This medication has to be administered carefully, since it has side-effects such as headache, insomnia, drowsiness and depression.

Drowsiness and depression quickly take hold of me. The only day I remember clearly is the first, when a nurse brings Valerian to help me sleep. It is the beginning of a long period of absence. For six months I lie in the hospital bed in a haze of Gestanon and Valerian. I wake only to eat and then fall immediately back to sleep. I barely move without feeling drowsy. It is like sleeping for six months.

'I think you're OK now,' Victor says at the end of this long blank time.

They take me off the medication and I pack my little bag and waddle out. I'm so relieved to see the blue sky above me, to feel the movement of air on my skin. I had become used to the heavy antiseptic hospital smell. I am grateful to be breathing fresh clear air again.

Our flat isn't as I left it. As I enter I'm overcome by a heavy stench of damp and cigarettes. Surely the windows haven't been opened since I left. The sofa is stained, the cushions are dirty and the carpet is grubby.

'Have your friends been here?' I ask Victor.

'Sure, some nights after work. We play cards, have a drink and listen to music,' he says.

I wonder how many women have slept in my bed. Already I don't trust Victor. But better to say nothing, I tell myself.

All afternoon I clean the flat while he sleeps off the effects of a double shift at the hospital. My feet ache. What I really want is to lie down with him and be held. For six months I have slept alone. I want him to wrap his arms around me.

When he does wake up, he stumbles to the kitchen and begins to cook okra stew and cut potatoes for the wedges for which he's famous.

'Some people are coming,' he says. 'Ghanaian friends. We'll eat and then play cards.'

I can't believe it. Already it's late. All I want is to spend my first night home alone with him. I begin to cry. I can't help it.

'Please, Victor, not tonight,' I plead.

'So now that you're home, I'm not allowed to ask my friends around?'

'Just not tonight.'

He's saved from answering by the arrival of Dr Frank and

some other Ghanaian friends accompanied by Romanian girls. When they see me, I am greeted with traditional hugs and looks of astonishment. It is as if these girls did not know that I existed. The attention doesn't last long. Soon they begin to eat from the mountain of food Victor has made. When they've finished, the pack of cards comes out and the games begin. Victor is in the thick of it, his booming voice mixing with their laughter.

They seem to know that I won't join them.

'I'm tired,' I tell Victor. 'I'm going to bed.'

He nods and turns to me for a moment. 'Are you OK?'

'Just tired,' I say, trying to smile.

But he has already returned to the game. He thinks I'm just seeking attention, but surely I'm justified in wanting his support? I want him to tell all these people to leave. I've been sedated in a hospital room for six months and all I want tonight is to be with him—just the two of us.

In the stale-smelling bedroom I cover myself with the pillow and the blanket and sob. Next door they go on drinking and betting and laughing. I feel hot and throw the blanket off. Sweat trickles down my back and breaks out on my brow. I feel pain in the lower part of my abdomen and wonder if it's the real food I've just eaten after so many hospital meals. Or perhaps I'm simply missing the drugs.

My head pounds. The noise in the next room seems to be mounting and mounting. Finally, my head spinning, I leave the bedroom and stumble towards Victor. He rarely drinks but tonight he has a whisky-and-ice beside him. His shirt buttons are undone and he's slapping cards on the table and talking loudly.

I see and hear it all as if through water or glass, at a distance.

'Could you please be quiet?' I try to ask, but I can't be sure that any sound has come out of my mouth.

Victor turns to me and his friends fall silent. His voice reaches me clearly although it sounds a million miles away.

'If you don't like it here, you can go back to the hospital.'

I say nothing. I feel as if I've been struck. I simply turn around and place one foot in front of the other to get back to the bedroom. As I lower myself onto the bed I wonder how on earth I got here.

And then I realise there's something wet and hot between my legs. I'm bleeding.

I am rushed to Brancovenesc Hospital. The same female doctor who called Victor in to ensure that I was a virgin is treating me now. She feels for the baby and her worried look makes my heart beat faster.

'The baby is on its way out,' she says to Victor. 'The legs are already engaged.'

She shakes her head and I know they won't save my baby now.

They take me to the delivery room. In my short life, I've known nothing worse than this pain. There is no peace between contractions. It's just one long, pointless agony. They leave me alone in a small dimly-lit room. No nurses come to check.

Victor goes to his room to lie down before his twenty-four-hour shift. I bear the suffering alone.

When I feel my baby emerging, I call a nurse. Suddenly the pain passes. The nurse walks around the bed and stands close to me. 'Have a look,' she says. She points to a metal trolley and tray with the tiny body of a baby boy on it.

I can't believe I have lost my baby.

'It weighs 900 grams,' the nurse says.

She walks away. For a long time, all I can do is stare numbly into space. Were the injections given to me meant to ease the physical pain of giving birth or my emotional pain? I don't know. This is my first time. The memory of the tiny body of the brother I buried flashes before my eyes. I am about to reach out and touch my own baby when the nurses come back and pick up the tray. I know what they will do with it; they will put it in the incinerator with all the other rubbish. Burial is not a concern of theirs. Neither am I.

I remember the monk's prediction: a dark girl. For a moment I feel comforted that it could mean I may have another baby one day, but then I begin to cry loudly. The grief of losing my baby is deeper than any I have ever experienced.

The nurse wakes Victor and he comes to me. He is also weeping. 'I'm so sorry, Hellen,' he says and I know that this time he means it.

After that, they sedate me again.

In the morning I wake and reach for my stomach. It's flat. The memory of my pregnancy tears my heart.

Victor is remorseful. When he takes me home, he leads me to the bedroom and tucks me in. He strokes my hair. 'Hellen, there will be other babies,' he whispers.

Cornelia comes to visit. She sits on my bed. We don't talk about it.

'How are Mama and Tata?' I ask. It's now widely known that they have disowned me for the dishonour I've brought them.

22

Humiliation

Our neighbour Florica comes to my home. She sits down with me, but I can see from her preoccupied look that it's not because of me that she's come.

'Lenuta, your mother is in Hospital Nine,' she tells me.

I've heard of this place. Mental illnesses are treated in that hospital.

'Come with me and visit her. It's not far. She wants to see you.'

My heart feels hard and closed towards my mother. Why should I visit her when she has turned her back on me?

'What's wrong with her?' I ask.

'She had a nervous breakdown,' Florica says. 'You know why. It's because of what you've done.'

I shrug and return to my cleaning. 'I didn't put her there; she put herself there. She brought it on herself.'

Florica knows better than to argue with me when I've made up my mind. I can see that she's disappointed in me. I haven't seen my parents for almost eighteen months.

Soon I'm pregnant again. I'm taken to hospital from time to time, but this pregnancy is different. I'm stronger and somehow I know my baby will survive.

Living with Victor makes me feel that I don't belong anywhere. I am set apart, different. Until I'm legally married, I cannot share Victor's privileges such as carrying foreign currency or shopping in stores designated for foreigners.

'You look beautiful,' Victor says to me one day over lunch at the Lido Hotel.

I feel beautiful. My hair is long and I am in a maternity dress that one of Victor's friends has brought me from England. It is navy blue and covered with tiny white-and-blue cornflowers. It's really meant for later in my pregnancy but I'm so excited to have it I wear it now.

Everything will be fine this time.

After lunch, Victor catches a taxi back to the hospital. As I walk towards the tram stop a man comes up behind me and grabs my arm. 'Come with me!' he orders.

This is how things happen in Romania. This is how people disappear.

I try to pull away but he flashes an ID card which shows that he is from the secret police.

'What have I done?' I ask, terrified.

I've heard of people disappearing and never being seen again. The more paranoid Ceausescu becomes, the more people vanish. There are spies and hidden microphones everywhere. It has reached the point of madness. Those who work as spies are recruited from the villages and trained by the government. They are often brainwashed. God help you if you fall into their hands.

I follow this man to a small office upstairs in the hotel I've just left. There are other men like him there, plainclothes agents.

'She's going out with a black man,' explains the man who arrested me.

They look me up and down with curiosity. 'Can't you find a handsome Romanian guy?' asks one. 'Look around—maybe you can find one in this room.'

I keep my mouth shut.

'Empty your handbag and your shopping bag,' says another man. His face is harsh, and I guess he is from rough peasant stock. He looks at me through his small dark eyes as if I'm a prostitute.

Among my things are some American dollars that Victor has given me. I know it's illegal for Romanians to carry foreign currency. They ask for my ID card but I don't have it with me.

'Are you working? Or a student?'

I answer that I'm neither. 'I'm pregnant and waiting for approval to marry and leave the country.'

'Hang on—so he hasn't even married you?'

'*His* name is Dr Victor. He works at the Brancovenesc Hospital. Everyone knows him,' I tell these ignorant men. They begin insulting me. I know it's useless to argue so I remain silent.

When they've had their fun, they take me down into the basement, a windowless dimly-lit room filled with about twenty women, young and old. If these men in charge are to be believed, these are the prostitutes of Bucharest. More particularly, they are women who go with foreign men and who have been picked up in hotels and restaurants just as I have.

I sit down among them and begin to cry. I wonder how Victor will find where I am. How on earth can I get out?

'I haven't seen you working,' says a woman when the men have gone.

'Where did they pick you up?' asks another.

'I was having lunch with my husband. I'm pregnant,'

I tell them. They believe me at once and regard me with compassion.

It's they who deserve sympathy, however. Some of them, I find, have been here for days and days. There are chairs but the floor is bare cement. There is one toilet in the corner and the air is foul. Every now and then one of the girls is taken out and questioned about the men she sees: who they are, how much money they carry, and who they work for.

I'm beginning to feel ill. I know I can't spend even one night down here. I rub my stomach with my hands, terrified that I could lose this baby too.

The next time a man comes to fetch one of the others, I approach him. He is older and seems kinder than the rest.

'I'm not a prostitute,' I say. I give Victor's name and place of work. 'He's one of the best doctors in Bucharest. We've already lost a child and we wouldn't want to lose another.'

Half an hour later, the man returns and rescues me. 'Don't mention to your husband what has happened,' he tells me. I am led out to the street. They don't return my American dollars or my handbag.

I walk slowly to the hospital. Victor is called. He looks worried.

'Where have you been? I've been ringing the flat.'

I can't pretend that nothing has happened. 'Just after you left me, they picked me up off the street,' I tell him. 'They locked me in a basement with prostitutes.'

'I don't believe it,' he says. 'How dare they?'

He sits me down and as soon as his work is finished, he takes me home.

The next morning we return to confront the men at the office where I was taken. The same ones are there but today they look at me blankly.

'Why did you arrest my wife? Why did you take her handbag?'

'We've never seen this woman before,' they tell Victor. 'Why would we take this lovely woman's bag? She's been telling you stories. Maybe you should keep a better eye on her.'

I know when we turn our backs they will laugh. I'm lucky Victor believes what I've told him. He holds my hand tightly as we leave.

23

Elsie

Faith is the bird that sings when the dawn is still dark.
Rabindranath Tagore

On 18 March 1976, my first real live baby is born. As I expected, she is a beautiful little girl. Her face is as small as my palm. Her eyes are just like her father's and her cheeks are chubby. She is pale and bald and beautiful. She is cuddly and curious. She is perfect.

I am beside myself with joy. Victor names her Elsie. This time he stays with me throughout my whole labour, pacing up and down, terrified that something will go wrong. At first Elsie struggles to breathe, her chest cavity working hard, her tiny throat contracting and expanding. They take her from me and put her in an incubator.

'Nothing to worry about,' Victor reassures me. 'It's just a precaution.'

Part of me doesn't believe him. I am sedated to help me rest, but I get up and walk, holding onto the walls, to the incubation room so that I can see her and know they're not lying to me. No one tries to stop me. They couldn't. This baby will survive, I tell myself when I see her. She is mine.

When I've watched her for as long as I need, watched that tiny life unfolding, I go back to bed. At peace.

My father comes to visit. For a moment, I think I'm dreaming. He stands by my bed and takes some small red apples from his coat pocket. He holds them out to me and then he walks away. I hold them up to my nose and smell their scent. I remember when I was a child that I would climb the fence to wait for him to come home from work, his pockets full of apples.

'I need my sleep,' Victor says when I bring Elsie home. He makes himself a bed on the sofa.

Elsie is colicky. I place her beside me in the bed so I can calm her cries and feed her when she needs it. She cries and cries, full of all the tears in the world. Finally I begin to understand what my poor mother went through. How fortunate she was to have Mama Draga, Auntie Ana and Auntie Ileana living in the same house with her. How comforting to have all those other pairs of arms to help rock and soothe me.

I think too of the cradle Mama Draga had for me and I wish I had one here for my Elsie. Instead, I lay my daughter on a pillow resting on my legs and rock her endlessly, the rhythm of mothers everywhere. As soon as I stop rocking, she begins to cry again.

Once I woke to hear Elsie crying louder than usual. I must have fallen asleep. To my horror, I find she has fallen to the floor. I'm terrified. I lift her up and hold her tight. Her tears stop. She looks up at me and smiles her gorgeous smile. She forgives me.

Nights become days and days become nights. I barely sleep. I love sitting up and breast-feeding Elsie; it fills me with so much happiness. I don't want to lose these precious quiet moments as I stroke her head while she feeds. But I'm worried I don't have enough milk. If only there were someone here, older and wiser, to advise me. I feel I have no one, no other woman who understands. It's just Elsie and me.

I feel myself sinking into a deep postnatal depression.

One evening, Victor arrives home from work and I start crying. I want him to listen to me and to empathise.

'Stop this nonsense,' he says.

So often I've heard him advising his patients' husbands, warning them of the signs and symptoms of postnatal depression. And here I am, suffering with it right before his eyes and he's refusing to hear and see me.

Elsie is all I have. I promise myself I will be there for her. I wished for children and that wish has been granted. I must be strong.

24

Black and White

Where there is anger, there is always pain underneath.
Eckhart Tolle

For me a party is a reminder of the lack of affection and respect I get from Victor. He loves loud music and dancing and enjoys flirting with Romanian girls. He treats me as if I barely exist. Most of the time I sit alone watching the others. I don't drink, I don't smoke and I don't dance.

Everyone knows who Victor is, what a great doctor he is. His kindness and compassion towards the women outside his own home is boundless. They adore him. What he gives to the outside world, he denies me. There's nothing left. I feel that I'm being punished, but I don't understand why. I'm doing everything I can to please him but it never seems enough. Part of me wants to run away to find myself again, my self-respect and pride, my happiness and joy, but I am bound to this relationship. I have a daughter now. I am a mother and I need to protect her. It's not about me any more. I take second place.

Victor is rarely around. He returns home for short periods to have a shower and something to eat before going to bed. We no longer sleep together. I know he must work long hours in the emergency department and study for his final exams, and that he needs his sleep. He spends his spare time with friends.

I don't miss sharing a bed with him. Elsie is enough. She is all I want, though now I am suffering something new.

'Where did you find this chocolate baby?' someone says in the street. On a tram, a man doesn't stand up to give us a seat, even though I am holding Elsie in my arms while the tram lurches along. 'She's slept with a black man. She doesn't need my seat,' he says to another passenger.

Anger and hurt rise inside me. How dare he! Who is he to judge me?

I decide that Romanians are hypocritical: nice to my face but critical behind my back. Of course, it's even worse for Victor. People are grateful to him for his professional skills and his kindness, but outside the hospital, most Romanians will have nothing to do with him.

These days, I need Victor more than he needs me. The less confident I feel, the stronger he seems to become. The balance of our relationship has shifted. I no longer seem interesting to him and I feel lonely and sad.

I am desperate. I wash his shirts and scrub every surface of our little flat. I try to keep Elsie quiet when he comes home so that she won't irritate him after another long day at work. I cook the food he wants. I wear the clothes he likes. Even so, all his friends and our neighbours continue to insist that he will leave me.

'I don't want to live in a white man's country,' he tells me. I nod, understanding better now.

'When I was a boy,' he says, 'I once played a game with other children where we folded a piece of paper as small as we could, and then hid it. I was such a smart boy I decided to hide it in my ear.' He grins. 'I pushed it in as deep as I could, but then it began to hurt. I told my father and when he looked into my ear he could just make out the tiny piece of paper deep inside. He took me to the doctor, a white man. The doctor sat me down and used an instrument to reach inside my ear. It took him a long time but finally he got the paper out. "You're a stupid boy," he said to me. Right there, in front of my own father, he slapped me.'

Victor's eyes are fierce with this memory of childhood humiliation. I know he thinks the doctor would never have dared slap a white child.

Another painful story I try to forget.

Deep inside me, I know that when Victor looks at me, a white woman, I am a reminder of such prejudice and hatred. I try to be loving, hoping this will save us.

One day Victor and I are walking home from a restaurant near the hospital. Before long, we hear a man behind us calling me insulting names, muttering about how I am 'walking with a black man'. I glance behind us. The man is in his early twenties, short and skinny, rough-looking. Although Victor pays little attention to his own clothes, he is always tidy and clean.

We walk on. Victor is silent but I can feel his whole body tense. Even though his skin is dark, I can see the blood rising to his face.

The man swears and jeers. 'Whore,' he says. 'Slut.'

Victor and I glance at one another. I can see a venomous rage in his eyes that I have never seen before. Without warning, Victor spins around and strides towards the man. He strikes him, then hits him again and again, in the face, on the body, until the man falls to the ground, bleeding.

From where I stand, frozen, I see Victor bend down and

say, 'My name is Dr Victor and I work across the road, in the hospital.'

There is blood all over the pavement. The man lies perfectly still.

Victor returns to me and we walk on without a word. When we sit together later that night, eating our meal, I ask how he could do something like that. But he just looks at me and says I don't understand.

I protest. 'I do understand. I've been abused too.' I pause. 'I know what humiliation feels like.'

He won't accept this. He thinks I can just melt back into my own world, my white world.

I push my plate away and think that no matter how hard I try, our relationship may never work.

25

Our Wedding

When government approval for our marriage arrives, we take it to my parents for my father's signature. They say little, just lead us inside and sit us down at the kitchen table. My mother sits beside my father, and they face Victor, Elsie and me. My mother smiles at Elsie and I feel she wants to hold her beautiful granddaughter but is too proud to ask.

Pride, I tell myself, defines my mother.

'Would you like to hold Elsie?' I finally ask. Instantly she rises, comes around the table and scoops up our baby. She gives her a kiss and I see her eyes filling with tears. It's been six months since Elsie was born, and Mama is finally holding her first grandchild.

She goes back to her seat beside my father, cuddling Elsie in her arms.

'I don't have a pen ...' begins my father. Victor smiles and hands him one. My father's hand shakes as he writes his name.

'I'm doing this for my granddaughter,' he says. 'She needs her father.'

Elsie is the bridge between my parents and me as I was a bridge between Mama Draga and my father. Bridges can span two different worlds. Elsie is the image of her father just as I was the image of my father.

The wedding is planned. The night before we marry, I have a dream that Victor has died and I am spreading flowers on his grave. I wake suddenly and hear his snores rumbling in from the living room. Whatever I dreamed, he's very much alive.

We marry on 22 January 1977, a cold day. My white dress is long with a fitted bodice. It is lovely, all I ever imagined. I wear a veil and sheer embroidered gloves. A cape around my shoulders keeps me warm. My white shoes have fashionable high heels. My sister brings me a bunch of lilies as a bouquet.

'You look beautiful,' she tells me—but I don't feel that way.

I look at my face in the mirror and see that it is tense and sad. Worse, I look into my eyes and see no sparkle there. Right now, getting married is not what I want to do, but what I must do.

First there is a civil ceremony at the City Council. It is a typical Communist ceremony: cramped, charmless and bureaucratic. Victor and I are asked to step forward and an official asks for our documentation. I can't believe that I have forgotten my birth certificate.

Victor turns to me. 'You stupid idiot,' he says, for everyone to hear.

Tears well up in my eyes. Dr Frank rushes to our home to fetch it. The wait is unbearable. I try to be calm and pleasant.

When Dr Frank returns, the formalities are conducted and a wedding certificate is issued.

After the civil ceremony, we travel in a Mercedes Benz to the Orthodox church, a majestic old place with an upstairs gallery. Eighty people have been invited to celebrate with us:

friends of Victor's from the Ghanaian community; doctors, lawyers, dentists and their wives, girlfriends and families. The only friends I have left to invite are Tamara and her sister.

Victor's best man walks me into the church. As we step inside, the organ begins to play so loudly that the walls, the very air, throb with sound. Through the music I hear another distinct noise. I realise it's the sound of my father weeping.

Victor and I walk towards the three priests who are surrounded by candles and whose faces look soft and benevolent. Although Victor is Anglican, he is marrying in the Orthodox church to please my father. I am Catholic but I was not consulted about this. The decision was made by the two men in my life, my father and my husband.

'We will have a proper wedding,' Victor said. 'I want to show all of them that I will honour my promise to marry you.'

As I step closer to the priests and to my husband, standing with a wide smile on his face, I wonder if my father's sobbing is a sign of relief that I am now as respectable as I will ever be. I turn and glance at him and see Cornelia and my brother Gheorghe beside him. My mother hasn't come. The wedding would be too much for her.

The church ceremony is long: two hours. We step out into the freezing air and pose for photographs. All around me people are chattering and laughing. They kiss my cheeks and congratulate me.

'Mrs Victor,' they say. 'Congratulations, Mrs Victor!'

I try to smile but I don't really know how I appear. I'm envied by some and pitied by others. This is not what I imagined feeling on my wedding day. In the photographs, I clutch a small posy of flowers in my gloved hand. Around us are more white flowers, twined around poles where candles burn. I remember their fresh smell. I am the bride. I am meant to be joyful, overflowing with tears of love but my smile is tight, forced. Beside me, Victor in his smart three-piece suit is all smiles, charming and gregarious. His cheeks shine with happiness.

My father is the first to leave the wedding photo sessions. He holds his hat the way he always does when he's nervous. I know this is not the wedding he dreamed for me.

Where is my mother? Where are all my friends? I smile because it is done. It is not a smile of love or joy. I do what is expected. I must let everyone think it's all perfect.

The guests arrive at my father's house where my mother, despite her mortification, has busily been preparing food. My father is expansive now, proud to be the host, to see the beautiful foreign cars pulling up outside his home. Ferentari is not an affluent area and all the neighbours come out to stare. No one around here has seen so many foreign people in one place at the same time.

I cannot wait to take off my wedding dress. It's long and elegant but I'm stifling inside it. In my room, I fold it into a box and pull on a loose, bright traditional Ghanaian dress. I feel comfortable wearing it.

Music is put on the record player. Victor, the dancer, is already twirling a friend's wife around my parents' living room. Even in my comfortable new dress, I cannot dance. In fact, I'd like the guests to leave, but of course the party is only just beginning. I force myself to move around the room, talking to everyone. Everyone except my husband.

Cornelia helps my mother serve the food. We have a special Romanian dish called beouf salad, stuffed sour cabbage rolls and roast pork with red wine. No one would realise Rosalia is the mother of the bride. She doesn't greet the guests. It's almost as if she's been hired as a caterer.

My father chats and makes jokes. Cornelia laughs and dances and calls everyone by name. 'How does Cornelia know them all?' my father asks. She has been forbidden to come and visit me so he can't understand how my sister knows all Victor's friends.

I shrug my shoulders and watch my happy sister dance. I wish I could share her delight.

26

The Earthquake

Bucharest is devastated by an earthquake. As if I needed another reason to leave Romania!

The city was designed by French architects and for a time it was a cultural centre full of writers, artists and musicians and known as the Little Paris of the East. That was before Ceausescu and Communism ripped the city's soul.

On 4 March 1977, the earth rises to destroy what remains.

Victor is still at work and my mother is looking after Elsie while I am at my friend Tamara's, helping her sew clothes. She works at Bucharest's biggest fashion house, where only the wealthiest people, the elite members of the Communist Party, can shop. Tonight she has a big order to finish and I am helping her cut patterns and create the garments. I'm getting better at this and she welcomes my help.

Tamara has no children and lives in the centre of Bucharest in a beautiful old apartment with high ceilings and ornate balconies.

'Stay the night,' she urges. 'It's getting late and this way we can get more work done.'

I'm happy to have one night away from home. Since our wedding, Victor and I have been arguing a lot.

I ring Cornelia. She is staying overnight at my apartment. 'Do you mind if I spend the night at Tamara's place?' I ask. She says she'll be fine on her own.

'I'll be back early tomorrow,' I say. Then I call Victor and my mother to let them know where I am.

Tamara makes up the spare bed, we eat a quick dinner and then go back to the workroom to do more sewing. As we cut and stitch, something makes me change my mind. 'You know what, Tamara? I've decided to go home after all,' I tell her. I don't really know why.

'But I want you to stay!' Tamara says. Her husband is away on a job and she enjoys having company.

'I just feel I need to go home.' I ring Victor and tell him.

'Why don't you walk over to the hospital and we'll go home together?' he asks. 'I'm tired. I want to get out of here too.'

It's not a long walk and I'm pleased to be out in the fresh air. Spring has come, there is a hint of it in the warm evening air. When I arrive, Dr Frank is there with his car. He offers to drive us home. Victor sits beside him and I take the back seat. It's just after nine.

All of a sudden the car begins weaving all over the road as though the driver is drunk. I have no idea what is happening.

I look out the window, and to my astonishment, I can see buildings swaying. I don't understand how this can be going on. In an instant, my curiosity turns to terror. I know that something is horribly wrong with the world. I scream and in the front seat, the men shout. Dr Frank stops the car. Suddenly all the streetlights go off, leaving the buildings in darkness. Out of the pitch blackness I see a ghostly red arc in the distant sky, like a flaming rainbow.

People are crying and wailing all around us. It's like Hell.

'What's happening?' I shout.

Victor and Dr Frank reply together, 'It's an earthquake!'

We sit in the car for what is probably two minutes but it feels like an eternity. Then everything is suddenly still and silent.

In the back seat, I am shaking uncontrollably.

'Should we get out and walk?' Dr Frank asks Victor.

'I think so. There might be after-shocks. We can get the car in the morning—if it's still here.'

We climb out and reach for one another. I hold tight to Victor so that he can steady me. I'm worried about Cornelia.

Nearby a woman comes running out of her apartment screaming, 'The water pipes! The water pipes!'

'What does she mean?'

'The pipes must have burst. They'll be spraying hot water everywhere,' says Victor. I see that the woman is wet and in agony. Her skin looks burnt.

'We're going to die! We're going to die!' shouts another woman. Others are screaming and tearing at their hair.

No buildings have fallen down in the area where we live but there is broken glass everywhere. There is the smell of smoke in the air. Finally we reach our apartment, only to find the door jammed shut. The men kick it open and Cornelia runs towards us, unhurt, but shaking. Everything around her is smashed. Cupboards have spilt their contents onto the floor. Glass and crockery lie shattered. Our chandelier has crashed down from the ceiling.

Cornelia is sobbing. 'Lenuta, everything began to spin. I thought I was sick. I thought I was fainting or dying.'

I hold her tight by the elbow and lead her out into the street. Soon, Victor and Dr Frank join us and we return to the car and drive to Ferentari, where more people are running through the streets screaming and wailing. Here there is no power. The traffic lights are not working. But, to my amazement, all the houses, new and old, are still standing.

When we open my parents' door, we find my mother sobbing and pressing Elsie to her chest. She has been terrified on her own. My father is away driving his truck.

'I'll stay with you,' says Cornelia and begins to help her pick up what has fallen and sweep away the broken glass.

'Hellen, Dr Frank and I need to get back to the hospital,' Victor tells me. 'There will be work to do.'

I nod. Of course they must go there.

Then I think of Tamara and wonder about her old apartment in the centre of town. What might have happened to her?

'I'll come with you,' I say, quickly kissing Elsie and hurrying back to the car. From the hospital I can easily walk to Tamara's house and check that she's unhurt.

When I leave Victor and Dr Frank and venture out on foot through the city centre, there is carnage and rubble everywhere. I stumble over dead bodies. Buildings have collapsed and there is still smoke and the smell of fresh blood in the air. There are blocks collapsed on top of one another leaving people exposed in what's left of their rooms, clinging to whatever they can find to stop from falling. I see a body hanging out of an apartment. I see handbags, shoes, clothes, toys, food, furniture, household appliances, lying in piles everywhere. Cars have been crushed. Sirens wail and people stagger around, stunned, talking wildly. It's dark. The air is thick with gas, dust and smoke. I step on something soft. A stomach. It's impossible to avoid the bodies. I don't even know where the streets are any more. Fires are burning brightly and there is an eerie glow across the city.

I'm worried about Tamara in her old block. I'm desperate

to reach her. Fire engines are outside her building and police are on the stairs trying to open doors and release people who are trapped. Water streams from the doorways.

Then I see Tamara sitting on a pile of rubble, holding her head.

'Tamara! Are you hurt?' I run to her and wrap my arms around her.

She sobs but asks me about myself, about Victor and Elsie.

'We're fine. We're all safe,' I tell her. I glance down at her legs and they are covered in burns. Welts are appearing.

'The hot water was rising so fast I couldn't get out. I climbed on a table to avoid it. But I'm fine. I'm fine,' she says. Her eyes are wide and I can feel her fear.

In some flats, she tells me, the scalding water rose up to a metre deep.

'Thank God you left,' she says, and now her eyes hold mine. 'The entire wall collapsed on the spare bed I made up for you. If you'd been lying there, you would have died.'

I take her hand and squeeze it. We are alive and we are grateful.

A man sits near us amid the rubble with a Maltese terrier in his lap. 'Just before it happened,' he says, 'my dog started barking. He wanted to go out. Animals know when these things are coming. That's my building.' He points to a heap of fallen bricks.

In all, the earthquake kills 1424 people in Bucharest and injures more than 11,300. Many buildings are damaged and over thirty collapse. Tremors are felt throughout the Balkans as far as Ukraine and Moldova.

The following day the authorities announce they will keep any unclaimed bodies for two days only, because the weather is warm. After that, anyone unidentified will be buried in a mass grave.

Ceausescu jumps on a plane from Lagos where he has been negotiating with the Nigerian military dictator. He visits the scene of the earthquake and extends the time to search for survivors. He praises the emergency services and rejects foreign aid. 'We'll do it alone,' he says, although we residents of Bucharest would be grateful for foreign aid. We need medicine and food.

His regime uses the devastation as an excuse to rebuild the city according to their Communist vision. They construct the Centrul Civic as a memorial to Ceausescu's Communism. They pull down the beautiful Ienei Church. 'Earthquake damage,' they say. So this night of terror and destruction benefits some.

27

Leaving Romania

Two months before we are due to leave Romania, I come home from a walk with Elsie. I open the door, my baby asleep in my arms, and see my father sitting on the sofa with my husband. Before they see me, I stop and listen from the hallway.

Victor says, 'You need to have a talk with your daughter and tell her to respect her husband and do what she's told. She needs to learn how to shut her mouth.'

My father doesn't reply. From where I stand, I cannot see his face, just the edge of his shoulder.

'She's been rude and obnoxious and rebellious,' Victor continues. 'I'm warning you: if she goes on like this in Ghana, I'll pack her bags and send her back to you.'

His voice, low but clear, reverberates in the little flat. I wonder what my father will say. Finally, he says, slowly, 'I'll be happy to have her back.'

I realise that being outspoken is foolish. Being legally married is not a guarantee that my daughter and I are safe. I wonder if Victor could take Elsie from me and leave Romania?

I know I am walking on eggshells. I am outraged by the men's little discussion. I need to leave Romania for Elsie's sake.

Then I make a firm decision. If I ever return, it will be in my own time and for my own reasons. I will not be handed back and forth like a lost parcel.

I decide it is time to appear. 'Hello Victor. Hello Tata. What are you doing here?' I smile as if I haven't heard a word.

I make another decision. I vow to myself that once I leave Romania, I will never be the woman either of these men wants me to be.

In the weeks that follow, I am careful not to rock the boat. My thoughts move more and more to the life we will live in Ghana. I wonder if my husband is growing apprehensive about bringing home a white wife. I have no idea what this might mean for him. Stories circulate in Romania about African men having several wives or even exchanging their wives for camels. I made my views clear to Victor about second wives. All he did was laugh.

I have not been back to my beloved Cluj since I was taken there by force by my parents. I want to see Mama Draga, Auntie Ileana and Auntie Ana before I leave the country, and I want them to meet Elsie.

I fly to visit them and show them my beautiful toddler. 'This is Elsie,' I say.

Auntie Ana turns away and begins to make tea. She considers me a disgrace and the look on her face tells me that we are not welcome. I feel deeply hurt. Then my grandmother bends down and touches Elsie's thick curls. 'Come outside and see the river where your Mama used to play,' she tells her gently.

Later, when Elsie is sleeping, Mama Draga tells me what she really thinks. 'Lenuta, I'm worried for you. Are you sure you want to go all the way to Africa with this man? Is that what you really want? It's not too late to change your mind.'

'I want to go,' I say.

'But the men there have many wives. You can't live like that.'

Not that again! I laugh. 'Mama Draga, things have changed. It's very different now. Victor is a doctor who has worked in Romania. Everyone respects him.'

She is practically wringing her hands. 'But you don't know where he comes from. You don't know what it's like there. Come back here to Cluj, to us, where you were always so happy.'

The life I dreamed of, living in Cluj and working as a professional woman, is the furthest thing from my mind now. Elsie's future is far more important. Romania is not the place for us. As though reading my mind, Mama Draga adds, 'We'll look after Elsie. You can go out and get a job.'

She's not preaching. She's begging.

My eyes fill with tears. I have heard that Mama Draga used the same words to persuade my mother not to leave Cluj, twenty-one years ago. Mama didn't listen and followed my father to Bucharest. I don't want to listen either.

I now understand my mother. She wanted to prove everyone wrong, to prove that she could make a life with my father. Her pride would not let her give in.

Why aren't I learning from the past and listening to my grandmother? I search within myself for my own answer. Is it fear of the stigma of forever being labelled a slut or a whore? No—it's more. It's fear of the stigma my daughter will have to endure for the rest of her life if we stay here.

I gaze at my kind, stony-faced Mama Draga, her long years of work and hardship etched into every wrinkle. Her hair is tied back beneath the same black scarf she always wears. The

Mama Draga with her children.

Mama Draga.

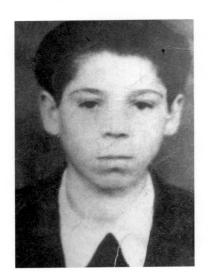

Mama Draga's only son.

My mother.

Mama Draga with her sisters.

Mama Draga's house.

My father in 1953.

With Auntie Ana.

Auntie Ana.

Petre, my paternal grandfather (left).

Fataluta and Petre, my paternal grandparents.

Petre, my paternal grandfather.

My father (on chair, middle).

My father holding me (left) and my mother holding my brother (right).

My brother.

My mother holding my sister on the left, my father, my brother and I on the motorbike.

In front of our house in Bucharest from left, my friend holding my sister, my brother and me.

Aged eighteen in 1972.

Wedding photo in front of the church. My father is in front holding his hat.

With Victor at the marriage registry office.

With Victor at a friend's party.

At our farewell party.

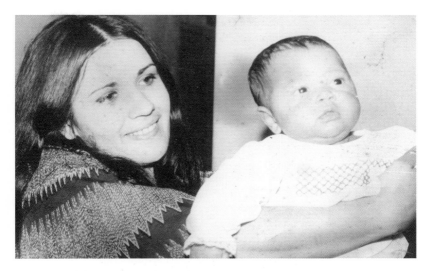

With Elsie aged three months in 1976.

William in 1979.

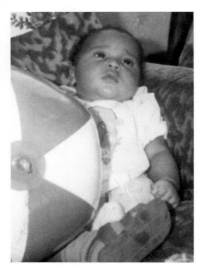

Nancy in 1980.

William in 1982.

Elsie doing her homework,
Romania, 1984.

From left to right: Nancy, William and Elsie in 1984.

fingers of her hands, spread open, urging me, are dry and cracked.

'How can I stay here, Mama Draga? Romanians will never accept my baby.'

She has no answer to that. From that moment she seems to accept my decision, but I know I have disappointed her deeply. She holds me to her, silently, and a memory from long ago fills my heart, a stab of intense fear: the fear I felt when I left my grandmother at the end of every summer holiday.

'Have courage, Lenuta,' were always her last words before I went back to Bucharest. I know that this time I need more courage than ever before. I am going to Africa, far, far away My grandmother's strength, warmth, and boundless love will carry me along any path I choose. I know her indomitable spirit will always be with me.

Back in Bucharest, I feel excited once again. I have great expectations. Perhaps Victor and I will be able to leave all our troubles behind us. He will be a specialist, an important man. We can have a big house and I'll have more babies—maybe as many as ten.

I don't dare ask Victor the questions I really want to ask. Are there electric lights in the streets? Will we see monkeys and other wild animals? Do poor people live in mud huts?

We go to a function at the Ghanaian Embassy. I examine photos of the capital, Accra, displayed on the wall. It looks like a modern city. The substantial colonial buildings and new office blocks have nothing to do with camels and wives being exchanged in chaotic marketplaces.

'Tell me about your family,' I ask Victor when we get home.

Once again, he says little. 'They're great. They'll love you. You'll be as happy as can be.'

I always want to know more, but that's all he'll say. I feel there is so much more personal information that he could tell me, though I just nod my head. At least I'll be free of the ties binding me to my homeland. Wherever in Africa I find myself, it cannot be worse than Romania.

'You look beautiful,' Victor tells me as we drive to our farewell party that the Ghanaian Ambassador has organised for us. I am wearing an elegant white hat with a wide brim.

There is true warmth in this small Ghanaian community. When we arrive, all of Victor's friends are there, nearly one hundred people, talking loudly and laughing as if they are back in Ghana. I think they are trying to prepare me for my new life.

None of my friends or family come. I have no friends of my own any more. It's time to leave Romania.

We feast on delicious Ghanaian food and I'm swept along with excitement as I contemplate my future. The farewell goes on long into the night.

This is the first time I really enjoy being with Victor at a party. This night he is different from the man I've known since I moved to his apartment. He offers me the love and concern that first attracted me to him. It's as if we were back in 1973, the year we met. He is extremely attentive, making sure that I am not left on my own. He is kind and respectful.

I lie awake in bed afterwards thinking of the contradictions in his character, the soft side and the hard side, the warm and the cold.

I feel no sadness about leaving my country. My father and Cornelia come to the airport. My mother cannot bear to come and say goodbye. Victor moves off towards the departure gate while I linger with my father. 'Elsie, take my hand,' I hear Victor say. 'Hellen, it's time to go.'

I hold my weeping father close but feel no loss. I no longer feel as if I belong here. My love of Cluj, my nostalgia for my childhood, they have disappeared. I am already uprooted.

I step towards Cornelia and put my arms around her. Finally something inside me stirs. 'Goodbye,' I whisper. Only my sister is still important to me. I kiss her wet cheek and follow my husband.

Victor and I begin our stopover in England through different gates, me on my Iron Curtain passport and he on his Ghanaian one.

London is huge and rich and cold. We marvel at the large buildings and opulent department stores. I've never seen anything like this, not even in the movies. How extraordinary, I think, that all these banks and shops are owned by people like us. But how can an individual own a bank? In Romania, only the government has such power.

We pass an ornate fountain. The marble is clean and shiny, so well maintained. I stand and stare. It seems to me to be hundreds of years old. Back home, Ceausescu destroyed most traces of our past.

I will have to stop calling Romania home, I tell myself.

I feel more relaxed than I have in a long time. I realise it's because not many people stare at us in the street here. In London, it's not uncommon for Europeans and Africans to walk together.

On our flight from Heathrow to Ghana's capital, Accra, most of the passengers are Ghanaian. I begin to understand what it is like to look different. But somehow I don't feel white among them. Instead it feels as if something is lifting, some barrier that stands between who I am and what I can really become.

Above Accra, I look down and am stunned by what I see.

Everyone at home has told me that I'm going to a jungle. 'It will be primitive,' they warned. But what I see below is a galaxy of lights, a big airport and marker lights twinkling along a wide landing strip bordered by roads and buildings that seem solid and new.

On the Gulf of Guinea, Accra has existed since the 1400s. It became a valuable port for ships from all over the British Empire and for decades was a centre for the slave trade with Portuguese, French, Dutch, British, Swedish and Danish traders all building forts on the coast. When in 1873 the British conquered the northern city of Kumasi, Ghana was declared a crown colony and in 1874, Accra was taken too.

In 1957, Ghana was the first African state to become independent. Since then its people have been led by both military and civilian governments. Compared with some of its neighbours, it is stable and secure.

Beside me, Victor shifts excitedly in his seat. It's been thirteen years since he was last here. I know he's wondering how he'll be received with his new wife and daughter.

'What do you think?' he asks me as the plane touches down. Out the window we glimpse the terminal, impressively large and white. Already there is pride in my husband's voice.

'It looks beautiful,' I say. I don't want to reveal my surprise.

I turn to Elsie and take out the special comb I keep to brush her hair. She is in a lovely white dress I have saved for this moment. I have watched her all through the flight so she doesn't dirty it. I'm wearing white too. Even my handbag is white, and my hat. My hair is long and smooth and I comb it over my shoulders. My heart is pounding. I'm about to meet my new family.

As we land, the passengers clap and burst into song, overjoyed to be home.

I have reached my destination, I think, the place where I will spend the rest of my life. Until this moment I have focused on leaving Romania. As the clapping and singing die away I realise that I am about to be immersed in a whole new world, vast as an ocean. I've tried to plan, to control my destiny, but now I must depend on others.

My future stretches before me and I cannot see the horizon.

I am almost twenty-five.

28

My New Home

As I leave the aircraft, I clutch the rim of the big white hat which the hot wind is threatening to lift from my head. For a moment I recall how in Cluj I would parade my hats for Mama Draga and Mrs Giurgiu in the shade of the walnut tree.

Africa greets Elsie and me with a blast of humidity and heat. Accra's air is thick and raw, with an earthy smell I have never experienced before. It is so heavy that it puts pressure on my heart and I find that I'm squeezing Elsie's tiny hand tightly. As we pause at the top of the steps leading down to the tarmac, she wrenches it from my grasp and begins to tear at her white cotton dress. She tugs at the buttons, gazing up at me with big, desperate eyes.

'It's hot, Mama! It's so hot,' she cries. Victor doesn't notice. He is already running down the steps.

I struggle to contain her. She has torn the bodice and a couple of buttons have been ripped off. She's trying to tug the dress over her head.

'Elsie, please stop it,' I plead. 'It's just hot. You'll get used to it.'

I hoped to present a smartly dressed little girl to Victor's family, a well-behaved and brought-up child. Now she is half-naked and clearly out of control. The humidity and heat are too much for her. 'No, Elsie. You have to keep it on,' I say firmly. I lift her up and we move down to the tarmac.

Ahead of us, Victor is entering the terminal, but instead of hurrying after him, I stop on the very bottom step. I have planned to make my first step on African soil with my right foot. In Romania, this means good luck for a new beginning. But I am clumsy and I stumble and for a moment, I feel as if I'm caught between two worlds, two lives.

When I do step, I can't be sure which of my feet touches Africa first.

Victor has stopped, waiting to see what's holding us up. I shake off my confusion, smile and hurry towards him. I follow him inside the terminal and find, to my relief, that it is air-conditioned. We enter the country with no fuss, showing our documents and walking straight to the arrivals hall.

I see that there is a crowd waiting who are all waving and shouting Victor's name. When Elsie and I arrive behind him, for a moment no one even notices us. 'Victor! Victor!' they shout. I hear words in a language that means nothing to me, and I hear the word, 'Doctor!' called over and over.

Victor has paused in front of an elderly man and three women. The man, dignified and handsome for his years, is dressed in smart western clothes. I sense that this is his father. They embrace and then Victor turns around and draws me forward. Elsie and I step closer. 'This is Hellen and our daughter Elsie,' he says to the four people, who stand and nod. Now, using Romanian, he tells me, 'Hellen, this is my father. You can call him Papani.' Then he points at each of the women in turn. 'This is my mother, this is my mother and this is my mother.'

Mama Draga's words echo in my head. 'But you don't

know where he comes from. You don't know what it's like there.'

I cannot move. My ears are bombarded by shouts and cries. The three women watch me and I stare back at them, confused. Finally, when I can speak, I turn to Victor and in Romanian I ask him, 'Who gave birth to you?'

I've asked him before whether his father has more than one wife but he has always avoided this question. 'Shut up,' he says softly in Romanian. There is malice in his voice. I know better than to make a scene.

As Victor catches up with his four parents, I examine each of the women in turn. All wear traditional Ghanaian dress. One of them strongly resembles him. She is pretty and smiling broadly. Her mouth moves as she chats to Victor while examining Elsie and me, curious about everything from my shoes to my hat to my daughter's curly hair. There seems to be a hint of mischief in her face. The woman beside her has a long, thin face and seems severe. The woman closest to Papani is tall and graceful. She seems soft and loving. I like her immediately.

Victor speaks warmly to them all. He doesn't seem to favour one over the others.

For a second, I want to turn around, climb back on the plane and return to the world I know. I can't stop a feeling of dread. I don't want to be in a new world where women must share their men. My fear is that, like my mother, I am destined to become one of many. Given Ghanaian society's acceptance of polygamy and extramarital affairs, I'd be expected to play the loyal wife and bear my husband's infidelities with good grace.

I know I could never do that. From this very moment, I begin watching Victor closely, looking for signs.

Behind Papani is a group of about fifteen people, all

wearing traditional dress. I assume they must be Victor's close relatives. The women are crying. Overcome by emotion, Victor rushes ahead towards them. Soon he is smothered in hugs, kisses and tears. Elsie and I arrive behind him again and suddenly everyone is greeting me too, all speaking at once. Some use English, some their own language. Victor is not beside me to translate so I have no idea who is welcoming me. I just try to smile and nod as I present Elsie to them. All the while my mind is spinning.

Everyone begins to move outside and it's as if we are carried along on a wave of energy. I worry about our bags but can only assume that someone will take care of them. I don't want to lose sight of Victor.

We step out through the main entrance and leave the air-conditioning behind us. Another gust of hot wind hits me and then I see a sight I could never have imagined. Before us, a crowd of two hundred or more people are gathered on the lawn. They are dancing, singing and drumming. Women's bodies are moving and shaking. The beating drums sound tribal, somehow terrifying. The singing is beautiful but raucous and wild.

Two chairs have been set out on the lawn. Victor and I are led towards them. Elsie's hand is rigid in mine. I see her little head moving back and forth as she tries to take everything in. She seems afraid. She begins to cry. I bend down and give her a hug and a kiss to reassure her that we are safe, that this is just a welcoming party.

The drumming and singing rise to a crescendo, raw and powerful. You might think a king or a president had arrived. A ritual seems to be unfolding. I am seated on one of the chairs and Elsie stands near me, clinging to my dress. She is so overwhelmed that tears run down her face.

Victor sits down beside me. 'You must take your shoes off,' he tells me. Women approach and our feet are dusted with white powder. I can focus on nothing. I'm at the centre of some ancient ritual that I don't understand.

Victor says, 'They are cleansing us.'

'From what?'

'It's for luck. And for future prosperity now that I've finally come back.'

His family crowd around us, moving and swaying as one. The thick air is suffocating and the pounding rhythm of the drums is deafening. 'This is my mother, this is my mother and this is my mother.' It seems to haunt me. It's all so confusing: the noise, the smell, the vivid colours of the clothes, the charcoal paint on people's faces, the rhythm of the dance. It's all bewildering: first the airport, big and clean and modern, and now this ancient ritual. But I love the free spirits and joyful expressions of these Ghanaian women. I wish I knew how to join in.

The drumming goes on and on but eventually the crowd parts for us and we are led towards the road where cars and trucks are parked. I look up and see streetlights high on poles. The road before us is smooth, not covered in potholes as it would be back in Romania. And then I see the car that will take us home.

'This is Michael,' Victor says, pointing to his brother who will be driving. He is younger than Victor. Like his father Papani, he wears smart western clothes, trousers and a shirt. He is a handsome man of medium height and build, and from the beginning, I notice that he has an air of contentment and self-confidence that Victor lacks.

Michael is trying to explain something to me but my face must show that I don't understand English. 'Victor's mother's people are Krobo and this is their welcoming ceremony,' Michael says, as Victor translates for me. I realise she is the pretty one who was examining Elsie and me so closely, curious about everything.

As we drive away, I turn to look out the car's rear window. I can see people packing up their drums and beginning to pile them into the trucks that have brought them here. Elsie's hot little head is buried in my shoulder, her nose pressed into my neck beneath my hair. I know she isn't asleep because I can feel the tension in her body. I rub her back to soothe her. 'It's all right,' I whisper.

We drive along a wide smooth avenue with palm trees on either side. Above us, the night sky is filled with stars. I am amazed at how modern this city is and how clean it seems. Suddenly I see a strange yellow glow along the side of the road. It is the glow from rows of kerosene lamps made of old cans. We are at the edge of a vast slum. The shacks are tiny.

'Can I wind the window down?' I ask Victor.

'Of course,' he says.

When I do, a powerful smell blows in, a mixture of wood smoke, kerosene and sewage. It is a smell so intense I can feel it moving up my nose and into my mouth. 'Oh my goodness!' I exclaim and put my hand to my nose.

Victor turns around and sees the look of horror on my face. 'Don't worry. Just wind up the window. These people are like your gypsies. They don't live in a civilised way.'

'You mean they have a choice?' I ask. 'Your politicians must drive this way from the airport all the time and see what's going on. Why don't they help them to live better?'

Victor shrugs. 'Because politicians are just like the rest of us who don't have to live there. It's not our problem. You'll get used to it.'

I close the window, press my face to the glass and watch the little yellow lights glowing in a rolling procession.

29

Papani

We are on the way to Papani's family compound for the Ga tribe welcoming ceremony. He has left the airport before us.

Papani comes from Jamestown, part of the British area of Accra. Ga men, I discover later, have a reputation for being gentle, but deep down, they are as brave and proud as any other tribe. Educated Ga men are known for having taste and charm, for dressing well and winning good jobs. Many have been educated at boarding schools in England or at the elite Achimota School in Accra and so speak English perfectly. Papani seems more English than the English.

Ga men also honour their heritage and their traditional way of life. In Ghana, the traditional way to clean teeth is, I discover, to chew on a 'sponge', a wooden toothbrush of a design that dates back thousands of years. Even a man who has been educated in England can be seen chewing on his sponge in public; it is accepted.

Jamestown has slave connections. When I finally go there, I feel an eerie energy around the beach, especially in the evenings. The mist above the sea is white and dense. I wonder if my sense of foreboding is connected with the souls of those thousands who were enslaved, who perished during raids or while in chains awaiting ships. Perhaps these spirits are still floating above the waters.

Papani lives in Mamprobi, a suburb not far from the sea. A cool breeze is blowing and I can smell the salt of the water and the drifting aroma of fried fish.

As we drive into his compound he approaches, eager to welcome us home. 'Hellen!' he greets me, arms outstretched. 'And Elsie.' His English is slow and clear and his voice deep and resonant. He stands tall and trim.

Papani is warm but reserved and I feel that he is the type of man who will never say a word without carefully thinking it over.

My daughter is sleeping and so I carry her in my arms. 'Welcome, little girl,' says Papani, stroking her hair. Already I feel part of his family.

In the compound, the Ga welcoming festivities begin. In front of the two houses, beneath a vast spreading mango tree, two chairs have once again been placed side by side. They face rows of chairs in which guests are now seating themselves. The people gathered here are quieter and more restrained than those from the Krobo tribe we met at the airport.

Although I keep my face calm, interested, and polite, I am angry with Victor. Back in Romania, I asked him many times about his family, but he has told me nothing that can help me handle all this. He might have prepared me better. Fortunately, no one calls on me to speak or act.

Papani leads Victor and me towards our thrones. 'Sit! Sit!' he urges. I sit and cuddle Elsie. I glance up and notice that tiny lizards are running up and down the branches of the mango tree. Will they fall on me? I try to make myself as small as possible in my chair, praying that nothing lands on me.

Once we are all seated, an old man dressed in traditional Ga clothes comes to bless us. He is thin and almost blind. He sprinkles our feet with schnapps from a bottle. As he does so, he chants in his language. Of course, I can't understand a word.

Finally the festivities are over. Michael leads us to his car.

'Come again soon,' Papani says, hugging me goodbye and squeezing my hand tightly.

As we drive, Victor and his brother speak quietly together. I say nothing. It's been a long day, perhaps the longest of my life. Thankfully, Elsie is still asleep on my lap.

Because Victor will be working in a government job at Ridge Hospital, we will be given a house to live in. Since it isn't ready for us, I am grateful for the clean and quiet hotel room that has been provided. When we are finally left alone, I make no attempt to engage Victor in conversation. I'm simply too tired. I just lie down and sleep.

When I wake, for a moment I forget where I am. Elsie is sitting up in bed beside me, her curls tousled and her eyes bleary. 'Mama?' she says. 'Where have all those people gone?'

Victor comes out from the bathroom where he has showered, and is dressing. He seems nervous. I haven't realised he is starting work today. I imagined we might have some time alone to adjust to our new life together.

'You might as well unpack,' he tells me. 'We'll be staying here for a little while.'

He comes close and sits on the bed beside me. There must be fear in my face, or at least confusion. He wraps his arms around me and holds me tight.

'I'm OK,' I tell him. He touches my cheek and I know he understands that all this is hard for me. Sometimes words are not needed.

I turn and see that Elsie is watching us closely. By the look on her face I can tell that she has never before seen us behave intimately. I burst out laughing, filled with optimism about our new life.

When Victor leaves, suddenly I realise that I have no idea how to do simple things like get something to eat or make a phone call. I don't even know where Victor works or when he'll be home. This is the first time I have stayed in a hotel room and I have no money and speak very little English.

'Mama, I'm hungry,' Elsie announces. What am I to do? I remember the hotel brochures I saw on the table last night. I fetch them and try out my few English words after I've rung the number on the cover. 'Milk,' I say. 'Bread.'

They must understand me, or perhaps Victor had spoken to them as he left, because soon a breakfast tray arrives carried by a cheerful boy. He puts it down and winks at Elsie as he leaves. Later, while she plays, I unpack our clothes and hang them in the wardrobe. I bury my face in them because they smell of Romania.

Elsie and I dress and leave the hotel holding hands. When we step outside it's into the same heat as the day before. The neighbourhood seems safe and green, with large houses surrounded by gardens entered through big gates.

I have no map so we don't venture far. Down the road is a shopping centre and I lead Elsie inside, hoping that it will be cool. It is nothing like shopping centres back home in Romania, not least because it's full of Ghanaians, serene and beautifully dressed. I see displays of attractive dresses and shoes, apples and potatoes laid out in perfect rows, bottles of cow's milk, cheeses and yoghurt. Everything seems of good quality—and expensive. I can't imagine shopping here.

The Ghanaian women smile at both of us. There are

European women here too, and when we pass, we glance at one another without speaking, wondering about each other's stories and what brought us all here.

'Are we shopping, Mama?' asks Elsie.

'No. We're just looking.'

Later, we find our way back to the hotel. We both fall asleep.

When Victor comes home, he sits beside me and holds my hand. 'How was your day?' he asks. I am comforted by the familiar hospital smell he brings with him.

'I was lonely,' I tell him. 'I want to be busy. I want our own house. I want to cook and do the washing.'

'But you'll have servants to do all those things for you,' he says. 'You should learn to enjoy your leisure.'

I know I need to work. I need to be busy to take my mind off my doubts and fears about the future.

Elsie and I have been taking anti-malaria tablets since before we left Romania. But a few days after we arrive she starts to shiver, even though her body is hot with fever. I lie with her on the bed, stroking her and trying to get her to sip water.

Throughout the day her condition worsens. When Victor comes home, I run to him in fear.

'We must take her to the hospital. Quickly!' I tell him.

He examines Elsie. 'She'll be fine,' he says. But I insist we go at once.

We take her to Korle-Bu Hospital, a teaching hospital connected to the medical school of the University of Ghana. It was built in the 1920s but has expanded and developed over time. It is a large white building, well-equipped and well-run. I feel that with the care we can receive here, all will be well with Elsie.

I sit with her all night while the staff tries to cool her body by wrapping her in icy towels. Around us, in every bed and even on the floor, lie children, all suffering from malaria. If a person is bitten by an infected mosquito it can affect the blood supply, possibly causing brain or kidney failure. Malaria can appear with flu-like symptoms and progress quickly into a high fever which can lead to convulsions.

Victor leaves us at the hospital. He says he needs to go home and rest before his next shift. I struggle to communicate in English with the nurses and doctors. I'm the only European here. Although everyone is kind and willing to help, I don't fully understand what they are saying to me.

I feel so alone and wonder what will happen to my daughter. It is only three years since I lost my first child. Now my beautiful daughter is ill. I pray that she will survive.

By morning, Elsie's fever has passed. She is weak but her temperature is back to normal. The whole experience has made me think, why am I here?

30

Family

Days pass. Victor works long hours, since not only does he want to establish his reputation at the hospital, but he is also working at setting up a private clinic in his mother's town of Somanya. I am mostly alone, and with the passing of each week I grow more lonely and alienated. Sometimes Papani takes Elsie and me into Jamestown for a meal or back to his Mamprobi home to spend time with his family. He lives in one of the houses in his compound and Michael lives in the other with his wife, Felicia.

Papani is kind to me although we can barely speak together. I have a smattering of English and am picking up some words of Ga but I feel as if I'm separated from everyone by my inability to understand and speak English. It's like living on the other side of glass. I can see what is going on but I can't participate. Elsie learns the language more quickly than I do.

Victor knows what I'm going through. 'You'll get there,' he encourages me. His natural warmth and compassion are what keep me going. I take in his words and try harder. Adjusting to a new way of life was never going to be easy, I remind myself. I will find life here completely different from faraway Bucharest.

One place I do love to go is to Makola Market. As soon as I enter, I feel energised and positive. From the early 1920s the stalls and shops have been at the heart of Ghanaian trade and are a focus of city life. They are vast mazes of alleys, extending for blocks, crowded and bustling. TroTros—the vans and trucks used for public transport—weave in and out of the crowds. The ground is uneven. Cars honk and flies buzz.

I love the noise and smells, the smiles of the many women traders and the way they proudly carry their produce in bundles of all sizes on top of their heads. They sit beneath bright umbrellas, surrounded by their wares. A lady in a huge sun hat and striped dress rests among her baskets of yams, smiling peacefully. I wonder what she thinks about, sitting there all day.

I love the children who run around my ankles, peering up at me and chatting to Elsie as if she understands every word they say. Their lives are lived between mini-mountains of fruit, headlands of vegetables. Everyone is selling and everything is for sale: sunglasses, tools, coloured beads and bracelets, used bike tyres, pots and pans, baskets of smoked fish, fresh beef, mutton and goat meat.

My favourite fruits are sweet, rich pawpaw and aluguntugui, called soursop in English, thorny on the outside and creamy on the inside. It's hard to find, so it is always a treat. The huge round tomatoes remind me of those in Mama Draga's garden when I was a child. Green plantain and yellow bananas are heaped in baskets. Chillies of all shapes and sizes are separated into piles by a woman whose hair is braided close to her scalp. There are stacks of tinned fish and bottles of oil. Women gather loads of shopping to take home to their families.

One day after venturing down long alleyways, I find

women selling beautiful textiles. Here, rolls and rolls of the bright traditional Kente cloth are for sale, woven and printed in brilliant shades of red, orange, green, yellow and blue. Fabric rolls rise in walls that are a feast for my eyes.

Kente cloth was familiar to me in Romania. It is hand-woven on treadle looms and comes in strips just four inches wide which are then sewn together to make garments. Kente is more than just material for clothing. Each weaver gives every piece of cloth a meaning: philosophical, historical, even divine. Its colours are significant. Kente cloth is important to the person wearing it. I run my hands over the fabric. Kente cloth truly speaks to me. It is gorgeous, warm, vibrant. It is Ghana.

One of Victor's 'mothers', Papani's third wife, whom I call Auntie in the Ghanaian tradition, has given me a simple blue batik fabric to make a local Ga outfit. Felicia, who is a seamstress by trade, sews it into a stylish Kaba and slit for me. The Kaba is a fitted top with puffed sleeves and the slit is a long, fitted skirt. There is an extra piece of cloth, a kind of shawl, which can be draped over the shoulders, wrapped around the head or used for carrying children on your back. It doesn't take me long to learn the art of bending down, putting Elsie on my back and wrapping the fabric around her to bind her to my back.

As soon as I put on my Ghanaian dress, I feel free and more at ease. The faces of the local women light up when they see me pass, even more so when I carry Elsie tied behind me. At last I start to feel part of this exotic place.

What does it mean to be a Ghanaian? They are proud of being the first African country to gain independence from European rule. Their land is rich with gold, diamonds and cocoa. The black star of their flag symbolises unity, identity and destiny. There are many languages and many tribes unified in one nation.

And here I am among them. It's not just that I am white. Here I am the odd one out in a place where tribe, family and history mean everything.

I wish Victor and I could spend more time together. Most evenings he is out seeing his old friends, leaving Elsie and me to eat our hotel food alone as we sit on our bed in front of the television. I have begun to hate living in this hotel.

My only joy is our visits from Papani. Once again, he has picked us up and brought us back to his compound. Elsie exhausts herself playing in his yard. Although the language is a barrier, my pleasure must shine from my face. Plates heaped with food are spread out before us. It is so nice to eat with the family in their home.

'You like the food here in Ghana?' Papani asks me with a twinkle in his eye. He already knows the answer. There isn't a single Ghanian dish I dislike. I love the shito, which is a hot fried sauce made with shrimp, onion, oil and chilli. You can only eat a little bit at a time, it's so hot. We eat it with kenkey, corn that has been left to go sour and then wrapped in leaves and boiled into dumplings. Sometimes we eat shito with fish and gari, dry, ground cassava. I also love the deep-fried fish and palm soup.

'Come again whenever you want!' says Papani kindly as we leave.

I feel at home at Papani's. I like to be part of a family, even one as different as this. I like the smells of cooking and the movement of people as they go about their daily lives. I'm becoming restless. It's not in me to be a woman of leisure.

When Michael drives Elsie and me back to the hotel, I feel my heart sinking as we stop at the entrance. 'Can we come again and see you soon?' I ask him.

'Sure, Hellen,' he says as he waves to us from his car.

When Victor comes home I ask again about our own house. 'When will it be ready? I can't live like this.'

'Let's just wait and see,' he says as he pulls off his shoes and lies back on the bed.

These words 'wait and see' are so common in Ghana. I hear them over and over again.

The next time I am at Papani's, I ask him in my broken English, 'Please, Papani, can we come and live with you?'

He claps his hands then cuddles Elsie. 'Yes, of course,' he says with a big smile.

When I am bathing Elsie later that day, I see how she is changing here in Ghana. Her skin is darker and her feet are growing tough from running around without shoes. Often when I look at her, she is frowning, perhaps because of all the new things she doesn't yet understand, the new language and new ways of doing things. Her will is growing stronger too. She's more defiant. She is certainly my daughter.

When I tell Victor I want to move to Papani's house, his face shows only amazement. 'You want to? Is that what you really want?' He's not unhappy. He spreads his arms wide. 'If it will make you happy, do,' he says.

Because Victor was in Romania for thirteen years on a scholarship, the Ghanaian government allowed us to bring in three tonnes of European goods. We have shipped furniture, a washing machine and other electrical equipment that we brought from Germany. I was already married to Victor when he ordered these goods, but I wasn't allowed to choose them. 'You don't know what's best,' he tells me.

As my dowry, my father bought a lounge suite and a dining set with a sideboard and cabinet. He didn't have the money to pay for it all at once, so he did so in instalments. In Oltenia, my father's homeland, girls are always given a dowry when they marry and he was proud of what he managed to give me.

Everything is stored, waiting at Papani's house, so there are only our suitcases to move from the hotel. We are going to share the second house on the compound with Michael and Felicia. We are given two small rooms and an enclosed verandah with a separate entrance.

Felicia is kind to me. Her smile is always warm when we pass one another in the yard, but I still can't speak with her. My English isn't good enough.

At least I'm back in the real world where I can do my own washing and ironing. I want to learn Ghanaian cooking, and so I carry my pots and food over to Papani's house where I use the kitchen and take lessons from Auntie.

'Hellen!' Papani beams. 'What are we making today?'

Auntie is a wonderful teacher. Even though we don't understand one another she nods encouragement and hands me a spoon to taste what we're making. She doesn't criticise the way I chop vegetables, as Victor does. She shows me the best way to pound cassava and to dry-roast the peanuts that we crush for soup. With Auntie, everything is fun.

One day, while Auntie and I eat peanut soup we've just made, I find myself hot with nausea. I know this feeling; I'm pregnant again. I push away my bowl and try to smile politely.

When Victor gets home, I lead him to the bedroom and tell him my news in private. He nods, and for a moment I cannot read his thoughts. Panic floods me until he says, 'That's good.'

But there's a gulf between his words and his actions. Something is wrong. These days he is busier and busier in

Somanya, setting up his clinic and spending time with his mother and all his Krobo relatives from there who welcomed us. Some nights he even sleeps at his mother's house rather than coming home to us. And even when he is with us, he seems tired and remote. The hope I had that he and I might find a way to be happy here is draining away.

It's only with me that I see this lack of spirit in Victor. With others, he is the charming, vibrant and lively man I once knew.

I ask him questions that are spinning around in my head. 'You're not as intimate with me as you used to be. Do you still love me? Has something happened?'

Victor shakes his head. 'You think too much, Hellen. Your feelings are sending you crazy, just as they did when you were last pregnant.'

Maybe he's right. I try to act sensibly. I try not to think.

The following weekend, Elsie is helping me carry the clothes to hang out to dry when I see Papani speaking heatedly with Victor. It's strange that Papani, who never raises his voice, is upset and almost shouting. Victor is angry too, and I know he won't tolerate advice from anyone, even his father. As I watch, my husband throws his hands up in the air and walks off. He leaves for Somanya.

I know this has been about Victor's long periods away from home. The less I see of my husband, the more care and attention I receive from Papani. Sometimes he seems like the true father I never had.

I hardly ever speak with my family back home. It's expensive and complicated to ring them. First I must go to the post office in Accra and book the call. Then my parents are contacted about the time of the call and, at the agreed hour, they must go to the post office in Bucharest while I go to the one in Accra and make the call. I do write to them but I avoid letting them know about my fears and difficulties.

I am in turmoil. There is something going on I don't understand. I leave Elsie with Felicia and her servants and go for a long walk along the beach near Papani's compound. I watch the fishermen throw out their nets and then haul them in, hand over hand. On the beach I watch the glimmering, moving bodies of hundreds of dying fish. Women are scattered across the sand selling black-eyed beans and fried fresh-caught fish. It could be a scene from hundreds of years ago. Watching it, my loneliness and fear recede—at least for now.

31

Shock

I am five months pregnant. My baby is growing and I feel blessed by my pregnancy.

One day Victor asks me for the key to the post office box. 'But I enjoy collecting the mail,' I say. I walk there a couple of times a week, sometimes more often. It gives me something to do. Besides, I'm always excited to receive a letter from Cornelia telling me what she is doing back in Romania. 'Why do you want the key?'

'Because I want to collect our letters from now on,' he says.

I don't argue. Perhaps he wants to save me the effort of another task now that I am pregnant, but if so, why doesn't he say? As the weeks go by my curiosity deepens to suspicion. To calm myself, I walk more and more frequently along the beach. I watch the local women in their vivid outfits as they sit beneath umbrellas or sun-hats and fan the pots of food they are selling. I imagine their lives to be so much simpler than mine.

A local man has died, a distant family member, and Victor and I are expected to attend his funeral. Because of the intricate web of tribal connections, there is always a funeral to attend. Sometimes it seems as if everyone in Ghana is related.

I know that, pregnant and emotionally fragile, it will all be too much for me. In Ghana when somebody dies, their bodies are frozen before being laid out for the elaborate ceremony. It lasts a whole day and night, with music, dancing, food and drink for a traditional burial.

'Victor, I prefer to stay at home,' I tell him. He nods although I can see he is displeased. He doesn't like it when he thinks I'm not making an effort to fit in with his world, into his traditional customs.

On my own during the day I feel at peace and have time to think. I plan a letter to Cornelia.

I look for a pen but can't find one. Then I notice Victor's briefcase in the corner of the bedroom. Surely he will have a pen. I open the case. Immediately I find an envelope addressed to him, both his name and the address of our post office box written on it in a hand I don't recognise. The writing is very neat and precise. I open the letter without a single qualm. Victor is my husband. We should have no secrets.

As I read, blood rushes to my head. *Dear Doctor* the letter begins. My eyes move to the end, where I see a name, *Naomi*. I glance back to the top and see that the sender's address is a boarding school.

Thank you for a wonderful weekend. I really enjoyed it and I hope you did too. Thank you for the lovely exercise book. I look forward to the next weekend.

But it is the last line that really opens my eyes: *Love for ever, Naomi.*

My head spins as I read the letter over and over again. I am trying to understand, trying to be sure of the tone. This Naomi must be a young schoolgirl. Victor is nearly forty now. Is he really courting her with stationery items?

I don't want to misjudge my husband but there is a horrible heavy feeling inside me. Could they have slept together? My hands are shaking. I start crying and I can't stop.

I walk to Papani and hold the letter out to him.

'What's the matter, Hellen?' he asks me, taking it. He can see how upset I am. He reads it in silence, then looks up at me with sad eyes.

'History is repeating itself,' he says.

He gives me a hug. I feel his boundless compassion. I know then that all my nightmares are coming true. I have been right in suspecting something. It feels like the end when it should still be the beginning. I feel weak. I can't talk now and so I take the letter back from Papani and walk away. I forget there are steps in front of me and suddenly I fall forward, on to my stomach.

I'm terrified that I've hurt my baby. I roll over and lie on my back, rubbing my stomach and trying to feel if everything is all right.

'It's OK,' I whisper. 'Everything is fine.'

Papani runs to me, lifts me up and carries me to my bed where I lie still and breathe deeply. Before long, I feel the baby kick and push against me.

I steel myself for a confrontation when Victor returns home. When he walks in, I don't waste time on small talk. I have come all the way to Ghana to be with him and he owes me an explanation.

'How dare you have an affair while you're married to me?' I say. He pretends to be surprised but I hand him the letter. He glances at it then glares back at me.

'You know, Hellen, if you don't like it—there's the door.'

My last traces of reason and calm have deserted me. My emotions take over. 'How dare you?' I shout. 'How dare you treat me like this? I'm your wife and I'm going to have your baby.'

'Here in Africa, two wives is nothing. You white people just have affairs. You lie and cheat. At least we're honest.'

'What's honest about this?' I yell. 'So now you're going to marry her?'

'No one's saying that, Hellen. Calm down.'

There is no possibility that I will calm down about such an outrage.

'I said if you don't like it, there's the door,' he repeats. 'Maybe you should join the women on the docks.'

This is an insult. I know what he's talking about. According to gossip, some white women are servicing the white sailors passing through the port of Accra. There is nothing more offensive Victor could have said to me. I can barely believe he could utter the words. Again the blood rushes to my head. I draw myself up to my full height.

'When you took me as your wife, you didn't take me from the gutter or a slummy dockside,' I tell him. 'You took me from a decent family and a decent home. When I met you I was a virgin.'

He turns and walks away. I cannot stop weeping.

32

A New Start

The next day, Victor goes away again. He spends many nights at his mother's house in Somanya, returning only briefly. When he does, he sleeps in the other room. What can I do? I have no money of my own. No choice. Nowhere to go.

I have breakfast with Papani and Auntie. I cannot stop crying. Papani reassures me that everything will be fine. He will seek help from the family elder in Jamestown, the ancient robed man who poured schnapps on our feet the day of our arrival. It is the custom here to seek help from elders like him in times of trouble.

Papani calls a family meeting chaired by the elder. Victor and I are seated next to one another. Everyone speaks Ga, of which I understand only a few words. The word I hear recurring is *obroni*, which means 'white person'. I learned its meaning when little children ran after me calling out *obroni*, *obroni*, like a game. It's not a rude word, not like being called black in Romanian.

The girl, Naomi, is not mentioned. I know polygamy is accepted in Ghana but she is still in high school and only seventeen. At forty, Victor could be her father. In the world

I left behind, this difference in age would have brought disapproval, but here, it seems a younger wife is a source of pride.

Papani translates for me. It is hard for the family elder to come up with a solution to our marital crisis as in their cultural tradition a man is allowed more than one wife. He tells Victor that since he has married a white woman, he must learn to respect my culture and customs.

I could not ask for more. Victor has his head bent down and avoids eye contact with the older man. I know that he doesn't like what he is hearing. He says nothing and promises nothing. I understand his silence very well. I know he will defy me as I defied my own mother. I promised her nothing too.

One day Victor comes to Papani's with the news that our house is finished. This ought to be a time of rejoicing but we move in with scarcely a word to one another. The house is in an area called Osu, a central district known as the West End of Accra. Here there are restaurants and modern office towers, clumps of waving palm trees and the bustle of a modern city. There are large white houses behind white walls with palm fronds peeking above them. The road is wide and flat with grass growing alongside it.

Our home is beautiful. At the front of the house there is a huge mango tree on one side and a big grassy garden on the other. The house itself has two storeys with a bathroom above the garage. There is a master bedroom, a children's bedroom and a guest room. The master bedroom becomes Victor's room and the guest room becomes mine.

There are also separate quarters for servants and their families. They cook their own food and seem to have no life beyond their work.

I am not used to the idea of employing people to wait on me. I have done my own housework all my life and find it hard to let others do it for me. I've also seen the way people treat their servants, shouting at them and acting as if they are second-class citizens. 'Tsst, tsst,' people say, snapping their fingers. The word 'please' is seldom used. Everyone behaves like this, Ghanaians as well as Europeans. It is a shock for me to see how dismissively people can treat one another.

One of my servants is Ashia, sent to us from Somanya by Victor's mother. She is Krobo too, and beautiful, with high cheekbones, her hair arranged in tiny plaits. She must be only seventeen, but I learn at once that she has wisdom and a kindness beyond her years.

'Are you happy here, Ashia?' I ask her as she works diligently, cleaning the floor.

'Working for you is a good job, Madam,' she tells me. She laughs and scrunches up her nose. 'If I wasn't working for you, I would just be waiting until a man chooses me for his wife.'

I love her free spirit.

She speaks more English than I do and she teaches me as we walk to the market together. It's almost as if she's my little sister. I'm so pleased to have someone I can confide in, although I know Victor would not approve of his wife befriending a servant.

'Why do you dress like a Ghanaian woman?' Ashia asks me.

As usual these days, I'm wearing a long traditional Ga dress and a scarf over my head. Elsie is tied up on my back where she is happy to watch the world go by. I wonder if Ashia is embarrassed to walk with me dressed like this. Perhaps she would prefer me in white women's clothes.

'I feel comfortable,' I tell her, shifting Elsie on my back. It won't be long before I'm too big from my pregnancy to carry her this way.

'You make a good Ghanaian woman,' Ashia says, laughing.

I look forward to my trips to the market with Ashia. I enjoy buying our food, cocoa butter to nourish my skin, and things we need for the new house. I can easily get caught up in the friendly bustle of commerce.

Ghanaian women watch us curiously as we pass by and it occurs to me that in fact Ashia is proud that we're here together, side by side. All the other white women use cars with drivers, or catch taxis. But when I'm with her, I think I'm the one who should feel proud.

Now that I'm pregnant, the smell of the market is overwhelming. The alleys are full of hanging animal carcasses, displays of smoked fish, and pigs' trotters soaking until they rot in salt water. Their sharp aromas mix with the stench from the gutters. I try my hardest not to be overcome by nausea.

'*Obroni! Obroni!*' shout the female stallholders when they see me coming. They are sitting with their wares, sometimes chewing the teeth-cleaning sponge, as they wait for a sale.

I have become a familiar face to them and I feel that they respect the way I've embraced their culture. They hug me and offer me goods, then won't take my money. I insist on paying. I know I have more than they do.

When we've finished our shopping, Ashia and I go to the outer edges of the market, to the stalls that sell cooked food. Early in the morning you can buy breakfast: porridge made of sour cassava or maize. There is waakye, rice with black beans, sold with shito, the pepper sauce people use on everything. Vendors, messengers and buyers move around pushing barrows and carrying sacks or boxes on their heads. For someone from Eastern Europe, the wild colour of an African market is a treat. All the women make an impact with their vibrant outfits. Print patterns vary from region to region but the colours are similar: navy blue, red, purple, yellow and pink. The colour is so bright it's almost shocking.

Ashia and I load up with good things. We talk and laugh. Here, like this, with her, I am completely at peace.

33

William

In June 1979, Flight Lieutenant Jerry Rawlings leads a military coup against the Ghanian government, citing corruption in both it and the military. Rawlings and his Armed Forces Revolutionary Council lead Ghana for 112 days. A 'clean-up' is conducted to root out corruption, including executions and shoot-outs.

Panic and fear grip Accra. A place known for its peace and stability is now under siege. Everyone's lives are in danger and shooting becomes part of everyday life. Between the rounds of gunfire, the once bustling city falls silent.

I fear for those I know and care about. Soon the sad news arrives that my friend's husband was among those shot.

Most people stay inside their compounds, using only phone calls to communicate. I keep Elsie close to me for safety. She does not understand where the noises are coming from or what they mean. She has never seen gun fights and neither have I. I don't know how to explain to her what's going on. I can't lift her because my stomach is too big. All I can do is wrap my arms around her and hold her tight.

Another burst of fire scares me so much that my waters break. The danger is that leaking amniotic fluid may cause bacterial infection. I am determined to give birth to a healthy baby.

I ring Victor in Somanya to tell him.

'Are you having contractions?' he asks me.

'Not yet. But I'm scared.'

'Ring me again when the contractions start,' he instructs. 'I'll come back then.'

As I hang up, tears start pouring down my face. As he spoke, I felt the coldness in his heart. It seems a long time since Victor was interested in our lives, Elsie's and mine. He doesn't ask how I am enduring a city wracked by violence. He doesn't check on me and our baby. I have had the tests on my own, walking the few kilometres to and from Korle-Bu Hospital. Now I am not only alone but frightened. Memories of my painful past experiences of giving birth flood back: my still-born baby on a cold metal trolley, Elsie in an incubator with tubes attached to her tiny body. There were always complications.

As I lie on the bed, I place my hand over my stomach and feel my baby move inside me. I pray for strength and courage to face the night. Elsie joins me and I hold her tight in my arms, falling asleep to the sounds of her breathing.

I rest and wait two more days. Finally, I feel the sharp pain followed by another sharper one that means my contractions have begun. I need help. There are no ambulances. I ring Michael. He comes to get me.

When we arrive at the hospital, they tell me my doctor has fled. 'Perhaps his name is on a wanted list,' they say.

My contractions are strong and frequent, but for some reason the baby isn't coming. The doctor who is called, a young obstetrician, wants to use the vacuum device. Then Victor arrives.

'No, no! You must use forceps,' he orders.

But the doctor isn't comfortable using forceps. 'There's nothing better than the vacuum,' he insists.

I'm in pain. I can't push and I just want it all to stop. 'Please, Victor, let him do his job,' I say.

But Victor won't listen to me. He is furious, treating my doctor like an inexperienced fool. 'You don't know anything,' he shouts. 'Let me show you how to do it!'

'Please, Victor—stop!' I plead.

Finally, with the nurses' help, the doctor manages to manoeuvre Victor out of the room. Through my half-shut eyes, I see him backing out the door.

'If you damage my child, I'll kill you,' is his last threat to the doctor. When he is finally gone, the doctor closes the door, takes the vacuum and helps my son emerge.

William is born at Korle-Bu Hospital on 11 June 1979. His head is pear-shaped.

'I told you,' Victor shouts at me when he sees William. 'I told him to use forceps!'

I say nothing. I touch my baby boy's cheek. All I can see is how beautiful he is. Besides my love for him, I feel grateful that my pain is gone.

'What an idiot that doctor was!' says Victor. 'What a fool.'

For me, the doctor was a gentle and caring man who treated me with respect. I look up and gaze into Victor's angry eyes. I'm beginning to realise that in Ghana there are at least two kinds of men. There is the serious, proper, trustworthy type and there are those like Victor, charming, the centre of attention but full of ego and always needing to be in control.

I nurse my son and wonder which type of man he will become when he grows up.

When I arrive back in Osu, I find Victor's mother bending

over a wood–fire in the yard, cooking food in one of the beautiful red pots I brought from Romania. The flames lick and blacken the shiny surface. It will take hours to scrub them clean. She stirs her food with a wooden spoon.

'She's come to help you with the baby,' Victor tells me.

'You mean that she's going to live here?' I ask incredulously.

'Not with us. With the servants.'

Until now, his mother has only come on short visits. It's not long before she takes over my entire house. Now it's as if I hardly exist.

I've now heard the family story about Victor's mother, or Ayawo as she is called. She has never been Papani's wife; it was just an affair. Papani decided to end the relationship but he insisted that he raise Victor.

At the age of two, Victor's mother gave him to Papani, who brought him to his home in Accra to join the rest of his family. After that, Victor's upbringing was in the hands of a stepmother.

But now his birth mother calls him 'my son, the Doctor' as if she is solely responsible for what he has made of his life.

When I try to cook or clean or bathe my own children, I feel I am blocked at every turn.

'I am cooking you rice,' I tell Victor.

'My mother is cooking me yam,' he says.

If I cook yam, she cooks fufu. And Victor always makes sure he eats her food, not mine.

My mother-in-law snaps her fingers at Ashia and shouts her requests. She looks at me as if I am unsuitable for her god–like son and I know she wishes Victor hadn't married a white woman. She is intimidated by me and at the same time she despises me.

Of the three tonnes of household goods that we have shipped

to Ghana, Victor has still hardly let me unpack anything. A fridge, washing machine, freezer; all these things would now be useful. I have been given permission to unpack only the crockery, cutlery, cooking pots, pillows and linen, as well as the furniture I set out in our living room. It looks stunning.

There is a gas stove already in our home so I don't understand why my mother-in-law insists on cooking on an open fire in the yard.

'Please—use it,' I tell her when once again I find her blackening my pots. She doesn't even acknowledge me. I ask her again, my voice louder this time. When there is still no response, I turn to Ashia.

'Please explain to her that the pots are not for use in the fire. She can cook inside on the gas stove.'

Ashia speaks to her in Krobo. But she answers by waving her arms and casting an arrogant look in my direction.

'What does she say?'

Ashia is slow to respond but I know she won't lie to me. 'She says, "My son, the Doctor, bought the pots with his own money, not yours."'

I nod to myself and go back inside.

'I'll wash them for you,' Ashia says, following me. I watch the pots become ugly and feel the same is happening to me.

'The food tastes better that way,' Victor says when I challenge him about this.

Maybe he's right. I don't know because I am not invited to their meals. More and more of Victor's extended family from Somanya seem to live with us now. They come in droves and they sit together at the servants' table, eating, talking in Krobo, joking and laughing.

Now that we are in our new house, Papani and Michael seldom come to visit. Victor has decided to use our yard to make a chicken farm so the house is constantly full of his relatives who tend the birds: sisters-in-law, cousins-in-law. Everyone constantly comes and goes.

To escape their noise, I walk on my own on the beach. I sit on a rocky headland while the waves crash below. It's my refuge and the noise of the water helps drown out my unhappiness. William is too young to know what's happening and I don't like to cry in front of Elsie. I feel that I've been pushed to the very edge of my world.

'Please, Victor,' I demand over and over again, 'do something about your mother.'

She no longer sleeps in the servants' quarters. Instead, she has moved into Victor's room and actually sleeps with him in his bed.

'She says she has heart palpitations and must have a doctor near her,' Ashia explains.

'She needs me,' says Victor. 'Who are you to say she shouldn't do as she wants?'

Part of me wants to laugh. I can't understand how his mother can spend the entire day without a doctor on hand but then be totally dependent upon one at night. It is beyond me.

'I'll bathe Elsie,' Victor's mother announces, lifting her up and carrying her away before I have a chance to protest. My daughter screams. I follow Ayawo, grab Elsie out of her arms and head back into my house.

I discover that my mother-in-law and her family, like all Krobo people, eat cats. One morning I look out the window and see Victor's brother, the chicken farmer, put a cat in a sack and stab it with a knife until it's dead. Most likely it is one of the strays that hangs around the chickens.

He skins the animal and then hands it to Victor's mother.

She carries it inside. Later the air around the servant's quarters is filled with the awful stench of peanut soup with cat meat, the Krobo delicacy they love.

I storm into the kitchen. 'My children aren't eating that!' I shout. I'm terrified of toxoplasmosis.

Victor screams back at me, 'This is our traditional dish and my children are Ghanaians!'

Victor's mother stares at me as if I'm mad, throws up her hands, yells in Krobo—and then turns back to the bubbling soup.

When I take the children to visit him, Papani tells me, 'You're getting too thin.' I shrug. I can hardly bear to eat. Unlike me, Victor's mother is big and strong. She is also very beautiful, with fine features and light honey-coloured skin. When I read in the Bible of Delilah, it's my mother-in-law I imagine. She showers for what seems like hours, rubbing limes cut in half into her skin and under her arms. She dabs herself with perfumed powder and dresses carefully in traditional clothes. Her make-up is always immaculate, her big eyes outlined with charcoal. She walks proudly.

'Let's try and start again,' Victor says when he comes home one night.

'What about Naomi?' I say.

Victor waves his hand as if throwing away rubbish. 'That ended long ago. She's nothing to me. I made a mistake and I'm sorry. This time I promise to be faithful.'

I consider what he says. On one hand, I want to forgive him and start again. On the other, I remember all too clearly my father's infidelities. My mother said she forgave him. And she often reminded him about his other women, making it clear she didn't really forgive or trust him. He never changed.

I think that if Victor is truly remorseful I must forgive him completely.

We make love in Victor's bedroom for the first time since I found the letter. Even though I've made the decision to be here, my sense of betrayal remains. His deception has destroyed my passion and desire. I feel I have nothing, absolutely nothing to give him. The feeling of electricity I once found so tempting has gone. I simply feel empty.

When it's over, I return to my own bedroom.

The next morning, I pass Victor in the hall as I'm on my way to breastfeed William.

'Hellen,' he says, stopping me.

I look up into his eyes, and I know from the coldness I feel inside that we will never make love again. I think he knows this too.

'I'll be a good mother to our children,' I tell him and then I walk away.

William can feel my sadness. I stroke the top of his head gently as he tries to feed. I have hardly any milk but he refuses anything from a bottle. Soon I have no milk at all, a reflection of my misery, I think to myself. My baby loses a frightening amount of weight. For a week all he takes is glucose and water.

'What can I do?' I ask Victor when he comes home.

'You're the mother. Don't you know by now?'

My mother-in-law takes William from me in order to give him a bath. I'm too tired to resist but I hear him crying. When I go in, I find her pressing a hot towel to the soft part of his head in an effort to make it more rounded.

'Please don't,' I beg, holding my arms out for my son.

As I lose more and more weight, sickened by sadness, my mother-in-law seems to assume even more power over my home and my children. One day, when I'm sitting under the mango tree watching Elsie play, my mother-in-law comes up very close to me. She clicks her fingers for Ashia to approach and translate.

'What did she say?' I ask when she has said her piece in Krobo. Ashia looks uncomfortable, but finally she tells me.

'She said, "You look so thin and so small—like a child!"'

'Tell her I'm unhappy. I feel sick and can't eat.'

'She asks what you have to worry about. You're the first wife. You are here and she—Naomi—is there,' Ashia says.

Blood rushes to my head. Dizziness and nausea overtake me. The thought of accepting a second wife overwhelms me. My mother-in-law is telling me that I'm lucky, that being the first wife is an honour that can't be taken away.

What would she know? She has never been a wife. She has several children to different men. I know that she was raised in a well-to-do family where a woman's education was not valued. There would have been an expectation that she would be married off and cared for by a man. I wonder if she's disappointed with the way her life has turned out.

But Ashia is still translating. 'She says you must remember that you have a beautiful, luxurious house and a husband who is a doctor.'

I don't think I'm fortunate. My whole being is crying out that I have made a terrible mistake.

A week later William accepts formula and my appetite returns too. I find I crave Romanian food. I haven't missed it since arriving in Ghana, but now I want to eat sarmale, the cabbage rolls stuffed with minced pork and beef mixed with onion, spices and rice. When I cook, its smell fills the kitchen. I call Papani, who's visiting, to come and try it. I eat and eat. He enjoys it as much as I do.

When Victor arrives home from work, he waves his hand in front of his nose.

'It stinks in here. What is it?'

He lived in Romania for thirteen years and he knows exactly how sarmale smells. 'Its good.' Papani says. 'Will you have some?' But Victor simply leaves without a word.

The next morning I lie in bed, not fully awake. William is in his cot next to the window and Elsie is beside me. I feel a sensation in my stomach. I'm pregnant again. I find Victor in his room dressing for work.

I tell him. I see that he is stifling a laugh but then he looks at me and sees that I am serious.

'Give me a urine sample and I'll take it to the hospital lab.'

I wait for his call. This can only have happened on the one night we slept together, the night that I now know was our last.

Victor rings me from work just before lunch. 'It's true,' he announces. His voice is agitated.

Despite everything, a wave of joy washes over me.

34

The Break

William is so underweight that he can't be immunised. When he's just nine months old, he catches measles.

On one of the few mornings when Victor is at home, our son's temperature shoots up so high that I go into Victor's bedroom. 'He's burning up,' I say.

But when he examines William, he is dismissive. 'It's a common enough illness,' he says. He holds his son briefly in his arms and then puts him back in his cot before he leaves for work.

I go downstairs to make William's bottle but when I come back, I find him cold and still. I stretch out his arms and I touch his cheek but there's no response. I'm distraught. I'm convinced he's dead. There are no ambulances and I have no car. Victor has insisted I don't need to learn to drive.

I run out of the house into the main road holding my baby in my arms and screaming for help. A driver pulls over and asks me what's wrong.

I'm panicking, blind, desperate. 'My baby's sick!' I cry.

The kind driver takes me to Ridge Hospital where Victor works. William's little body is tight and unmoving in my arms and I can't tell if he's breathing or not. A paediatrician sees us immediately, puts an oxygen mask over William's tiny face, gives him intravenous medicine to reduce the fever and sucks mucus out of his nose so he can breathe.

'It was a convulsion,' he explains when William is breathing normally again. 'You did the right thing to bring him here.'

As I hold William, stroking his tiny arm, Victor throws open the door. He looks at me in horror. I realise that my feet are bare.

'How can you come to the hospital looking like this? You've disgraced me,' he says. I say that our baby was dying. Again, he is dismissive. I could argue with him—but there's no point.

After I return home with William, I notice Ashia is not her usual cheerful self. My mother-in-law has just gone back to Somanya. No one tells me why. I don't even know if or when she's coming back. As usual, I'm the last to be told.

Then Ashia, dressed in her best clothes, enters my house looking for me. She stands before me, very straight and formal, and takes a deep breath. Her eyes meet mine, then glance away.

'Madam, I have come to tell you that the doctor is preparing to get married. He will take a second wife,' she says. She watches me closely, worried by how I will react. 'Everyone knows except you. I decided I couldn't wait any longer to tell you.'

So my mother-in-law has gone home to prepare for the wedding! I nod my head and breathe slowly in and out. Who is Victor marrying? Could it be that girl, Naomi? Would he really marry a schoolgirl?

Ashia has more to say. 'Madam, since I've known about this, I haven't been able to look you in the eye. You've been good to me. You've treated me like a sister but I have deceived you—like everybody else.'

Suddenly I realise why she is dressed in her best clothes. Her bags are packed and standing in the hall. By defying her Krobo elders and telling me, she has broken the rules. Now she must leave or risk punishment at the hands of her family.

I cry and cry and then, consumed with rage, I telephone Victor in Somanya. 'How dare you marry a second wife? How dare you not tell me this?' After a moment of silence he hangs up. A few hours later he storms into our compound and heads straight for the servants' quarters.

'Where is she? Where's Ashia?' I hear him demanding. Thank goodness she's already left. I can only hope he'll never find her.

When he finally enters the living room, I explode with rage. 'I told you that if you take a second wife I will leave!'

'And I told you that if you don't like it, there's the door— and there's the dock. If you don't want that, I'll pack your bags and send you back to Romania.' He glares at me. 'Alone.'

Alone. His eyes are already full of hate. He would keep our children here. It is the Ghanaian way.

'If I go back, it will be on my own terms,' I say.

Then I get up and walk out. As I pass him I feel a new strength for what I know will be a battle ahead of me. Suddenly I know what I will do. I will divorce Victor in a court of law and then leave Ghana taking my children with me. His behaviour in taking a second wife, while accepted in traditional Ghanaian society, is not condoned by British law. I know I have grounds for divorce. I can see freedom ahead.

Victor hires two new servants, a young maid and a houseboy, both from Somanya. I have little to do with them. He rarely sleeps at home now. He leaves me little money for the children's needs. He also begins to lock up the food. Every few days he doles out what he thinks we'll need before securing the rest.

When he drives away one evening, I go into his bedroom and look through his papers in search of our marriage certificate. I cannot find the document we signed together.

I haven't revealed to my parents what is happening. 'Everything is wonderful,' I tell them in my letter. I ask my father to send me a copy of our marriage certificate. 'I'm so happy,' I say. 'William is growing bigger every day and Elsie is so much fun.'

I don't want my parents to know what I'm going through. I don't want to tell them yet that I want to divorce Victor and need the certificate. Apart from worrying about it all, they'll say, 'I told you so.' They will also be ashamed of what I'm planning. In their minds, divorce, even from a man they didn't want me to marry, is humiliating. If it happens, I'll be the first divorcee in my family.

I know that I need a lawyer. I visit some, but I can see that they think I'm crazy and all of them make excuses to avoid taking me on. Perhaps because Victor is known and respected, they don't want to represent me. What I want has never before been done in Ghana. If I win, I'll be the first white woman to divorce a Ghanaian on the grounds of adultery.

When Papani comes to see me, I explain it all to him. 'I want a divorce,' I say. Papani shakes his head unhappily but of course he isn't surprised. He's known all along what Victor has been up to, and he has been disappointed.

'Can't you stay with him, Hellen? Can't you try?' he says. But he looks into my eyes and understands how deeply hurt I feel.

'Think carefully before you act,' he says.

It's the same old story here: *Do nothing. Wait and see.*

A few days later Michael arrives at the house. Papani must have been talking to him. Michael hands Amartse's business card to me. 'He is a lawyer, he will help you,' he says.

I examine Amartse's credentials and find that he studied law in England so is accustomed to the European concept of a marriage and to the legal consequences of adultery. He understands how it can constitute grounds for divorce. It will still be hard. Ghana may be ruled by British law but the tradition of having more than one wife is not only permitted, it is honoured. We will be up against conflicting traditions.

After Michael leaves, I can't help wondering why he's doing this. I've always liked him and respected him as my brother-in-law, but Victor is his half-brother. What is happening?

Nevertheless, I ring Amartse's office and request an appointment. 'Is tomorrow morning a good time for you, Madam?' the secretary asks.

'I'll be there.'

35

Finding a Way

The next day when I wake up, I feel as if the children and I are now on our own. Elsie is almost four, William is seven months and my next child is waiting to be born. I ask one of the servants to look after Elsie and William for a few hours. I take care with my appearance and put on a pretty dress. I resolve to use money from my weekly allowance to take a taxi so that I look presentable when I arrive at the lawyer's office.

It is the time of year when the dry harmattan winds are blowing into Ghana from the Western Sahara, bringing huge gusts of heat. Dust covers everything, the people, the countryside, the city, creating a cloudy haze that makes it hard to see.

The taxi takes me to Amartse's chambers and when I enter his office, he extends his hand and smiles warmly. I like him immediately.

'I'm delighted to meet you, Mrs Victor,' he says. 'I will try to help you if I can.'

'Thank you. I'm grateful.'

Amartse is a sophisticated lawyer whose English is perfect and whose chambers look just like those in England that I have seen on Ghanaian television. There are shelves of law books and framed certificates on the walls. His furniture is solid and tasteful. Everything is perfectly maintained, just like the man himself.

My confidence is shaken by his first question. 'Mrs Victor, you're a beautiful lady. Are you having an affair?'

I try not to let my jaw drop. 'Do I look like someone having an affair? Can't you see I'm pregnant? With Victor's child?'

There is a slight pause between us.

I speak firmly. 'I didn't marry my husband to be ignored by him and treated without respect in my own home. Why should I be cast aside while he marries someone else? I won't spend the rest of my life bound by this custom. I need a divorce.'

Amartse will not meet my eyes. He seems unsettled by what he has said. 'Leave it with me. I'll think about what you say and call you if I decide to take your case.'

As I leave, I feel I've failed to discover what kind of man he is. I can't make him out.

Then, two weeks later, he calls. He sighs heavily and I expect bad news. 'We need to meet again. When can you come to my chambers?'

We arrange to meet the following morning. Victor is in Somanya. I toss and turn the whole night, as restless as William.

When I arrive Amartse says, 'I'll be honest with you, Hellen. Victor and I went to the same boarding school and I have a lot of respect for him. Michael wants me to take the case so that I can make Victor see sense and stop the whole thing from going public and dishonouring the family's name.' He looks directly at me. 'I've spoken to Victor.' I wait, wondering what might have passed between them. 'He told me he doesn't want you any more. He says you've lost your mind, that you're mad. He told me to do whatever I think is right.'

I try to control my breathing and stay calm.

As Amartse continues, I have the feeling he has rehearsed this speech. 'It's hard for me to oppose a fellow Ghanaian, someone I know. But I've also listened carefully to you, Hellen, and I want to help. You have the right to bring this case forward and achieve justice for yourself. I will take the case. I understand you have no money to pay me so I will take it pro bono.'

I cannot believe my good fortune. I cry and thank him.

The next time Victor comes home to dole out our food, I stand in the doorway and watch him fiddle with the padlock and then measure out our corn meal, dried beans and rice for the week. I watch him count out some notes with which I am to buy necessities for the children. Not a word is spoken between us.

Our baby is growing inside me and I am now quite large. I wonder if he notices.

The following day, I have an appointment with my specialist. It's the custom to bring a gift, perhaps meat, rice or sugar, and I realise I should have asked Victor for some extra food. If I take it out of what he has left for us, by the end of the week I'll have nothing to feed the children.

One of Victor's Krobo brothers manages the chicken farm in our compound. I ask him if he'll give me a few chickens. 'Madam, I cannot,' he says. 'The doctor counts the chickens as well as the money whenever he comes.'

So I have to use the money Victor has left me to buy two chickens from our own farm. I ask one of our neighbours to help me by pretending the chickens are for him. This means I have no money for a taxi to the hospital. Trotros, the bouncy and unstable public mini-buses, are risky for someone in my condition. Even though it's a hot day, I have no choice but to walk.

When I arrive, I bring the chickens to the specialist. He tells me that everything is fine and that the baby is developing well. 'But take it easy,' he says. 'You're looking thin. I hope you're eating well and resting.'

I nod.

The next time I meet with Amartse he looks stern. 'Victor has hired Robinson to represent him,' he tells me. I wait for him to explain what this means. 'Robinson is much older than I am. He wins his cases using his own well-tested methods. We're going to have a fight on our hands.'

'We will win,' I say firmly.

I can see that Amartse is worried. 'They're going to claim that you have lost your mind, that you're unfit to look after the children. Tell me truthfully, Hellen, do you feel stable?'

'Yes,' I say. 'Sometimes I get emotional and say what I feel, but you can see for yourself that I'm not mad.'

'Good. They've got no evidence against you. Remember that. All you need to do is show that you are stable.'

Victor and I meet in Amartse's chambers with our lawyers beside us. Robinson is over fifty, tall and skinny. He is also a Ga man and from one of the best-known families in Jamestown.

We discuss the issues: my grounds for divorce and our complaints against one another.

'She doesn't know how to look after my children,' Victor says. 'She can't even get my son to eat.'

Victor knows exactly which buttons to press. I can't control my fury. Before I know it, I'm screaming at him. 'How dare you? I do everything I can. Who is the one awake all night? Who is the one who took William to hospital when he nearly died?' I'm raging inside.

Robinson and Victor smile as they rise from their seats.

'See? You've got a nutcase on your hands,' Robinson tells Amartse, snapping his briefcase shut.

When the door has closed behind them, I put my head in my hands and sob. For a while neither Amartse nor I say anything.

I remember the anger I felt as a child when my father's mistress took my red cardigan from me and refused to give it back. 'See?' she said. 'She's out of control.'

I remember my fury when she told my father lies in front of me. I completely lost control over my emotions then—as I have just done again.

'I'm so sorry.' I lift my head from my hands and look at Amartse, who has taken on my case despite everything. I am so grateful to him. He's offered to help me fight his own customs and traditions, to assist a white woman in his own country. I wonder if he thinks, deep down, that I really *am* mad.

I hope not. I need him to trust and believe in me.

Amartse seems to be hiding a smile. 'At least there was no judge here to see that. But, Hellen, if you burst out at Victor again in anger, we could lose the case. And then he can send you away. Without your children.'

He knows that my Ghanaian visa must be renewed every two years, and for that I will need a letter from him to confirm that I am his wife and that he wants me to stay in the country. If my visa expires, Victor can send me back to Romania with a one-way ticket—just as he warned my father.

I know if that happens, I will never see my children again.

Suddenly Amartse is serious. 'I want you to go home and think about the risk you're taking,' he says. 'If you choose to go on with the case, remember that from now on you must behave like the most dutiful of wives. Do you understand?'

'Yes I do,' I reply, hoping that my voice sounds strong and convincing.

He continues, 'That means you must keep your temper under control and do what a good wife does: cook, wash, iron and look after the children. Be a dutiful wife and a good mother. Do you understand?'

Once again, I answer that I do. 'I want my children and I'll do *anything* to win custody of them and my freedom.'

'Please, Mrs Victor, I want you to go home and think. Take time to think properly.'

'I don't need to think. I know exactly what I want and you've made it very clear what I need to do to achieve it. I promise to do what you say.'

Promise for me is a sacred word.

I thank him and walk out, agreeing to come back with my marriage certificate. The paper that gave me the freedom to leave Romania is now the very same paper that holds me as a prisoner in Ghana. I feel as if I am in a cage again. I find it hard to breathe.

Outside the chambers, dust from the desert blows into my face. As I walk home, I think of the promise I have made to my lawyer to be a dutiful wife. I must do it for my children.

'She must do all my housework,' Victor tells the servants after the meeting. Then he reminds them every time he visits. He even brings his dirty laundry in a bag, all the way from Somanya, for me to wash—everything, including his underwear, by hand.

I make sure that each garment is beautifully washed and pressed so that when he collects his clothes there'll be nothing to criticise. The house is immaculate. Even my tablecloths are starched. At last I am the perfect wife.

36

Nancy

On my way home from a visit to the obstetrician, I'm climbing a steep rise. My back is wet with sweat and all my muscles ache. I'm worried that I am stressing the baby, that he or she will be struggling to breathe, just as I am. Then the sky darkens and it starts to rain. I'm caught in one of those tropical downpours that instantly leads to wading through streams of swirling water. The palm trees bend in the wind and coconuts splash into the fast-moving currents.

Within seconds, I'm drenched. I must look a sight, pregnant with my red polka dress saturated and clinging to me. My hair is sodden and plastered to my shoulders. I've always been scared of thunder and lightning and here I am out in the open.

Suddenly I hear a car brake hard behind me. The screeching is carried away by the wind. I tense and clench my eyes tight, preparing to be injured. I turn around and am shocked to see Victor's face glaring back at me through the windscreen. He tilts his head and gives me a sarcastic, mocking smile. He puts his foot down and swerves around me, charging off through the downpour.

I'm so dumbfounded that I can't move. Nobody has ever treated me like this before.

I am now completely focused on divorce.

Victor phones to say he is coming for lunch. It's as if he's booking a table at a restaurant. I decide to make palm nut soup which is a beautiful deep red colour. I will also cook fufu. I ask the servants to bring me the large wooden bowl and the huge pestle they use to pound the cassava. The pestle is as tall as I am. I sit on the wooden stool, place the bowl between my legs. I lift the pestle with both hands, lower it into the bowl and start pounding. Pregnant Ghanaian women do this all the time—and so can I.

When Victor arrives home, everything is ready. He sits at the head of the table waiting for me to serve him. All day the servants have been lingering awkwardly in the kitchen, uncomfortable that I'm being made to do their work and, as a white woman, cook the dishes they have eaten all their lives.

I pour the soup and carry the bowl to the dining area. I place it carefully down in front of Victor. There is a bowl of fufu beside it and water to drink.

'I wonder if it tastes as bad as it looks,' he says. I look straight into his eyes and smile. I keep my promise. He will never make me lose my self-control again.

I say nothing, and as I turn around, I hear him rise behind me. He picks up the soup bowl and smashes it to the floor. Red soup splashes all over me, the table and the floor. Worse, it splashes over the upholstered dining chairs from the suite that my father bought.

When they hear the crash, the servants come running from the kitchen. 'Go!' Victor shouts. 'She must clean it up herself.'

I hurry back to the kitchen and get a bowl of water, soap and a cloth to clean up the mess. I keep my head down and continue to say nothing. Though I am eight months pregnant, I must control my feelings.

Victor sits at the table and watches as I scrub. Bending and kneeling is hard, but I need to remove the stain as quickly as I can. Palm nuts stain indelibly.

I turn my back on my husband. I don't want him to see the salty tears of pain and humiliation running down my cheeks. I feel that behind me he is rejoicing. I try to swallow my tears to make them disappear, but the well seems bottomless.

Suddenly, I sense a white light passing through my body, and all my sorrow and heaviness seem to float away. I feel strong. I know I have to be for my children.

I stop crying and scrub in silence. I focus on my children. Nothing else matters. In a few weeks my baby will come into the world.

I hear Victor get up, go back to his car and drive away. But I don't stop scrubbing. I'm sad that my father's gift, the only thing in the house that I consider mine, has been spoiled.

I have decided to have the birth induced on 11 June 1980 on William's first birthday. My son is still not walking properly. He is continually underweight and often sick. When I fell pregnant so soon after his birth, it was hard for him. I lost my breast milk when he was only a few months old. He refused to drink formula, for a whole week surviving on glucose in water. He will only eat two spoonfuls of mashed potatoes. If offered any more, he will spit it out.

I check myself in to Korle-Bu Hospital. Here, everyone knows that I am Dr Victor's wife. Victor's professional reputation remains high. As a doctor he has it all: a good bedside manner, patience, kindness, compassion and, above all, wonderful surgical skills. He has never caused a post-operation infection, for instance, and is extremely particular about his incisions. When he operates, the cut is always a fine line, something in which he takes huge pride. In his daily life, such skills can become obsessions. Every vegetable in a cooking pot has to be cut a certain way, to a particular shape and size.

'Is Dr Victor coming in?' I am asked. I tell everyone that he is, but the truth is, Victor doesn't know I'm about to give birth. The first and last involvement he has had with this pregnancy was taking a urine sample for testing six months earlier.

This baby is mine alone.

I settle into the delivery room, a drip with intravenous fluid is attached to my arm to help bring on the delivery. The contractions are not strong and the baby shows no signs of wanting to be born. I may need to rest overnight and start again tomorrow.

I hear that Victor has been seen on the ward and has been speaking to my doctor. Once again, he is trying to exert control. The nurse reminds me that she has been instructed to remove the drip and take me back to my ward. I beg her not to remove it. There is still some fluid left. She respects my wishes and wheels me back to the ward. As I am watching the last drops disappearing from the bag, my waters break. Straight away, strong contractions start.

I start screaming, 'My baby is coming!' The nurse rushes back in, takes a quick look, and then runs for the mobile bed to take me into the delivery room. They put me straight on the bare metal table and hurry down the corridor. They struggle to open the door to the delivery room.

It's too late. I give birth to my daughter there, in the corridor.

'A beautiful girl, as white as you are,' I'm told.

When I ask the time, I'm told it's ten minutes to midnight. My baby girl will share her brother's birthday as I'd hoped.

When I look at her face, I know her name. It's Nancy.

The nurse rings Victor to congratulate him. The following day he pulls back the curtain and walks straight to the cradle next to my bed. He picks up Nancy, gives her a kiss and puts her down again.

Then he hands me a small parcel. I take it and immediately throw it back at him. It falls to the floor and opens. A baby's bottle and a few tiny pieces of pink clothing fall out.

'I don't need them,' I scream. Victor turns and walks out.

I look at my daughter and make her a promise, 'I will always provide for you. We don't need Victor. Let him go to Naomi.'

For three days I lie in the hospital with Nancy beside me. She is a soothing presence, placid and content. I am fascinated by how beautiful my little girl is. She is perfect.

Then, back home, when Nancy is four weeks old, I am struck by malaria. I have lost a lot of blood during the birth and am quite weak. I hold onto the wall as I struggle to reach our bathroom near Victor's bedroom. Suddenly I realise he is in there. He must have come in late the previous night. He emerges. Perhaps he will help me? But he just strides down the corridor without giving me a second look. He leaves for his car with a bag of clothes that I've washed.

I could be a stray dog, left to die on the side of the road. His lack of humanity shatters me.

A few days later, I'm feeling better but I am still feverish and having trouble breathing. I'm hanging Nancy's nappies on the line when I hear Victor's car screeching to a halt in the driveway. He climbs out and I can see that there is another person with him, a woman. Without being told, I know that this is Naomi. She leans against the car checking her appearance.

Victor goes inside, no doubt to drop off still more washing, pick up another bag of clean and ironed clothes and dole out our supplies for the week. It reminds me of Romania during the latter part of the Ceausescu dictatorship, this food rationing. One day I spill our rice ration. It scatters all over the floor but I must scoop it up so that we won't run short.

I leave my washing basket in front of the kitchen door and find that I am walking towards Naomi. I can't help myself. She sees me approaching and her eyes widen. In Ghana women sometimes fight over a man. I wonder if this is what she expects from me.

I draw myself up to my full height in front of her. I see that she is young and pretty but that there is a hardness to her face which I don't like.

Suddenly words come out of my mouth. 'I don't fight over rubbish. I'm sorry for you because you're still a young girl, still at school. What he has done to me, he will do to you. And it will be worse for you.'

Then I turn away. I feel unsteady and my heart is racing. I can't go into the house while Victor is there. Instead, I run through the gates of our house to Eunice, my neighbour. She lives across the road with her husband and their three girls. They are an ideal Ghanaian family, happy, principled and successful. I know she cares.

'What's wrong?' she asks me when she sees my stricken face.

'Naomi, the girlfriend, is there with Victor.'

Eunice is angry. She wraps her arms around me. 'Don't worry. It might feel as if they're giving you poison—but you know later they will drink it themselves.'

My head spins. I am falling, falling. I'm hot and cold, my body tingling with pain.

I come out of my faint lying on the ground on a blanket. Eunice is cooling my head with a damp towel while one of her daughters holds my hand and rubs my chest.

'What happened?' I ask.

'It's just the malaria, dear Hellen.'

I struggle to sit up. Across the road, Victor and Naomi stroll to the car and drive away.

37

Preparing to Escape

Victor and I sit at separate tables during a mediation process in the family court. The room is small and square with a low ceiling and the atmosphere is oppressive, as fans whir listlessly overhead.

Warring couples sit in rows of seats like an audience, waiting their turn. I suspect that there are also spectators among them, people curious to see a white woman taking a local man to court.

Normally, Ghanaian women are respectful of their men, but when their anger surfaces, they really lose control. I witness women rising from their seats and screaming at their husbands. It shocks me that there is so much anger bottled up inside them.

Victor and I cannot behave like this. We're considered upper class, respectable. I know that for my husband even attending this court is humiliating. He always arrives wearing his hospital clothes. I know he wants to show everyone what a responsible and successful professional man he is.

Robinson, Victor's lawyer, is stiff and stern. I have never seen him smile. When he looks at me, I feel like his enemy. Does he really believe I'm mad? He has a big battle to fight, since he knows I am the first European woman to file a divorce case against a Ghanaian man on the grounds of adultery, according to British law.

By comparison, Amartse is gentle and seems driven by a need to help me. I can read concern on his face.

As I sit and watch, I breastfeed Nancy. When I'm finished, Victor makes a great show of taking her from me, kissing her and stroking her face before handing her back. The magistrate watches us carefully.

'Why do you think you should have custody of the children?' he asks me.

'Because I am their mother. I care for them and nurture them. I love them more than anything on earth.'

The magistrate turns to Victor and repeats his question. He spreads his hands flat on the table. 'Because she has lost her mind. And because I am a doctor and she is nothing,' he says.

When I hear his words, anger wells up in me so that I feel dizzy. The room spins around me. I think of all the things I gave up for Victor: university, family, friends. I think of the moment he trapped me. But if I show what I feel now, I'll risk losing everything. I stay silent and merely glance at the magistrate. I can see that he, too, is horrified by Victor's words. Even Robinson looks shocked.

'How can you say that about your wife?' asks the magistrate. For a moment, Victor's arrogant armour is pierced. He knows he's let himself down.

After the hearing, Amartse tells me that he is proud of the way I behaved. 'But remember, it won't take much to lose in court—and you know what will happen if you do.'

Victor is furious that I am disgracing him by dragging him through this process and threatening to take his children, the pride and joy of any Ghanaian man. I've heard that he has had to postpone his wedding to Naomi. A traditional wedding to a second wife against the backdrop of divorce is a shameful thing.

'If you weren't the mother of my children, I would have had you killed,' he tells me after one of the mediation sessions, quietly, so that no else one can hear. He doesn't spend time with the children. He rarely even greets them. Since I have often seen the vast compassion he has for his patients, I wonder again how a man's public and private lives can be so different.

When I go next door to Grace's house, she and Eunice are the only ones in whom I can confide. 'Hellen, is your marriage so bad? Isn't the alternative worse?'

No, it's not. My conviction that I am doing the right thing continues to grow. I know I want my children and my freedom, more than anything. I want a way out of this spiral of unhappiness and misery. I am determined to win.

My emotional pain is wearing me down. Victor's words echo in my mind again and again as I wash and fold his shirts: *She is nothing. She is nothing.*

I often feel I am nothing and it's destroying me. I weigh forty-eight kilograms and the malaria won't leave my body. I can't focus on the simplest thing. Sometimes when the children are asleep, I stare at the wall for what seems like hours. Even when they are awake and need me, I'm barely there. Increasingly I leave them to the servants.

It's more and more difficult to haul myself out of bed. I begin to spend all day in my pyjamas, not even bothering to comb my hair. In the mirror I can see that I'm not the woman Victor married. Why has this life of cruelty and isolation descended on me?

For the first time I feel that I have no strength to climb that mountain that my grandmother always talked about. Then I see my children, Elsie and William, playing in the yard and I look at Nancy in my arms, so peaceful and sweet. I know that no one will love them and care about them as much as I do. I am their mother and a mother is irreplaceable.

I recall the night I sat by my window in terror, fearing my own mother would walk down to the shed and end her own life.

I take a deep breath and gather my strength.

38

The Promise of Heaven

In the midst of this depressing period, I wake from a nightmare. In the darkness, Mama Draga, my beloved grandmother, was moving through a black hole in the wall. It was shaped like a coffin. I heard her begin to cry. I saw tears flooding her face.

In the dark night I try to make sense of the dream. I recall the day I walked out of the church with her and asked if she was scared of Heaven. 'Oh no—I'm looking forward to it. It's death that frightens me,' she said.

And when I asked where Heaven is, she pointed at the bright blue sky and told me that's where it is. Why did I see a black hole in my dream instead of a bright blue sky? I toss and turn. There is no way I will get back to sleep now. The clock ticks loudly and slowly. There are several hours until daybreak.

I wonder how quickly I can book an international phone call to Romania. I will need to wait days before it comes through. Too long. I close my eyes and memories of my childhood in Cluj come flooding back to me. I begin to cry. I was her most precious granddaughter; she was my rock.

Apart from my children, Mama Draga has provided the only real joy in my life. She protected me for as long as she could. She helped me grow wings to fly. She taught me how to love and is certainly the source of any courage and strength I have.

A few days later the international call comes through. 'Lenuta,' says my mother, softly, from so many miles away.

'Did Mama Draga die?' I ask.

'How do you know?

'I had a dream. She passed through a black hole, the sign of death.'

'She passed away a few days ago. I've just come back from her funeral. She died peacefully.'

My last promise to Mama Draga is that I will share her unconditional love, warmth and comfort. I pledge that I will pass it on to my children.

Now it is I who must become the rock.

39

Divorce

Amartse calls me to his chambers to tell me that the date for the divorce has been set: 18 March 1981, Elsie's birthday. We have been waiting for over a year for the final hearing. I try to persuade my lawyer to change the date. I have promised Elsie a party with her friends from kindergarten.

'I am sorry, Hellen. We must make the most of our luck in being granted a female judge. She'll know how you're feeling.'

I take Amartse's advice. I trust his judgement.

The day before the hearing, Amartse and I have a final meeting. I like being with him in his office. He gives me strength. We sit facing one another on his leather couches and discuss the case in detail.

'You do understand what you're doing, Hellen, don't you?' he says, seriously. 'It's not too late to change your mind.'

'Yes, Amartse, I understand. There is no chance that I will change my mind. The divorce must go ahead.'

Like the good lawyer he is, Amartse goes through everything point by point. 'You know that Victor can afford to send the children to a very good private school. You won't be able to do that.'

'I love my children and I will give them my very best. I know I can do it,' I say.

★

That evening I begin to prepare for Elsie's party. I decorate the room and bake a cake. While I'm frying plantain chips, Victor and my mother-in-law arrive from Somanya. They sit and talk with Victor's brother, the chicken farmer. They make food and eat it together in the servants' quarters, laughing and singing. It seems a joyful occasion for them.

It's late when I hear Victor enter the main house, shower, and go to sleep in his bedroom. Finally, after tossing and turning I fall into a deep, dreamless sleep.

The next morning, my bedroom door is opened abruptly. I'm dressing. Victor stands and stares straight into my eyes. He is looking smart in his hospital clothes. There's a bittersweet smile on his face. It's as if he's warning me to consider the consequences. I want to say something to him but I turn away. This is the last time I will remain silent, I tell myself.

The court for this hearing is in a British colonial building with imposing pillars and steps sweeping up to the entrance. It seems to stand in defiance of Ghanaian culture. British notions of justice and the rule of law seem not to register with many here when it comes to marriage. Instead, the wisdom of elders is sought. But today, for me, this court is a symbol of being treated justly.

I recall the day five years ago when I gave birth to our first daughter. I remember the fear I had carried for so long that I would not be able to be a mother. I recall my friend Petronella's words of reassurance, 'Don't worry. You may never have children—but I'm sure you'll have a happy marriage.'

Well, now I have three beautiful children and no marriage.

I have decided not to wear a Ghanaian traditional outfit. Instead, I wear a European-style dress. It shows how much weight I've lost. I'm almost twenty-eight but I feel and look fifty. All I want to do is survive this day.

It takes me an hour to walk to the court where Amartse is waiting for me on the steps. I can see that he too has slept badly.

'Have you seen Victor?' he asks at once.

'I saw him this morning, dressed for work.'

It's time to go inside. Although I'm focusing on my belief that we're going to win, there is a strange mixture of emotions churning within me. The past, present and future swirl around inside my head.

The courtroom feels hot. We sit right at the front. Amartse keeps looking at his watch and turning to the door where he expects Victor to appear. Time passes and there is no sign of either Victor or Robinson.

The Judge will sit behind a desk of dark polished wood in a seat that is as majestic as a throne. In front of it and below are smaller desks where court officials shuffle papers, type and make notes. Around us everyone is quiet and the only movements are the robotic comings and goings of the officials. Suddenly the enormity of the risk I'm taking looms before me.

'Be upstanding for Her Honour the Judge,' announces the clerk.

She enters, a beautiful woman, tall and slim, whose features are strong but not severe. I examine her face as if it will tell me what she has determined about my future.

'Please be seated,' she says. I see sympathy in her face. Her hair is cut in a bob and she wears her black gown over a simple white blouse. I admire her. I am sure she will be fair.

She leafs through the papers in front of her. 'I call on the petitioner and the respondent,' she says.

We look around again but neither Victor nor Robinson has appeared. Amartse and I rise. The judge nods at us then indicates where they should be sitting.

'Do you know why the respondent is not here?' she asks Amartse.

'We do not, your Honour,' he replies.

She nods and says she will adjourn the session for half an hour in case they have been delayed in traffic. We all rise as she leaves.

Victor is never late. I have come to know Robinson as someone who is always punctual. When half an hour has passed, the judge returns and we go again through the same procedure. Now I know for certain they are not coming.

'The court will proceed with the case in the absence of the respondent,' says the judge.

Before I can really take it in, she is giving her judgement. She declares that the marriage between Victor and me will be dissolved on the grounds that 'it has broken down beyond reconciliation'. She orders that I will have custody of the three children and that Victor must pay 600 cedis a month for their maintenance. Further, he must pay their school fees, provide clothing and pay medical expenses. Victor is also ordered to pay 500 cedis for the costs of the case.

I am overcome with shock and joy. But there is a condition—a huge one. I'm not allowed to take the children out of the country without Victor's or the court's permission.

But we've won. I can hardly believe, after all I've been through, that today was so easy. I have been prepared to be examined and cross-examined, to control myself against

208

every attack. Now in minutes, it's all over. I have nothing more to do.

After months of food rations and so little money, my future will be more than comfortable. And the children! The children are mine. The ban on taking them out of the country I will deal with later, I think.

I rise and bow. 'Thank you, Your Honour,' I say. She inclines her head.

Outside the courtroom I still can't believe what's happened. Amartse is obviously relieved that the judgement is in our favour. He asks me if I would like a lift home but I want to walk. I want to stride out and put it all behind me.

He nods and as I look at his gentle face, I wonder what price he will have to pay for his involvement in my case. He has gone against a fellow Ghanaian, a well-known doctor who was his schoolmate. Beyond that, he has set a precedent. Now European women can take their men to court and gain control of their lives and their children.

I walk home feeling free, free, free. Around me everything is suddenly brighter. The street seems wider, the sky bluer and more expansive. I realise that for months I have been walking with my head down, my mind crammed with dark thoughts. How wonderful it is to be happy again!

When I arrive home, I push back the furniture and hang up balloons for Elsie's party. I write 'Happy Birthday, Elsie' on a big sheet of white cardboard and stick it to the wall.

She arrives home from kindergarten surrounded by her friends, their mothers and their servants. I've never seen her so excited. She has chosen a pretty dress to wear and she walks around looking like a princess. The other mothers' servants hand around plates of Ghanaian snacks and we drink Fanta and Coke, treats we cannot usually afford. I put on music and the children dance with joy.

When everyone has gone and night has fallen, the servants help me clean the house. Then I climb into bed beside Elsie and William. Nancy is close by in her cot. I drift into a deep and peaceful sleep.

40

Alex

Each morning, the first thing I do after checking that the children are safe is look out through the window of our bedroom. I admire the lush green mango tree hung with fat orange fruit. This morning, rather than enjoying the wind in the leaves and the sweet fragrance of the mangoes, the reality of my situation strikes. I am now wholly responsible for my children's lives: their welfare, their happiness, their education. I am on my own.

This frightens me. I feel tears rolling down my face. How will I cope? I cover my head with the sheet and press my mouth against the pillow to silence my sobs. I don't want the children to hear me crying or to see how scared I am. What they need is security and comfort.

I remember Mama Draga's story of the cross we carry and start praying hard, my face still pressed against the pillow.

'God, give me courage and strength to carry the cross I have chosen.' After I repeat this a few times, I feel calmer. Surely I can trust God to help me in the coming months?

The stark facts of my life confront me. I have a year left on my Ghanaian visa. After that, Victor will be able to buy me a one-way ticket to Romania and send me away for good. I will never see my children again. In the coming weeks, I hear what he is telling everyone. His meaning is unmistakable. 'I didn't fight her in court because I didn't have time to waste. When her visa expires, I'll buy a one-way ticket and send her back.'

Victor has moved his mother into the house again. I'm sure it's because he wants her to spy on me, to see what I'm doing and planning. One evening I come across her trying to bathe William again. He is in tears, resisting her.

'They're my children, not yours,' I tell her. 'I bathe my own children.' She ignores me and continues soaping my son.

'I said that I bathe my own children.' I gently take William's arm and put my other hand on her shoulder, forcing her to acknowledge me.

'Don't pretend you don't understand me. This isn't your house. These are my children.'

Reluctantly, she lets William go and backs away—but her eyes tell me how much she despises me.

Another day she sits in the kitchen while Victor irons one of his shirts. No longer does this task fall to me. They talk together in Krobo while I warm milk for Nancy. For once, Victor's mother directs a remark at me. 'Hellen, when you go, leave the children with the Doctor. Here in Ghana women give children to the men,' she says in her broken English.

'In my country only prostitutes give their children to men,' I reply.

'Don't you ever speak to my mother like that again,' says Victor. I look him in the eye and repeat it. He lifts the iron and throws it at my head. Fortunately, he misses.

'Lucky for you that you're the mother of my children. I would surely have had you killed by now if you weren't,' he tells me.

I leave with Nancy's milk bottle held between my hands. They are trembling. I must control myself and not tempt fate.

I have seen none of the money the court ordered Victor to pay me. Often I feel as much a prisoner as before. 'I need friends,' I tell our neighbour Grace.

One of her acquaintances is a young woman called Gemma, attractive and lively, full of laughter and fun. She invites me to a party and introduces me to her women friends who all seem interesting. Some are married but others are still single. Several have lived overseas in London or other parts of Europe. They have experienced another life beyond their local culture and customs and express it through rebellion and sophistication.

I decide it's time to rebel against Victor's narrow views and expectations. 'Now that I'm free, I can please myself,' I remind myself among Gemma's friends when one of them offers me a cigarette. Though Victor would disapprove, I take it and light up, inhaling deeply. It tastes bitter but I force myself to keep smoking. I feel defiant.

Someone else offers me a drink but I refuse. One rebellion at a time is enough.

Parties have never been easy for me but these women are so warm. Everyone encourages me to consider staying in Accra. I tell them I need to renew my visa. Several promise to help and support me. The truth is that no Ghanaian woman likes her man marrying a second wife and these women are proud of me for having the courage to take Victor to court. They know from their own experience how lonely you can feel in a foreign land, and they understand how discrimination feels. Before the party ends, while others are still dancing and talking, Gemma leads me into a quiet corner.

'I think I have the answer to all your problems,' she says.

There is a big twinkle in her eye. 'Leave it to me.'

She calls me a week later. 'Good news, Hellen,' she says. 'A friend of mine knows a man called Alex. She's told him all about you and what has happened with Victor. Alex has a big heart. He wants to help you.'

'Help me? How?'

'He wants to marry you.'

I gasp in disbelief. I have just escaped one marriage. Why on earth would I want to entangle myself in another?

'He was told you need to extend your visa. He knows you want to leave the country but have no money. He can help you, Hellen. You must let him.'

If I agree to this outlandish plan, Victor can of course withdraw my alimony. In fact, it has never been paid. At the moment extending my visa is my priority.

I tell kind Gemma that I will consider her friend's offer very, very carefully.

Alex is one of Ghana's most successful men, an architect and civil engineer with his own company. He comes from a good family and he has a reputation for being proper and principled. When he was studying in Denmark, he met Greta and they married and returned to Ghana. They had three children together.

'What happened to Greta?' I ask Gemma.

'She got sick and needed an operation. She could have gone overseas to be treated but she loved Ghana so much she wanted to be cared for here. She died not long ago.'

I'm intrigued. 'Was she beautiful?'

'Oh—very. She was blonde, a lovely woman, but very western. She didn't dress Ghanaian like you. Alex was happy for her to live the way she pleased.'

Alex comes one night to take me to dinner. I'm waiting

outside but I know that behind me, my ex-mother-in-law is peering out the window, trying to find out what is going on. She knows I showered and dressed and kissed my children goodnight. I have no doubt that she will report everything back to Victor.

A car pulls up outside the gate, the latest model Jaguar. I approach the car and bend over to peer in the window.

'Hello—I'm Alex,' he says. I introduce myself, get in and the car moves off. At first it's hard to know what to talk about. I glance sideways at my benefactor as we drive. He has a strong-featured, square face. I cannot tell the tribe to which he belongs. I have been told he is older but I didn't realise how old. He must be in his late forties. On his finger he wears not one but two gold rings.

'So,' he says.

'So,' I reply.

The feeling between us is neither awkward nor romantic. It's businesslike. This will be an arrangement. I am on a mission to extend my visa.

Alex's car is immaculate but it smells of cigarette smoke. When he finishes one, he extinguishes it only to light another straight away.

We stop outside a Chinese restaurant, an imposing place I have seen from outside but never entered. When we've seated ourselves in a quiet corner and ordered our meal, Alex looks me calmly in the eye.

'I was told you needed help because your visa is about to expire. Tell me everything that has happened to you,' he says simply.

I lay everything out as fully as possible. He nods as he listens and when I finish, without hesitation, he says, 'I will help you.'

Even after this short encounter, I feel I can trust him. He seems a good man. But I still have to ask the question anyone would, 'Why are you helping me?'

He shrugs. 'Maybe I'm ashamed of some Ghanaian men who marry white women but don't respect their customs. Perhaps I think this brings shame on all of us.'

I wonder if he is looking for a new wife. 'Will you tell me about Greta?' I ask. Immediately his face tightens with sadness. I see from his eyes how much he still loves her even though she has been dead for more than a year.

'She was having an operation. It didn't seem life threatening. But she developed haemolytic anaemia, with her red blood cells breaking down, and needed a transfusion. They made a mistake. They gave her blood from the wrong group—and it killed her.'

Alex pauses and breathes deeply. He is clearly still upset.

'Greta was in one of the best private hospitals in Accra. I wanted her to have the operation in Denmark—but she wouldn't go. I should have insisted.'

We talk about happier subjects: our children. He has two boys and a girl, older than my three. I tell him about them. I talk about Romania and the dreams I had when I was young. He is a good listener.

We finish our food and they come to take away our plates.

'If I'm to help you, perhaps you'd like to see my house? We can have tea there.'

For some reason, I hesitate. There are so many things I need to consider. 'I should be getting back to the children,' I say.

'My home is close by,' Alex tells me. So I agree.

High walls encircle a substantial property. We drive in through a tall iron gate. The watchman nods to us as we pass.

'I like Muslim men to work for me,' Alex says. 'They are the most loyal and hard-working.'

We park in a double garage and Alex comes around to open my door, not something that Victor would ever do.

When I see Alex's house, my jaw drops. I've never seen anything like it, not even in the movies and certainly not in Ghana. The house is round and seems to be made entirely of glass. Everywhere I look I can see through to another curving room. Through the transparent wall of the living room, I see a central garden and a swimming pool.

Alex invites me to sit on one of his big soft leather couches.

'This is very beautiful,' I say. The room is enormous but decorated in a simple, tasteful way. There are tall lamps and Persian rugs.

When he offers me tea, he invites me into the kitchen. As I enter, I try not to show how amazed I am. It is huge with everything in its place and sparkling. I think of the small old kitchen at Victor's house and all our equipment still in packing cases at Papani's house. I return to the living room while Alex makes tea.

Despite the beauty and tranquillity of the surroundings, something doesn't feel quite right. Then suddenly, through the big glass window, I see a tall, elegant young Ghanaian woman walking towards the garage. Her hair is cropped short and she wears tailored pants with a tight, short jacket over a white shirt. Her head is held high and her back is straight. She looks like a model striding down the catwalk.

'Is anyone else here?' I ask later as we sip our tea.

'The children and the servants and my sister, who's visiting.'

The woman must be his sister, I think. Though surely she is too young.

After we have chatted for a while I tell him that I must get back to the children.

He nods and we leave our tea half-finished. He leads me through a large glass door and down the steps into the garden. As soon as I step outside, the smell of roses surrounds me and I realise it's the first time I've smelled that heady scent in Africa. They rise out of the darkness. Among them are black roses which I have never seen before.

'Yes, I planned the garden myself and I had them imported.'

Just then, I hear a woman's voice. 'Alex! Alex!'

I turn to him but he makes no response, just jiggles the keys in his hand and continues to gaze fondly at his roses.

'Who's that calling you?' I ask.

'What?' he says, turning as if he hasn't heard anything. 'Please, keep on walking. Don't turn round.'

My skin feels cold and I feel as if I have heard a ghost. I keep walking as instructed.

In the garage Alex opens the door of a white Peugeot for me. As we drive out through the gate that the watchman opens for us once more, I say nothing of what I've seen. I am trying to stay calm but I can't help feeling that there is some mystery in this big luxurious house.

We drive a few metres along the road when there is a muffled explosion from under the bonnet. Smoke rises. Alex brakes sharply and runs to my side of the car to help me out. The watchman also comes running and asks us if we are all right.

We're shaken but Alex reassures me that it's nothing serious, just a problem with the engine that could have happened any time.

'Will you see to this car?' he asks the watchman. 'We'll take the Jaguar.' He offers me his arm and leads me back to the garage.

'It was a sign,' he says.

'Of what?'

But he doesn't answer.

That night I can't sleep. A luxurious home like nothing I have ever seen before. A ghost. An explosion. Potential marriage to a man I barely know. Everything whirls around in my mind. For the moment it is overwhelming.

Once again, I am baffled by my own life.

41

Safe Haven

Victor has heard about Alex. When he confronts me, the look on his face is terrifying.

I know I must stand up to him. 'It was fine for you to bring your girlfriend to the house while we were married,' I remind him. 'Are you telling me that now we're divorced, I can't have dinner with a man?'

'Watch out,' he tells me. 'You're going too far.'

Despite the court's ruling, nothing has changed. I still haven't received any money. Victor still comes and measures out our food. My long-awaited freedom still seems far away.

Despite my misgivings, Alex seems to be my only way out. He takes me to dinner several times. Victor spends more evenings at home too so I'm sure he's keeping an eye on me. I'm terrified the two men will meet and fear how Victor might react. After the shame of divorce, the knowledge that I'm spending time with one of Ghana's wealthiest men is humiliating for my ex-husband.

'I'm scared. Victor keeps watching me and I can't bear it any longer,' I tell another friend, Mary.

'Come and stay with us. You'll feel safer. We have a spare room with a double bed,' she says.

I don't tell anyone we are going. I simply arrange for Alex to send his driver for us in the Jaguar. Elsie is at kindergarten and when I see the car arrive, I pick up Nancy and William and carry them out to it. The driver, Inosa, looks after my children while I run back inside and collect the bags I've secretly packed. I carry two out and then hurry back for two more.

Victor's mother has been in the servant's quarters, but when she realises what's happening, she runs screaming out of the house, crying and hitting her head. 'Where are you going? What are you doing?'

I understand her despair. After all, these are her grandchildren I am taking away. But I know that the longer I stay in Victor's house, the more I fear for my life. And my children need their mother.

Inosa drives off. The escape has taken all of five minutes.

Mary and her husband live with their children in a simple little house. The room they provide for us is about two metres by four.

'I won't let you live like this,' Alex says when he comes to pick me up soon after we move in with Mary.

'We're fine,' I tell him.

'You can come and live properly in my house, downstairs. I have private facilities for my guests who are always welcome. If you're prepared to let me help you by marrying you, I can also give you somewhere comfortable to live.'

I'm not sure why I don't want to move into his beautiful house. I think it's because I want to keep our relationship businesslike. But sleeping in a double bed in a small room with all my children is not easy. It doesn't take long for my resistance to weaken.

'You'll be entirely independent,' Alex reassures me. 'You'll have your own space, your own bathroom. Whatever you need.'

Within a week, I thank Mary for her hospitality and we move in with Alex.

Elsie and William wander around this vast glass paradise wide-eyed. It's lovely to watch my daughter's utter astonishment. I see her delight as she discovers the beautiful modern bathroom. She enters it full of curiosity. She can just reach the taps.

'As I've said,' Alex says, watching us fondly from the doorway, 'you can live your own lives. You can do exactly what you want.'

He also gives me an allowance. Ridiculous amounts of money. I've never seen so many cedis all at once. 'And this is the safe,' he says, leading me to a cupboard in his bedroom. It is built into the wall inside. He opens it and gives me the combination. Inside are neat stacks of notes.

'Help yourself whenever you need money,' he says.

I feel as if I'm in a different world.

The big house has four servants. 'Two of them do the washing and the housework,' Alex explains. 'The other two work in the kitchen. If you want something cooked, just tell them. Otherwise there's a set meal which we plan a month in advance.'

Normally, if I want fufu, I make fufu. If the children ask me for fried plantain, that's what we have. I wonder how I'll cope with so much organisation.

There's more. 'Use the driver whenever you need,' he continues. 'But I want you to sit behind, not in the front with him. And the watchman sits near the gate all day and all night so you and the children will always be safe.'

Although I still feel nervous and uncertain, how could I

not be grateful to this kind and generous man?

I come and go as I please taking Elsie to kindergarten or William and Nancy on outings to the beach. Sometimes I leave the children with the housemaid and visit Grace or Eunice.

Alex's three children, two boys and a girl, are older than mine and always seem to be studying or at school. I feel uneasy around them. They have not gone out of their way to welcome us. After several weeks, the topic of marriage is finally raised. 'When is your deadline?' Alex asks.

'My visa expires in May. There's still plenty of time,' I tell him, hoping to postpone it.

'Better to do it soon to avoid complications later,' he says. 'We don't know what Victor might be planning.'

I know he is right.

'How about January?' he suggests.

'Not January,' I say. I married Victor in January. 'Can we make it February?'

Alex nods. I have the feeling that he would do anything I asked.

On the day of our wedding, 3 February 1982, I wear a white dress and pull my hair up in a French roll. I examine my face in the mirror. I look joyless and feel empty. I try to focus on my purpose, my visa renewal. It gives me the strength to leave the room and join my husband-to-be.

Alex has never commented on the way I look, but today he rises as I enter the living room and takes in every inch of me. He smiles.

'You look lovely. Do I look all right?' he asks.

His suit is dark brown and his shoes as shiny as ever. He isn't wearing a tie.

'Very nice,' I say.

It is only five years since my first wedding. Is this really what I want? For now, however, it seems the only way.

I leave the children with the servants and we don't even tell them what we're doing. We are a small party: just Alex and I with Grace and Gemma, who will be our witnesses. I greet them both warmly when we arrive at the registry office. The room is sunny, neat and functional.

'Thank you for coming,' I whisper to them both and squeeze their hands.

'Anything for you, Hellen,' says Grace.

When the ceremony is over, the registrar tells Alex he may kiss his bride. He kisses my cheek in a kindly way.

The lunch the four of us have together is polite and restrained. I glance across at Alex and watch him as he eats. He is thoughtful and quiet, listening to us talk but rarely commenting. I'm beginning to understand how clever and sensitive he is, how attuned to others' feelings. Guilt washes over me. I worry that he is hoping this marriage will be something more than an arrangement to extend my visa and gain time to smuggle my children out of Ghana.

But I let it rest. After my initial doubts, I now trust Alex completely. He is a gentleman and I know he will never force me to do anything I don't want.

That night we eat dinner as usual with all our children and watch television. After I put mine to bed, I step out into the garden and the scent of the roses enfolds me. In the moonlight, they all look the same except the black ones which stand out, dense and solid. Their smell is rich and fragrant, filling the air.

I come back into the living room where Alex is staring at the television screen without watching the program. 'Thank you, Alex, for everything you're doing for me and the children,' I say warmly.

He smiles and nods.

I hope, for now at least, that this is enough for him.

42

The Juju Doctor

Every morning Alex heads off to his office and his children go to their high school. Inosa waits outside ready to take Elsie to school. He is short and thin and comes from a Muslim family in the north of Ghana. When I see him, so tiny behind the wheel of Alex's enormous car, I can't help smiling. He always has a big smile on his face.

'So long as you have my name, you will never walk anywhere,' Alex tells me.

Elsie loves being driven around like a princess. After we drop her at school, sometimes Inosa drives me to the expensive shopping centre. As Alex's wife, I no longer go to Makola Market. He prefers that our servants shop there. Occasionally I ask Inosa to drive me to the beach. Walking along the smooth white sand, breathing the fresh salty air, I no longer cry. I watch the waves crashing against the rocks, throwing up spray. The sight resonates with me. I have been hurled against the rocks of pain and deceit, by my father when I was a little girl and then by Victor.

At three each afternoon Inosa and I pick up Elsie. I sit with her while she does her homework. I bathe William and Nancy and we play together until it's time for dinner. These days, I don't do any cleaning, washing or cooking.

At five-thirty Alex comes home and his children return from high school. We sit together at the dining table for our only family ritual, dinner. Alex sits at the head near his children, facing me, Elsie, William and Nancy. Two servants stand ready to attend to us. The enormous table has room for many more people. We eat Ghanaian food with knives and forks, not with our hands in the traditional way as we did in Victor's house. We don't talk noisily as we did at Victor's either. Here there is only the sound of eating and the occasional polite remark.

Most of the time, Elsie loves this life. She sits up at the table, her elbows tucked in and her back very straight, acting 'like a lady'.

Victor is entitled to one weekend with the children every two weeks. I know he tells them lies about me. I know he feeds them cat meat. They spend more time with Victor's mother and Naomi than with their father. 'I hate you, I hate you,' William shouts after the first visit, pushing me away. It takes days for him to warm to me again.

I know what Alex thinks of Victor. For a start, he looks down on Krobo people. It doesn't matter to him that Victor is a respected doctor. 'You do not humiliate your wife. You do not let your pregnant wife walk to the hospital in the heat. You must respect and look after the woman you marry,' he says.

'You shouldn't send the children to Victor at all,' he continues. 'When the man starts to pay you maintenance, then he has some rights.'

He's right, but I'm determined to do exactly as the court has ordered. After dinner, Alex's children go to their bedrooms but mine crawl all over me on the sofa, laughing and playing.

Alex, drinking his coffee and watching television, says nothing, but I know he disapproves. However, he melts when Elsie sits next to him, resting her head on his arm.

'Tell me a story, Alex,' she pleads. You can see his mood lighten. He indulges her and she has learned how to exploit this. But he is still happiest when all the children are tucked up in bed. I feel differently. I am happiest with my children around me.

Then something strange happens. Pain, like a knife stuck into the right side of my body, strikes and will not go away. When I am lying down, I feel no pain. As soon as I rise, it stabs me and I must hold myself firmly and walk with my back bent. For a while, I don't say anything to Alex, hoping it will go away. But finally it's impossible to hide.

'What's wrong?' Alex asks me, his face full of concern.

I describe the pain, the way it is spreading over my body from my right side. 'Perhaps it's my liver,' I suggest. He insists I see doctors, the best in Accra.

'It's fine. It will pass.'

'My wife held her side like that before she died,' he tells me. From his face, I know that seeing me like this is reliving his nightmare.

Then he asks me a question. 'Tell me about the first night when you visited my house, the time the car engine exploded. Did you see anyone or did you just hear someone calling me?'

'I saw a tall, elegant young woman walking towards the garage. Her hair was cropped short and she wore pants and a short jacket. She walked like a model. I thought she must be your sister—but somehow she looked too young.'

Without a word Alex turns away from me and goes upstairs. Soon he returns holding a photo album. He asks me to look through it and tell him if I recognise anyone. I turn page after page and then suddenly stop. I recognise her. I point at the photo.

'That's her.'

Alex looks straight into my eyes. 'She is a family friend. She is *dead*!'

My skin feels as cold as that night when I heard her calling his name.

'We must go to a juju doctor for healing,' Alex says. 'We'll drive there tomorrow.'

I know there's no point trying to dissuade him. Juju doctors claim sick people are under the spell of black magic, and that they can heal them. In Romania there are similar beliefs. My mother once sought advice to try to break up the relationship between my father and one of his women. A gypsy woman came to our house and performed a ritual with chicken droppings, hair, ash and feathers. Not long after, my father ended his relationship with the woman.

It is a long way to the juju doctor, a couple of hours along a bumpy road. It's an excruciating journey for me. My pain seems to worsen the further we travel.

Finally we arrive at the village and Alex leads me to a round mud hut thatched with straw. Out here in the countryside, the air is hot and dry and dust cakes my feet and ankles. The sun is so bright it makes me squint. The pain in my side is like fire.

The hut entrance is low and Alex must bend so he doesn't hit his head. As our eyes adjust to the darkness, we see an old man who greets us and invites us to sit. He doesn't smile. In the corner of the room are pots and totems of straw and bark. I see animal skulls and bundles of cloth in the shape of figures.

I had imagined the doctor would be wearing clothes made

from leaves and bark. I'd expected a bone through his nose and a painted face, but this white-haired old man is wearing shorts and a T-shirt. His feet are bare. His eyes, however, are all that I imagined. As I sit, my hands nervously gripping my knees, I feel his eyes bore into me. They seem to see right through to my bones.

He circles and inspects me but doesn't come close or touch.

Alex watches him carefully. He is nervous too, afraid of what might be wrong with me. I know it disturbs him to see me suffer.

The juju doctor turns to Alex and speaks in a language I don't understand. I want Alex to explain what's happening but he's listening intently. The expression on his face worries me. The old man is clearly giving him bad news.

When the old man finishes, Alex turns to me. His eyes are sad like pits of darkness. He translates the juju doctor's words.

'He has told me to ask you to leave Ghana as soon as possible. He says the power of the black magic on you is very strong. He won't be able to break it.'

Alex is in shock and, even though I don't understand juju, I feel as if I am too.

'Did he tell you anything else?' I ask.

'Yes. He said that if we don't do what he says, the same thing that happened to Greta will happen to you. You will die too.'

Alex gives the juju doctor some money, thanks him and we leave. We barely speak on the long drive home.

43

The Woman in the Gutter

O ne day I am driving with Inosa through Makola
Market. I am lost in my thoughts. My days are now
preoccupied with formulating a plan to smuggle my
children out of Ghana. I have been losing weight with worry.
My body is thin and weak, my right side is still in pain but my
mind is completely focused.

I know I can get my children away from Africa.

As the car moves slowly through the busy, crowded market,
I stare absently out the window. Suddenly I see someone lying
sprawled in the gutter. As I look more closely, I'm sure this
woman is the European I've heard spoken about among the
people of Accra. It brings tears to some, while others simply
shake their heads grimly and say, 'It's up to us to choose our
own fate.'

Every time I hear people speak of her I feel a great fear. There
are so many parallels with my own life. People say a northern
European woman married a Ghanaian man studying in her
country. Together they travel to Ghana. They have children
together. After a while, he decides to take a second wife. She
is angry and when she refuses to accept his choice, he takes
their children away and casts her out of his life. Abandoned

and penniless, she has nowhere to live. She drinks to ease her pain.

'Inosa, please stop! I need to help this European lady.'

He pulls over. His eyes follow my own and we look at the woman lying insensible and dishevelled.

'Madam, she is lost. Don't worry about her,' he says gravely.

'Wait for me,' I say as I get out of the car.

I approach the woman. Her hair is long and matted, and even from a distance I can smell the rank odour. Gutters in Ghana run with smelly waste. Here in the markets they are full of dark sewage mixed with vegetable scraps, a toxic sludge. I cover my nose because the smell is unbearable.

The woman's clothes are torn and soiled. I bend down and try to shake her into consciousness. I want to help her but I have no idea how.

She doesn't respond to my touch. She makes nonsense sounds, delirious. Tears run down my face. I feel I understand why she has come to this. She could be me. We both bear the consequences of choices made when we married, young and innocent, into a foreign culture.

Love cannot conquer all. The reality lies before me, ruined.

'Madam!' Inosa appears beside me. He is embarrassed.

'What can I do?' I ask him. 'We must help her.'

But he is shaking his head. People are passing by, not stopping, I hear them whisper to one another, 'Look at that *obroni*!' It would be unthinkable to come upon a Ghanaian woman, drunk and lost, lying in the street. It is seen as weakness to fall so low.

I can barely see through my tears. I wonder about the woman's family. What about her children?

'There is nothing we can do here, Madam,' Inosa whispers.

I know he's right, although it breaks my heart to leave her

this way. Slowly, I follow him back to the car.

That night I tell Alex what we have seen. He bows his head. 'It shames us to let this happen. All we do is watch,' he says.

I feel a sudden rush of gratitude for what he has done for me. 'Thank you, Alex, for helping me.'

He lifts his head and looks right into my eyes. 'I needed to help you.'

I can see that marrying me has been a moral choice for him. He has chosen to open one cage and let one bird fly away. I was so lucky it was me he chose.

Encountering the woman in the gutter hardens my resolve. I must now pursue my plan single-mindedly. Getting a Romanian passport in my new married name is the first step. My children will be included in my new passport. It saddens me that my surname is now different from my children's, but my plan is predicated on the authenticity of my marriage to Alex.

Victor has not yet paid the alimony the court ordered. He just delays and delays. But now it is time to divide our joint assets and for that we must go to court again.

This time Victor and Robinson both attend. My ex-husband stares straight ahead, not meeting my eyes, disdainful and distant.

'She should get nothing,' Robinson tells the judge. 'My client worked to support the family during the marriage. She is entitled to nothing.'

Amartse puts forward my counter-argument. 'To manage a home and look after children is not nothing,' he insists.

The judge just nods his head. I can't read his face. I find it hard to believe that Victor is not prepared to share our assets.

'My client has documents proving his purchase and

possession of all that they own,' continues Robinson. 'As you can see.'

I watch as he pulls out shipping documents related to the car and household goods we brought from Europe. Naturally, they are all in Victor's name since the Ghanaian government paid for our relocation.

Then Robinson waves the shipping document claiming that Victor owns the suite of furniture which is my dowry, the same suite Victor stained with palm nut soup. I know it is only timber and fabric, screws and zips, but it is a part of my past and all I have left from my family.

I watch Victor, wearing his white doctor's uniform, cross the courtroom, pick up the Bible and swear that all these goods are his, paid for by him. I can't believe that this is the same man who attends church every week and sings in the choir. He is swearing on a holy book and lying.

The case is adjourned until I can prove my ownership of the furniture. No one believes I will be able to provide the papers, translated and validated. Romania is too far away.

I am determined to get the papers and the proof.

Meanwhile I get my new Romanian passport and then I renew my Ghanaian visa. Now everything is focused on our departure. I plan it carefully. I don't want anyone, particularly the authorities, to know that I'm taking my children out of the country.

'We'll make it look like a visit to see your family, to introduce the children to their grandparents. It's the most normal thing in the world. People will only be suspicious if you give them reason,' Alex tells me. He is such a comfort. My heart pounds, thinking that we may be stopped, but Alex is always calm and rational, speaking common sense.

I know my leaving will sadden him.

44

Myself Alone

Inosa picks me up and drives me to Alex's office.

'Is everything ready?' he asks and I nod. Together we walk to the Ghana Airways office and buy return tickets to Romania for William, Elsie, Nancy and me. It will be a seven-hour flight to London and then we will have to hurry to our connection to Bucharest.

The flight will take off in less than twenty-four hours. As I receive the tickets, my hands are shaking.

Alex and I walk back to his office. 'What are you thinking?' he asks gently. I look up at him and try to smile. I don't tell him that I'm terrified of what Victor would do if he knew. In Ghana, what I'm about to do is in contempt of the court ruling. If I'm caught, it could mean deportation without my children or perhaps even a prison sentence.

'I'm thinking how wonderful it will be to go home,' I say brightly. In fact Bucharest could not be further from my thoughts. Of course my family is excited that we're coming. They cannot wait to see Elsie again and to meet William and Nancy for the first time.

That night at dinner I almost choke on my food. I push my plate away. 'What is it, Mama?' asks Elsie. I smile and say something about a headache. The children still know nothing.

As he eats, Alex is silent too. Of course he is sad and nervous. He's worried for me.

After I put William and Nancy to bed, I sit for a while with Elsie and hold her hand. 'You're my eldest,' I say and she nods. 'So I need you to help me.'

Her eyes grow wide. 'What is it?'

'Tomorrow we're catching a big plane. You, me, Nancy and William. We're going to visit your grandparents in Romania.'

Elsie nods and thinks for a while. 'When are we coming back?'

'Soon,' I say. The lie makes me feel guilty but I have no choice.

'A plane!' Elsie says, excited now. 'Where will we sit? How long will the flight take? How high in the sky will we fly?' I promise that tomorrow she will find out, it's a surprise.

All night I toss and turn. Nausea washes over me in waves and my head spins with all the things that might go wrong. I remind myself that as soon as I've passed through immigration control at the airport we'll be safe.

The next morning I rise very early. I wake the children, shower and dress them and finish packing. Our flight is at seven-thirty. I'm a cauldron of emotions yet I know I must be steadfast and controlled.

William and Nancy are still too young to understand and they watch what's happening with curiosity. They don't ask any questions. They play at my feet.

Elsie, with her active mind, is a different matter. 'When are we coming back?' she asks me again. I know she feels my tension and suspects that I haven't told her the truth.

'Soon,' I repeat and promise to myself I'll apologise later for the lie. There will be a right time to explain it all.

'Are you nearly ready?' Alex asks.

'I need five more minutes,' I say. I have two large suitcases and some hand luggage. I try to think what I need to put in the cabin bag: Nancy's nappies, milk, a change of clothes, tissues, snacks. I will be travelling on my own with three young children. Elsie is just six, William not yet three and Nancy will soon be two.

As I pack, Elsie is on my mind. I know she loves her father. He gives her so little of his time but still she worships him. And then there is Alex whom she adores because he lavishes attention on her in his quiet way. I wonder how she'll cope without them. I hope I will be enough for her.

Then it's time to leave. Inosa opens the car door and we pile in. Alex and I sit in the back with the children between us. I have brought a blanket.

'Let's play a game,' I say. 'Why don't you hide under this blanket? You're not to come out until I tell you.' The children giggle and snuggle down, their arms around one another. Alex is tense.

Sometimes when cars slow down, vendors approach to sell bread and fruit. Alex is worried word will spread that a car containing my three children is approaching the airport.

'Can we come out now?' giggles Elsie, wriggling under the blanket.

'Not yet,' I say. They are tired of the game but luckily there isn't much traffic and we're soon entering the car park. We drive through the gate and I pull the blanket off them.

'Peek-a-boo,' I whisper. They giggle as they surface, laughing and blinking in the bright sunlight. My heart is hammering in my chest.

Inosa helps us with our bags. He shakes my hand. 'Goodbye, Madam. We will see you soon.'

'Yes,' I tell him. 'I'll be back.'

Alex accompanies us into the terminal. Elsie has begun to cry softly so he holds her hand. 'Don't worry. It won't be long before I see you again,' he tells her and the lie seems to calm her.

Porters take our bags. I carry William and Nancy and the cabin bag. 'Please Alex, go now,' I say, turning to him. I don't want him to be involved in what will happen next, what could be seen as kidnapping. I sit the younger children down on a bench.

'Look after them, Elsie. I need to talk to Alex.' I lead him away from the children and put a hand gently on his arm. 'Alex, you've helped me so much. You know how much I appreciate it. Now I need to do this on my own. I don't want trouble for you.'

We turn back to the three children sitting quietly together on the bench, their curious little faces turned towards us.

'I want to make sure you get through,' insists Alex.

'No. Go now. Trust me. I'll be fine.'

'Are you sure?'

'Yes.'

He kisses me on both cheeks. I feel his sadness.

'I'll call you as soon as we arrive at my parents',' I say. I watch him go, tears pouring down my cheeks.

'Why are you crying, Mama?' Elsie asks when I rejoin the children. 'We'll see Alex soon.'

'Yes, Elsie.'

I watch Alex walk away. Every few steps he turns and looks back, as though he can't bear to let us go.

There is now no time to waste. I hurry the children towards

the check-in and immigration desks. My pulse is racing. I clutch my passport with the all-important tickets inside.

'Good morning,' says the woman behind the counter. She is polite and her smile is warm.

'Good morning,' I say, handing her our documents.

She checks them carefully. 'And where are you going?'

I'm frozen with fear anticipating her next question.

My children and I have different surnames. I'm terrified that Victor has informed the authorities that I might try to leave. This fear has grown more and more in the last few days. Suddenly a flash of dread, of what life might be like without my children, strikes me. I feel as if I'm choking on my own breath. Then I realise that the official has asked me a question and is waiting for an answer. I know there's sweat on my brow and my lip. I hope that she thinks I'm just another European who can't handle the heat.

'I'm going back to Romania with my children to visit my parents,' I say, trying to keep my voice low and pleasant.

She looks at each child in turn. Nancy is in my arms and William at my feet, with Elsie holding his hand. 'How long will you be away?'

'Oh, somewhere between four and eight weeks.'

She smiles at the children. 'Rather you than me! It's going to be a long flight with three little children.'

I nod and smile. Then my heart leaps. She is actually stamping our passport.

'Have a good trip.'

We've made it through the first step. I pick up our passport and begin to walk towards the departure lounge.

Something makes me turn back to look for Alex. Yes, he's there, watching from the entrance. I raise the passport high in the air and wave. He waves back.

My relief is immense. It's as if the door of my cage has opened. Suddenly I remember my brother Gheorghe and the birds he used to keep in cages in our yard. One day I opened the doors to release them all, he was furious. But it was worth it to see them fly.

'Come on, Elsie!' I call. She leads William forward and he holds out his arms up for me to carry him too.

We wait in the departure hall. I'm nervous, I still don't feel safe. Only when we are in the air, turned towards London, will we be truly safe. Finally we are told to board.

'Let's go!' I say, trying to sound cheerful and calm. By this time I'm carrying both William and Nancy. On the tarmac the hot wind hits us, just as it did on my first evening in Ghana. I suddenly realise that I've left the cabin bag at passport control. I'm about to go and get it but change my mind. In Romania, it's bad luck to turn back when a course of action has been determined. Both my feet are pointing forward. I can't go back.

Two hostesses help me carry the younger children up the gangway while I hold Elsie's hand. Inside, we find our seats and then wait as the plane fills, agonisingly slowly, around us. Finally the cabin crew closes the doors and the captain announces take-off. I try to banish thoughts of the plane being halted at the last moment, the doors flung open and police boarding to take me away. As long as this plane's wheels are on Ghanaian soil, I'm still not free.

Beside me, the heads of my three little children bob and turn with curiosity and excitement. 'Are we going, Mama? Are we?' asks Elsie.

I squeeze her hand. 'Any second now, darling.'

We taxi to the runway and then, after what seems hours, we take off. My chest expands and at last I breathe freely.

From that moment I feel no more pain in my right side. Was the juju doctor right? Was I under a black magic spell? I will never know. All my feelings of being trapped, all the feelings that have weighed so heavily on me since the day I committed my life to Victor, suddenly disperse.

I don't know if I'm happy or sad. Memories flash though my mind. I arrived in Accra just four years ago on a hot and steamy evening and now I am leaving on this fine morning. I arrived with Elsie and now I'm leaving with Elsie, William and Nancy. I have suffered divorce and married again.

All this in four years.

I focus on the thought that I've succeeded. The children are here with me. I watch them playing together and feel tears rolling down my face. I reach out and hug and kiss each child. Elsie looks at me as if I've gone crazy.

The flight is full of friendly Ghanaians but I'm still paranoid and nervous. I speak to no one, not even the hostesses. When Nancy needs her nappy changed I don't want to ask for assistance. I do nothing. I'm afraid to draw attention to us or leave Elsie and William alone.

My mind has shut down. I just want this flight to be over.

After a while the children fall asleep. I should sleep too, to gather my strength. But I can't take my eyes off them. Their innocent little faces, their dark curls. My mind floods with images of them growing up, happy and content. How much do the children understand about what I have gone through? What will they remember?

My mind is full of noise. I want them to have what I never had: a contented mother. My childhood has taught me that an unhappy wife will never make a happy mother. I think about the separation from Mama Draga and Auntie Ana. Have I done the right thing to take them away from their father? Nancy and William are too young to understand, but what about Elsie?

Then I realise that my childhood may have been hard but it taught me to be resilient.

45

Temporary Home

My parents think we are coming back to stay. To them food and a home are all that children need.

When we land at Heathrow Airport, I ask Elsie to walk ahead of me while I carry Nancy on one arm and William on the other. Poor Nancy is crying. I don't know how I've managed to leave her sitting in dirty nappies for the whole seven-hour flight. I have to put William down in order to organise our luggage. He holds onto my skirt, stumbles and trips. Elsie, dragging one of our suitcases, also falls, with the case on top of her. No one offers to help us, a woman with three children and a mountain of luggage. No one takes any notice. So here we are, back in the big uncaring white man's world.

We continue walking, struggling with our bags, until we reach the departure gate of the British Airways flight to Bucharest. People are already boarding. I am so relieved that we have made it in time for the flight.

I take a deep breath, a breath of freedom.

Not long after we take off from Heathrow, my children fall asleep. I'm tired but I cannot close my eyes. One moment I sense freedom and the next I'm terrified, thinking that in a couple of hours, I will touch down on Romanian soil. I know these hours on the flight from London to Bucharest will be a memory I will always treasure as a constant reminder of how freedom feels. It is the first time in my life I have ever felt truly free.

'How long are you staying?' asks the man at Bucharest immigration control as he examines my Romanian passport.

'I'm not sure. We're visiting my parents.'

He nods and looks at each of the children in turn. He looks back at me then again at the children. I sense judgement in his gaze.

'Well, you can't stay more than three months,' he says abruptly. 'You've married a foreigner and are a resident abroad. Those are the rules.'

I must have a three-month tourist visa on my Romanian passport to be able to visit my own country.

'And if I want to extend my visa?' I ask.

I feel him watching me closely—or perhaps I'm paranoid. There is nothing illegal in what I'm asking. So why do I feel so anxious?

'You have to leave Romania and come back again. You can take a short trip. Go to Belgrade by the night train and return the next day.'

'Thank you,' I tell him and take back my precious passport. It's only now I realise that my blue Romanian passport which gave me the freedom to leave Romania also restricts the length of time I can spend here in the country where I was born. For the time being I have no choice but to obey the rules. At least we're over the first hurdle.

Now for the next. My parents, my sister and my brother are waiting for us just moments away. The children are practically asleep on their feet. Elsie is exhausted, William is on the verge of tears and Nancy's head flops against my shoulder.

'Not long now,' I say. 'Soon you'll be seeing your grandparents, Mamaie and Tataie. Let's keep going.'

Bucharest Airport is all dull grey walls and flickering lights. I have no sense of a homecoming. I know that our time here will be transitional.

We see the family waiting. My mother hasn't come. Elsie barely remembers who they are and William and Nancy have never met them. Even so, the children open their arms and run towards them. Cornelia sweeps up William while Elsie finds my father's arms.

'Lenuta!' Cornelia gasps. 'What has happened to you? I only recognised you because of the children,' she says softly over the top of William's head. Her eyes are wide and sad.

I know I am gaunt and exhausted. I now weigh forty-two kilograms.

I hug my father. I know I have let him down. He predicted this. I am conscious of being the first person in our family ever to divorce. He smiles but I sense he is ashamed of me. I've accepted my fate. Now I must explain it to my family.

As we drive home through the city, memories of being here with Victor flood my mind. I remember that day in the tram, holding Elsie, the time the man didn't stand for me to sit. God, not this again!

I cannot even find Romanian words to express all this. I've forgotten them. Victor forced me to speak English, then criticised my pronunciation. Alex helped me overcome my lack of confidence by encouraging me to take classes at the Institute of Languages in Accra. Now, surrounded by the Romanian language again, I feel lost. I can read street signs and understand what my family is saying, but even simple thoughts will often be hard for me to express. Perhaps I have suppressed that part of myself.

My mother is waiting for us at home. She has cooked a traditional meal of sarmale, sour cabbage rolls. She weeps as she bends down to pick up Elsie. 'How you've grown!' she says, squeezing her.

'Hello, Mama,' I say and kiss her cheek.

While my parents and siblings cuddle the children and organise our meal, I finally sit down and rest. I look around me. How small and backward everything seems! Once I was proud of this house with its cement walls and two big iron gates, the largest on the street. Now, after Ghana, it seems poor and badly kept.

The original house my father built from mud and straw back in the early 1950s, before he started his military service in Cluj, seems to be sinking. The windows, always low, now seem even lower. Maybe this mud house is sinking back into the earth from which it came.

'Why don't you live in the other house?' I ask my parents. The new house, built next to the old one, is more modern and made of brick.

My parents shrug and glance at one another. 'That's for guests. We're happy in our old house.'

As we sit for dinner, I see how tired the children are.

'I'll put them to bed,' I say, and lead them into the bedroom they will share.

'Mama, where is my bedroom?' asks Elsie.

'It's here. All of us will sleep together.'

'Where's my bathroom?' is her next question.

I explain that there is no such thing and that the toilet is outside in the garden. Tomorrow we will heat water on the stove and carry it to a wooden bath in the room at the back of the house. After they have bathed, we will tip the water onto the floor where it will make the mud soften for a while before it dries out again.

Elsie is not impressed.

As far as I know, the toilet must still be pumped out every couple of weeks with a hose-pipe and there are still no drains.

'It's ironic,' I whisper to Cornelia as we stand in the doorway and watch the children fall asleep. 'I suppose you all think that Africa is primitive. But you should see Alex's house. It's stunning, huge and new. The walls are made of glass. His kitchen is equipped with everything you can imagine.'

Cornelia shrugs. 'Then why aren't you there with him?'

So far I haven't told anyone here the truth about why I married Alex. I haven't been able to write letters or speak over the phone for fear the Romanian authorities will find out and take my passport and my freedom away. Ceausescu's Securitate is at the height of its powers, in total control. I might not just lose my passport. I could be thrown into prison as well. I know that this has happened to others.

Now, face to face with my sister, I can tell her the whole story. 'My marriage to Alex, it's an arrangement, Cornelia. Otherwise, Victor could deport me from Ghana and keep the children. When the time comes, we'll divorce and I'll find a new country for us.'

Cornelia's mouth falls open and her eyes widen.

'You mustn't tell anyone,' I say. My sister puts her arms around me and I realise that I am crying.

'Oh Lenuta, you're skin and bone,' she tells me, poking me with her finger as she used to when I was a teenager and went on a diet of vinegar. 'You're sick.'

I think perhaps she's right but I haven't wanted to acknowledge this.

We go back to the others and sit with them long into the night. My parents tell me stories about neighbours and old friends and I try to be interested. As I listen, I miss Alex. He would take us all back in a moment. I could escape Romania properly if only I could love him but I don't. Respect and gratitude are what I feel for Alex. He deserves to be loved.

As we say good night, my father puts his hand on my arm and gazes seriously at me. 'Lenuta, it's your fault that your children don't have a father.'

His words strike deep into my heart. I had expected this— only not so soon. After all, we've just arrived.

'I was in pain, Tata. I was unhappy.'

My father cannot understand. He believes a woman must be prepared to suffer in a marriage for the sake of her children. This is, after all, his own experience.

But I am not my mother.

'Look at your cousins,' he goes on. 'They're all married and they've all got fathers for their children. You know I didn't want you to marry Victor. But you made your bed. You should be prepared to lie in it.'

There's nothing I can say in response to such fixed, closed judgements. Tonight he has shown my children love, yet he's still capable of such harshness towards me. My resolve to move on as soon as possible is strengthened.

As I try to sleep, thoughts come to me of Accra: the people, the markets, the atmosphere. I miss Ghana already. I try to put it out of my mind.

46

Proof

When I wake the next morning, I've forgotten where I am. The ceiling, the smells, the light: everything is different. But here are my children, all three of them piled into bed with me. Then it all floods back and I remember that I've spent the night hugging them, holding them tight, so happy to have them here with me, safe. At this moment my happiness is boundless.

I doze. It's a luxury to slip in and out of sleep like this. Soon I can smell breakfast and hear my mother forgetting to creep about and beginning to bustle. I expect she is eager to see the children, to feed them and hold them. I rouse them and we gather in the kitchen to eat the breakfast she has prepared.

'Can I leave the children with you today?' I ask. 'There are things I need to do. Paperwork. Formalities.'

I am already planning my next steps. I want to locate all the papers that prove my father bought my dowry furniture and have them translated into English, then certified by a Romanian court. If I can do that and take them back to Ghana, I can prove that Victor lied in court. I want to avenge this insult. I will also divorce Alex and then the children and I can move on with our lives.

Over the next days I sleep and eat the kind of food I ate when I was a child. I can feel the flesh forming around my bones again. Although this is only temporary, I know that I am healing. That is what a home and family can do.

Every few weeks Alex calls. 'Hellen?' This time his voice sounds tense. 'When are you coming back?'

'When I've got the paperwork together.'

'Are you still thinking of divorce?'

'Yes. We'll divorce as soon as I get back.'

He is silent. I know he wants me to reconsider. I am now sure that he is in love with me.

'I'll let you know when I'm coming,' I say reassuringly.

'I miss you.' His voice is subdued.

'Take care, Alex.'

My father opens the door and the children race in. They are already using a few words of Romanian with their English.

'Did you have fun?' I ask, hugging them to me.

I know when they're with my father, people are afraid to make comments about their skin colour. When the children are with me, people often spit on them and call them 'black crows'.

When Cornelia comes home, she brings cheeses and fruit. The children run to her as she unwraps the package of food she has bought from the up-market Snagov Restaurant where she works. This restaurant is exclusive and secluded, a favourite lakeside destination for men who wish to entertain their mistresses in private. Romania is still a man's world.

Food is scarce because most of what is produced is being exported so we can pay off our national debt. Of course, there are always some who eat well.

Across the river from the restaurant is a luxurious hotel with another restaurant attached, heavily guarded by the

Securitate. This is where Ceausescu and his family can often be found living the high life. It is known as CC, 'Casa Comunista'. My sister, despite her intelligence and talent, is not permitted to work there. She tells me she has heard that Ceausescu's son, while drunk, climbed up on the restaurant table, pulled down his pants and peed into the sardines. 'They need more salt!' he shouted.

Cornelia understands how Romania works, from the inside. I tell her my plans. I need to return to Ghana alone to divorce Alex and to prove the ownership of the furniture. She promises to look after the children.

'Is a bit of furniture worth all this effort?' she asks. But I know that I must do this.

'What will happen about the children being taken out of Ghana?' she continues. 'What if the court charges you with contempt? What if they won't let you return?

'Please Cornelia—trust me. Be their mother while I'm away. I know what I'm doing. I'll be back soon.'

47

Geneva

What country will take us? How shall we get there? Cornelia has a friend who has given me the contact details of a woman in Geneva named Daniela who can help with information for Romanians like me seeking political asylum. It's a dangerous thing to talk about. Our government forbids and punishes defectors.

I plan to fly to Geneva, speak to Daniela, then fly to Ghana, divorce Alex and prove that Victor is a liar. After that I'll return to Romania to pick up the children. Then we can all leave for good. Only Cornelia knows the details of my plan.

Geneva stuns me with its beauty. It is so bright and clean, its lake sparkling in the afternoon light. I arrive at my contact's address but she's still at work. I sit on my suitcase outside her apartment.

When Daniela arrives, she smiles broadly, holding out her hand. 'Come in, come in. I hope you're not too cold.'

She is tiny, her dark hair cut in a bob around a lovely fine-featured face. I like her immediately. She has dedicated her life to helping people escape Romania to find a better life. I am fascinated by her and, as I am whenever I meet clever, independent women, I am impressed.

She leads me into her small apartment. It is clean, tasteful and sparsely furnished. She makes me tea and we talk. I ask her how long she has been in Geneva.

'I escaped Romania six years ago,' she tells me. 'I was lucky enough to go to university in Bucharest and so I speak French. When I came to Geneva on a short trip for work, I found it easy enough not to go back home. And now, when I'm not working here for the United Nations, I try to help Romanian refugees find freedom. There's a large network of emigrants, you know, and we all help one another build better lives.'

I nod. She gives me hope.

'So, Hellen, tell me your story.'

She listens carefully as I explain what has happened to me, her hands on her knees and her lips pursed in concentration. When I've finished, she looks me in the eye.

'You won't be happy to hear this, but I'm afraid you have no grounds for claiming political asylum here in Switzerland. The grounds of your claim are humanitarian. That's hard to obtain here.'

I take a moment to acknowledge my disappointment.

'But there's another issue too. Even if you could settle here, the racism here is silent but deadly. I know you and your children would suffer. This is a beautiful place, and advanced in many ways, but I don't think it's the place for your children to thrive.'

I knew that it wasn't going to be easy but I never thought it would be this hard. Tears come into my eyes.

Daniela is reassuring. 'Don't lose hope. You'd be far better off in the United States or Canada. Get a tourist visa and go directly to one of those countries. When you arrive, apply for asylum. Don't apply from somewhere in Europe or they'll send you straight back to Romania. Make sure you go on your own at first. Life is hard for the children in refugee camps.'

Now I know that it is crucial to get my alimony. Without it, I'll never be able to pay for a flight to freedom and for whatever follows.

Daniela clearly knows what she's talking about but I am uneasy. To fly across the seas and give myself up to the police or an immigration officer will be to put myself into the hands of people who may not understand the kind of mistreatment people suffer in Romania. In European refugee camps, surely the authorities will be more sympathetic?

'No,' Daniela says. 'There are people in those camps who have much stronger grounds for seeking asylum than you, persecution for their political beliefs, for example. Your reasons are social and emotional. You need a different level of understanding and compassion and you won't find it in the camps in Europe. The racism here in Geneva is just as bad as in Romania—even if they don't spit at you or call you names.'

She pauses and looks at me sympathetically. 'I'm sorry not to be more encouraging but I want you to be aware of how large the problems you face can become. Think carefully before your next move.'

She cooks me dinner and offers me her bed to sleep in. How kind she is! I want to be in a position to help people just as she does. I want to find my own true home, to really inhabit my life.

Daniela takes the next day off work to give me a tour of Geneva. She shows me the United Nations building where she works and takes me down to the lake. We sit over coffee and chat as if we're old friends.

'I like it here,' says Daniela, 'but the Swiss aren't warm like Romanians, nor as demonstrative. However everything is neat and well organised. Things get done and it's easier to be the person you choose to be.'

She shrugs and gives me a big smile. 'You win some, you lose some.'

I smile too. I know she's right and I feel her compassion. But I'm preoccupied, thinking about everything she told me last night. I hadn't anticipated these complications and I pray that I have the courage to face all the obstacles still in our path.

Here in this attractive café looking out over Lake Geneva, I close my eyes and for a moment I'm back in Ghana. I often have a dream at night: I'm standing on a dusty piece of ground and cannot decide which way to go. Left? Right? I feel panic of not knowing what to do. Yet someone or something always shows me the way.

I open my eyes and see Daniela's lovely forehead creased with worry. I don't ask her what she thinks I should do. I fear she will advise me to stay put and not risk the enormous cost of flights and months of separation from my children.

But staying in Romania is not an option. On that, I am firm.

When I leave, Daniela and I hug and kiss one another on the cheek. I thank her for her kindness and good advice.

'If you come back to Switzerland, I'm here for you,' she says.

From the window of the taxi, I look out at the city. It feels cold and alien and I'm happy to be leaving.

48

Back to Africa

Soon I am on the plane back to Accra, on my own this time. New fears loom: the possibility of being charged with contempt of court for taking the children out of the country and also finding the right way to face Alex to finalise our divorce. I don't even know where I'm going to sleep. I know I don't want to stay with Alex. I'm sure now of his feelings for me and I don't want to give him false hope. He deserves more than I can give him. The only real possibility is Eunice, my friend who lives across the road from Victor and Naomi. She doesn't even know I'm coming.

I close my eyes. I miss my children. At least I'm stronger now than when I left Ghana. I've put on weight and am sleeping better. I'm ready for the next battle. I will prove that I own the furniture and that Victor was lying. After that, I will burn it!

As I imagine my revenge, my feelings must show on my face. 'Are you all right, Madam?' asks the hostess.

'Yes, thank you,' I tell her. As the plane lands I feel rested, refreshed and ready for my legal battle.

The official at the immigration desk asks where my children are. 'I've left them with my parents. I'll bring them soon,' I tell him.

He crinkles his forehead as if he doesn't understand.

'Their grandparents are such a long way away. And Romania is a Communist country, so they can't come to visit. I wanted them to have more time together. Family is so important.'

My voice is confident. And I feel that confidence too. The official nods me through.

When I step out of the airport I can't take the smile off my face. The light and the warmth! Ghana has the power to make me so happy. After Romania, it is bright and glowing and vibrant. For a moment, I think I should come back and live here. The faces passing me are smiling and welcoming. There is so much here that I love. It is peaceful, without racism, and I would be financially secure.

No. The reality would be very different. I take a taxi to my old street in Ringway Estate. When I arrive, I look across the road to the house where Victor and I lived together when we were married. It is quiet and no one is around.

I turn to Eunice's house and open the gate. One of the servants appears and is shocked to see me. Then Eunice herself appears.

'Oh, my God! You're back!'

'Yes, I'm back.' I burst into tears as she puts her arms around me. She has been such a support. She is wise, quiet and thoughtful. Today she puts her arms around me and I let myself feel safe.

'What on earth are you doing here? Where are the children?' she asks.

'I've come to stay for a little while, if I can.'

'Of course you can.'

Her daughters come out and also throw their arms around me. 'Sit down, sit down!' they cry.

Eunice takes meat from the freezer and before long she has cooked a huge meal. I eat eagerly. It feels terrific to be eating Ghanaian food again, surrounded by friendly faces chattering all at once and eager to hear my stories from Romania.

When darkness falls, I step outside to really take in that enormous African sky. I've missed it. Then my attention is caught by what is happening across the road. Lights have been turned on and I see a woman moving back and forth in a window, straining to see across to where I stand. I can tell that it is Naomi. The blood rushes to my head and I feel sick.

Why does it bother me that Victor has another woman? A younger woman? Am I jealous?

When I go back inside, Eunice knows I am upset. She asks me why.

'Naomi is there.'

She shrugs her shoulders. 'Don't worry about them. No one is happy over there. I hear her and your ex-mother-in-law screaming and shouting at each other in Krobo every night.'

It doesn't make me feel any better to know that they're not getting on. Afterwards, in bed, I can't fall asleep for a long time. I miss cuddling up to the children.

Next morning I make a phone call. 'You're where?' Alex asks me, amazed.

'Accra,' I repeat. 'I'm staying at Eunice's.'

'Across the road from Victor's?'

I detect agitation and concern in his tone. I take a deep breath and say the lines I've been rehearsing. 'Alex, I rang to tell you that in a couple of days you'll be served with divorce papers. You deserve to know before that happens. I'll pay all the divorce expenses. And I want to thank you for everything you've done for me.'

I can't go on. I burst into tears. For a moment Alex is silent.
'Do you want to talk?'

'No,' I tell him. 'I just want my freedom.'

He is quiet again but before long he speaks in his calm,
gentle voice. 'Hellen, for as long as you have my name, I
don't want you walking about the streets. I will have Inosa
leave the Jaguar outside your house and I would like you to
use it until you leave Ghana.'

Alex is a lovely man. I thank him with all my heart.

Later I sit in the backyard at Eunice's while across the road
I listen to Victor's loud voice shouting in Krobo. I'm grateful
it is not directed at me. I am almost free, but guilt is pressing
heavily against my chest. I think of Alex and the emotional
pain I've caused him. I think of his kind heart. He helped
me open the iron gates of the cage where I had imprisoned
myself. Now all he has to show for it is a broken heart. His
sad voice resonates in my head.

I wish I could give him my heart and my love. I search
deep within myself but all I can find is respect and gratitude.

'Don't feel bad,' says Eunice, coming up behind me. 'He's
a grown man. He took you on with his eyes open.'

I turn to her. I know she is right but it doesn't make it any
easier to see Alex hurt.

49

A Lonely Christmas

I put on make-up and brush my hair. I wear a dress and high heels. I feel confident and happy. I am on my way to visit Amartse. But my first stop is the Canadian embassy where I apply for a tourist visa. My hand is shaking when I fill in the form and I'm sure they can guess that I plan to apply for asylum as soon as I arrive. I return the form and cross my fingers.

'Hellen!' says Amartse's secretary. She can hardly believe her eyes. 'Are you back for good?'

'Just for a short while.'

She rises and knocks on his door, calling that there is someone special here to see him.

'Who is it?' comes the familiar voice from inside. She opens the door and he sees me. He jumps up and rushes out to greet me.

'Hellen! What on earth are you doing here?' He hugs me and kisses me on the cheek.

'I'm so pleased to see you, Amartse,' I say.

When all the greetings are over he holds me at arm's length and speaks seriously. 'You do realise you're in contempt of court, don't you?'

'Yes. But I need to divorce Alex.'

'You could have rung me from Romania and I could have done it for you.'

'I need my alimony from Victor.'

'I could have done that for you, too.'

'And there's the furniture.'

'Dammit, Hellen! Still the furniture?'

I show him the translated documents.

'I don't understand. You came back for this?'

'It means a lot to me, Amartse. Victor swore on the Bible that it was his. He lied.'

He interrupts me. 'The judge already knows the truth. Just going to court will bring up the issue of contempt. Are you sure this is worth it?'

'Yes. I have to.' He knows by the expression on my face that I'm not going to give up.

'Fine. Leave it with me. I'll get dates set for the hearing.'

Meanwhile I feel lost without my children. I ring my family.

'Mama, when are you coming home?' asks Elsie. Her voice sounds tiny and very far away.

'Soon,' I say. 'As soon as I've finished everything I need to do here. Are you having fun, my beautiful girl? Are you happy?'

'Yes,' she says brightly and then she's off. I hear the phone drop and her feet pound as she runs away. I hear her shouting to William. I'm glad they're having fun although I miss them terribly.

My father picks up the phone. 'Lenuta?

'I'm here. The children are happy, Tata, aren't they?'

'Sure they're happy. Why wouldn't they be?'

I know how easily children can adjust to change. Or can they?

'Do they really feel at home?' I ask him.

For a moment he is silent and then he sighs. 'You're their home, Lenuta. They just want their mother.'

December 1982 is my first Christmas without my children. I miss them with all my heart. We speak on the phone and I hear that their Romanian language is improving.

Elsie cannot contain her excitement. 'It's snowing, Mama! Father Christmas is coming. He's going to bring us presents!'

They have never had a Christmas like this before. In Ghana, I couldn't even find a Christmas tree.

'We're going to church,' William tells me.

In some ways this will be the most exciting Christmas they've ever had. I hear my mother in the background calling Elsie and Nancy in from the snow.

That night I dream about my visit to the monk all those years ago. How can I explain why so many things he predicted have come true? Has having his words in the back of my mind directed me more than I think? Perhaps if I had never consulted the monk I would still live in Romania, be married to a Romanian man and have a professional career.

But I might never have had children.

Perhaps the monk's predictions have helped me accept my destiny. Does the Universe have its own plan for me?

What else did he tell me? 'You will travel very, very far. To the end of the world,' he said. So I know there is more to come.

50

Second Divorce

This divorce is much simpler than my first.

'How are you?' Alex asks me as he enters the court registry office where I stand waiting. He looks the same as ever, neat and perfectly dressed. I look into his calm, gentle face. I can feel his concern for me—but there is something else, something hard to read.

'I'm fine, Alex. And you?'

We both sit together and wait for Amartse to join us. It is hot and I wish I had a fan to cool my face. I suddenly realise my dress with its red polka dots is similar to the one I wore when, pregnant with Nancy, I encountered Victor that stormy day in his car. I picture how he drove off, laughing at me.

Alex is tapping one of his gleaming shoes in a nervous way. I glance at him again and see how sad his face looks. He catches me looking at him and for a moment our eyes meet. It occurs to me that he knows me better than anyone—certainly better than Victor, despite the years we spent together.

Amartse arrives and then the registrar, and the process begins. It is quiet and civilised.

'Are there any goods to exchange?' asks the registrar.

Alex's head is bent. He doesn't say anything but simply waits for me to respond. I remember that he was warned by his family to sign a prenuptial agreement. He refused because he trusted me.

'No. No goods,' I say.

When it is done, we stand and wait for the registrar to leave before turning to face one another. I want to say so much, to thank him for the goodness of his heart and his willingness to help me and my children. But I know that nothing I can say will heal his broken heart. He wants me to love him as much as he loves me.

I know I can't do that. I try to find the right words but all that comes out is, 'Thank you for the use of your car.' Then I hold out the keys.

He won't take them. 'Keep the car until you leave Ghana.' Then he nods to me and leaves.

Amartse shrugs and shuffles his papers. I know he thinks I've done the wrong thing. Alex would have been a good husband for me.

We cannot be the person others want us to be.

51

My Furniture

t is another stressful day. I call the Canadian Embassy and
learn that my tourist visa application has been rejected.

Next I go to court for the hearing on my furniture. When
I arrive at court and take my seat beside Amartse, he whispers
in my ear that we will be making our case to the same female
judge we had for the divorce.

'How did you manage that?' I whisper. He keeps a straight
face but I know he's hiding a smile.

Victor and Robinson are here and are sitting several rows in
front of us, close to the judge's desk. Even though they ignore
us, I can feel their anger.

The judge enters and we rise. Amartse explains our case and
she calls on me to answer some questions.

'Why did you take the children out of the country when
you knew you needed the court's or their father's permission?'
she asks me. 'Do you realise your action constitutes contempt
of court?'

'Yes I do,' I answer.

'Does that make you feel guilty?

'No, Your Honour, because I needed family and financial
support and I had none here.'

The judge leafs through our file. 'The ruling is that Dr Victor should pay 600 cedis a month into your bank account for the maintenance of the children, to pay their school fees and to provide for clothing and medical needs.'

'He hasn't given me any money.'

The judge turns her attention to Victor and calls on him to rise. 'Is this correct, Dr Victor?'

'Yes it is. I thought she would come and ask me for the money.'

'It's not up to the mother of your children to ask,' says the judge. 'How did you think she could look after the children— feed them, clothe them, buy shoes, medicine?'

At this, Robinson jumps up. 'Her new husband could do all that for her.'

The judge pauses briefly. 'If the plaintiff has married again, that's her business. It's not the responsibility of another husband to provide for your children, Sir. I see no contempt here. If you don't comply with your part of the agreement, how can you expect your ex-wife to do so?'

Then she turns her attention to the furniture. 'A suite of furniture was claimed in the divorce case as the sole property of Dr Victor.'

'Yes,' says Robinson. 'My client has documents proving he owns all their assets.' I watch as he produces shipping documents related to the car and all the household goods, including my furniture.

The judge turns to Amartse. 'Your client claims she has proof that the furniture was bought and paid for by her own father. Can I see these documents?'

Amartse steps forward and hands the translations to a court official who delivers them to the judge. When she has read what they say, she calls for them to be handed to Robinson.

He looks at each one and then hands them to Victor.

'Dr Victor, do you still claim that you are responsible for the purchase of the furniture?' asks the judge.

For the longest time, Victor is silent. Even from where I sit, I can see that his hands and the papers he holds are shaking. His lies have been brought to light. Finally he breathes out slowly and says, 'No, I am not responsible.' His voice is so soft I can barely hear him.

The judge rules in my favour. The furniture is mine. I hear her tell me that I can go and collect it but all I can hear is Victor's subdued voice.

The emotional pain I have been carrying is washed away in an instant. Perhaps it's wrong to seek this kind of revenge. Is it revenge or righting a wrong? Victor's treatment made me feel at fault for everything that went wrong with our relationship, all the agony of our marriage.

Now, at twenty-nine, I feel I have struggled for so long that I need this moment to make me believe in myself once again. I have established the truth and I am ready to leave Ghana.

I turn to Amartse. 'Can you please ask the judge if I may address her?'

His look tells me that what I want to say had better be good. 'Your Honour, my client would like briefly to address the court.'

The judge gives me a small nod. I rise and place my hands on the table to steady myself. 'Your Honour, thank you very much for listening to my case. I want to let you know that I'm content. All I wanted was for Dr Victor to tell the truth as an honest citizen should, especially a doctor. He can keep the furniture because tonight I'll fly back home to be with my children. Thank you, Your Honour.'

The judge nods her head, the case is closed and we leave. I don't look at Victor or Robinson to see how they have reacted. I just walk out of the room. I feel as if I've been released from heavy chains. I brush away tears, the result of years of suffering.

At last I am free. I belong to no man.

Amartse stands with me on the steps and puts his arm on mine to steady me. As we stand there, Victor passes. He stops and looks straight into my eyes. I see his mouth open and then I hear his laugh float into the turmoil inside me. It's an awful laugh—almost evil.

'You'll return begging me to take you back,' he says. He knows what the word *beg* means in Romanian, how humiliating it is.

'Victor—' I begin, surprised at how steady my voice is. 'I'm crying now and you're laughing, but your laughter will stop soon and then you'll be crying for the rest of your life.'

I don't know why I say this. I have no idea where it has come from. The truth is that right now I feel a flood of pity for him and almost want to protect him from his fate. He walks away from me and I think that I will never see him in the flesh again.

Nor will I ever see the furniture. For all I know, Victor sits on it every day with his wives, his girlfriends and his new children. Maybe he throws soup on it to punish other women. All I know is that every day it stands in his house, it will remind him of me.

When I say goodbye to Amartse, he puts his arms around me. I hold him tight.

'Thank you, Amartse.'

'I have a meeting or I'd have come to the airport to see you off. You don't have any other legal matters do you?'

'No, all is done,' I tell him with a smile.
We laugh together.

52

'Left Ghana for good'

The secret to happiness is freedom …
And the secret to freedom is courage
Thucydides

After court I return to Eunice's house. I shower and then sit down to eat the dinner she has prepared. It is banku, sour maize, and okra stew. She knows this is one of my favourite meals. As night falls, I pack my suitcase and put it in the car.

They all come out to say goodbye, Eunice, her husband and their girls. Tonight, Accra smells like the sea and the frangipani tree that grows beside their house.

'We'll miss you, Hellen,' she tells me. We are all crying, wiping tears from our faces with the backs of our hands.

'I'll come back soon,' I say unsure any of us believe this.

Eunice holds me tight and whispers in my ear, 'Please find somewhere good to live, to bring up your babies and be happy.'

I promise her I will.

As I reverse the car, I stop and look across at Victor's house. The lights are on. I imagine my furniture sitting in its usual place in the living room. But now I am at peace. I've finished what I came to do here. I have no more ties.

I have rung Alex to say thank you and goodbye. As I drive I say my silent farewell to Ghana: to the big sky, to the feeling of ease and acceptance and to the warmth of the people who helped me. I leave the car at the airport with the keys in the glove compartment, as Alex asked.

My passport is stamped by immigration, ready for me to leave, and I walk towards the departure hall. The flight is delayed and as I wait I think about my African experiences. I remember the heat of my arrival, Elsie tearing her dress, the chanting crowd. I hear Victor saying, 'This is my mother, this is my mother and this is my mother.'

I remember smuggling the children out of the country, the terror I felt. The last image that comes into my mind is of the European lady lying in the gutter. She presented me with a powerful lesson. I say goodbye to her.

I feel overwhelmingly grateful that I have come through it all. Now it's time to look forward. I wonder where my children and I will go. In Romania, I will have to pretend that I'm still married in order to keep my passport.

I open the passport and flick through it until I arrive at the page which reads: *Left Ghana for good*. In order to transfer my alimony of $US10,000 to the Romanian Foreign Exchange Bank, these words had to be recorded in my passport by the Ghanian Ministry of Finance. At the time, I asked the official not to include these words but that was his job. He didn't really understand the importance of *Left Ghana for good* in my passport.

If the Romanian authorities see these words, they will take away my passport and I will never be allowed to leave Romania again.

So many ways to be trapped.

I am relying on Amartse to finalise the transfer of the money. It will be enough for me to buy a house in Romania and be comfortable for a few years. However, if there are complications we cannot foresee, I will have nothing.

When we land in Geneva I change my clothes in the airport bathroom. I have brought a white dress to wear because I want the children to see their mother looking bright and beautiful.

On the flight from Geneva to Bucharest I can't eat or sleep. The plane feels fragile, buffeted by the air, unsafe. I can hear the metal creaking. It sounds as if the screws are loosening. A Swiss man is sitting beside me and when we hit turbulence, I clutch his hand. 'Do you think we'll be all right?' I ask.

He laughs and pats my hand. 'Please don't worry. I fly this route all the time.'

As I watch the hostesses spill the food they're serving, I can't stop shaking. Suddenly I feel hot. I know it is my period. I move a little and see blood on my seat. My white dress is stained. I can't believe this has happened. Why now?

The Swiss man has noticed too, and in spite of my embarrassment, summons one of the hostesses. He whispers in her ear and soon she returns with a blanket for me to cover myself.

When it becomes less bumpy, I walk to the bathroom where I put on the clothes I changed out of in Geneva. I bundle up the white dress and return to my seat feeling lighter, calmer. I smile at the Swiss man and he smiles back. I'm grateful for his quiet kindness.

I relax. All I want now is to see my children again. I've missed them so much during the short time I've been away and I worry about them, especially Elsie who is older and understands so much more. As soon as I hold them in my arms, I will be happy. Then we can move on.

When we land, I'm eager to pass as quickly as possible through immigration, to hold Elsie, Nancy and William.

The Romanian official flips through the pages of my passport. 'Where are your children?' he asks. His manner is cold and unfriendly. He knows he has power over me.

'They're here with my parents, their grandparents. I've come to pick them up.'

'How long are you going to stay here?'

'Perhaps three months?' I say.

As he examines the pages, I pray he won't notice the one that says *Left Ghana for good*. Finally he stops turning the pages, and stamps the passport. 'Here you are. Have a good holiday.'

I breathe a huge sigh of relief.

Bucharest airport looks the same: small, dark and old-fashioned. It resembles a shed or a hangar. Everything is old, counters and walls, carpets and doors. People seem stern, their faces cold and hard. The luggage carousel squeaks, stops, and then lurches into life again. I pick up my suitcase.

I hope that it won't be long before I leave Romania again. Next time for good. America is now my hope. As soon as the alimony is in the bank, I will apply for an American tourist visa.

I step out into the arrival hall. Prison again. It is hard to breathe. But here is Cornelia, jumping up and down and waving to me. She's on her own. She throws her arms around me.

'I was afraid you might end up in prison.'

At my parents' house, the children approach me slowly, shy and unsure. I know they feel I abandoned them.

'The neighbours told the children that you weren't coming home,' Cornelia confided to me in the car on the way to the house.

'Don't worry—I promised them that their mummy would be back soon. I tell them all the time how much you love them.'

I hold my children. It will take time to earn their trust again.

That night we all sit down together for dinner. As I hold Nancy in my lap, I tell my father about the furniture.

'You should have burned it,' he says.

'Yes, but that would have kept me away one more night. Now that I'm here with the children, I don't know how I managed to stay away at all.'

The children sleep with me, all in the same bed, their little arms and legs everywhere, our breathing falling into rhythm. I feel as if I'm whole again. I hope that we will all make the next step together.

In the following days, I worry constantly about the words in my passport: *Left Ghana for good*. I cannot risk passing through immigration control again with this so easy to notice. An officer with a more careful eye could keep us here forever.

My sister and I invent a game with the children. They watch me fill a bucket of water.

'Let's wash Mama's passport in the bucket,' I say. I watch them giggle, splash and dip, tearing the passport, ripping the pages. When the game is over, I fish all the pages out of the bucket and dry them, except the one with those words written on it. That page, I burn. Then I take what remains to the passport office. I tell them that I'm devastated my children have damaged such an important document.

I fill in a form. They tell me my new passport will take a few weeks to be reissued.

I wait and wait. I fear that Victor may contact the Romanian Embassy in Ghana and tell them that I am divorced for the second time and therefore no longer eligible for a Romanian passport. Perhaps he would do that out of spite. Desperation and fear breed paranoia. I know I am deceiving the Romanian government by maintaining that I am married.

I must hold onto my passport. It is the key to my freedom.

Finally on 23 June 1983, my new passport is issued. I flip through it with trembling hands. To my relief, the words *Left Ghana for good* are not there.

The new words are: Passport she entered the country with has been replaced as it was damaged.

I am free.

53

A Shattered Dream

In Romania, education is free as long as you hold a Romanian identity card. When you are issued a Romanian passport, your identity card is taken away. Because I have a passport, I must pay a ridiculous amount of money if I want Elsie to go to school.

Since I don't know how long we'll be in Romania, I decide to send Elsie to school. She comes home in tears. The other children call her *the black crow*. I organise a private tutor to come to our house, one of the teachers from the local primary school. She is a kind person. As I'm still waiting for my money to arrive, Cornelia pays for the tutor.

Cornelia also pays my fees for a cosmetology course. Since I dropped out of university, this has been my dream.

While Elsie does school work, Nancy and William play or go out with their grandfather. They climb up into the truck beside him, smiles of glee on their faces.

My father looks fondly at them. He adores them.

'Our Tataie has the biggest car in the street!' shouts Nancy.

'It's a truck,' William tells her.

I love the fact that my father is oblivious to their colour. God forbid if anyone calls them *black crows* in his presence. I have seen him go mad, shaking his fist and screaming threats at anyone who dares insult them. My mother is the same. With her own grandchildren, all her prejudices are forgotten. In fact, she is over-protective and would never leave the children with someone who doesn't care for them as lovingly as she does.

When we go into the centre of Bucharest, I'm anxious, expecting the next insult, spitting, name-calling. This is destroying the faith I have in people. Anyone broad-minded, anyone who can, has already left Romania.

Every day I feel the small-mindedness and racism of Romania strengthen my determination to leave.

'Soon we will leave here and go somewhere else,' I tell Elsie.

'Why, Mama?' she asks. 'We're happy here with Mamaie and Tataie.'

'There's somewhere better,' I tell her. I don't want to say it's a place where people don't spit on you and call you names. Somewhere we don't need to share a bed. A place where there's running water and a proper bath instead of a wooden bowl.

'Nothing has arrived yet, come back later,' I am told each time I make enquires at the Romanian Foreign Exchange Bank. I am expecting my alimony of $US10,000. After four long months and many unsuccessful visits to the bank, I ring Amartese.

'Please, Amartse, I need my alimony. Do you have a receipt saying the Romanian bank received the money? Can you send it to me?'

As usual, he does everything he can to help me and pulls strings. Before long, a receipt arrives in the post. I take it to the bank and hand it to the official.

'Oh,' he says, pretending to be surprised. 'What a coincidence! I think your money has just arrived.'

There are no coincidences in the Romanian Communist banking system. They hold your money, they use it and they don't pay interest.

Now my next step is to apply for an American tourist visa.

The American Embassy in Bucharest is an impressive building. I climb its marble steps and cross a huge garden. As I enter the office, I imagine I'm already in America.

I approach the pretty girl seated behind the reception desk. She speaks to a colleague in perfect English. I assume she is American.

'Excuse me?' I ask in hesitant English. She turns and speaks to me in Romanian. Her eyes are kind.

'I would like to visit the United States,' I tell her.

She nods. 'Do you have any relatives there?' She doesn't seem suspicious.

When I tell her I don't, she asks to see my passport. I tell her I'm Romanian but I am a resident of Ghana.

She nods again. I know being a resident of Ghana is not in my favour. She hands me an application form and photocopies my passport.

'You'll need to wait two weeks for a reply.'

The smile she gives me is warm and I thank her.

As I leave, I try to maintain confidence and the expectation of success.

This is it, I think to myself. I'm leaving Romania.

On the way home I visit Marieta, an old acquaintance. We call each other Cherie. Since my return from Ghana, she has become a good friend. We were brought up in the same area and lived on neighbouring streets. She is tall and beautiful and I love being with her because she is happy and confident.

Aged nineteen in 1973.

From left to right: my father, William, Elsie and Nancy in 1983.

My arrival in Australia in 1983.

My children's arrival in 1985. From left to right: Nancy, me, William and Elsie.

With a friend in Coogee in 1984.

At Luna Park in 1985, from left to right: Nancy, Elsie and William.

On an outing to the National Park, from left to right: my mother, William, me, Nancy and Elsie.

First Christmas in Australia, 1985.

First Christmas in Australia, 1985.

William and Nancy's birthday.

From left to right: Nancy, Elsie and William.

Left to right: Elsie, William and Nancy.

My father's arrival in Sydney with
William and Nancy.

My sister's arrival in Sydney.

With my sister on Labadi Beach
in Accra.

With William at Accra airport.

With William outside our old house in Accra.

On holiday in Fiji, from left
to right: William, Elsie and
Nancy.

With my grandchildren.

With my children, from left to right: Elsie, Nancy, me and William.

In 2013 at my 60th birthday party.

To our   dear Mum
The painting depicted on this card
is indicative of your strength and
illustrates how none of us could be
where we are today if it were not
for your uplifting love
and support

Have a beautiful
          birthday
          you certainly deserve it
Love always
                    Your children

At first she was Cornelia's friend but now we have bonded because she understands what I am going through. She married a man from the Congo and has children around the age of my first two.

The Congolese and Ghanaians didn't mix well in Romania and Victor discouraged our friendship. Marieta always had a mind of her own. She was too outspoken and seemed threatening to most of the African men who had married Romanian girls. Often we were strong and independent girls, however over time, ostracism and alienation eroded our strength and confidence.

While Marieta was still studying medicine in Romania, her husband moved to France so he could continue his medical studies. Now he lives in Paris with their children and Marieta travels back and forth on visits.

'You should have pushed Victor to work in Canada or England. Even Germany. That's what smart women do,' says Marieta.

I never tried. I knew that Victor was not the sort of man who could be pushed.

'Cherie, it's going to happen!' I tell her as she opens her door to me after my visit to the Embassy. 'I'm going to America!'

'Come in and tell me everything, Cherie,' she says.

I'm so excited I can't contain myself. 'Oh my goodness, Cherie, what changes there will be.' I hold her hand.

'Are you sure you can do it?'

I don't doubt it for a moment, so when the letter arrives telling me that my application for a visa has been rejected, I can barely believe it. I am shattered.

'What?' Cornelia asks me.

I haven't moved since I opened the letter. Finally I find

the words. 'They say my grounds for the US tourist visa application are not strong enough.'

She doesn't know what to say to make me feel better.

I know that no one can solve this difficult problem of a visa but me.

Depression grabs hold of me. It pulls me down.

I sleep and sleep.

54

Josefina

When are you going to hand in your passport?' my father asks me. I feel as if he's watching me closely. He simply cannot understand why I don't use the alimony to buy a big house in Romania, find a job and settle here. I know he suspects I want to leave again.

'I'm not ready to do that yet,' I say.

He looks at me as if I'm crazy, crazier even than when I married a Ghanaian man. My mother, moving around the kitchen, says nothing. I think they must sometimes wonder what kind of daughter they have raised.

I need to renew my visa regularly. The quickest and cheapest way is to go to Belgrade by train, which I can catch at ten o'clock at night, leaving my children with my parents. I reach Belgrade the following morning, renew my visa, go shopping for all the things we can't get in Romania, and in the evening, take the overnight train back. I go every three months.

The officials come to know me but the questions never stop. Where are you going? Where are your children? Where is your husband?

I smile and answer straightforwardly so there is nothing they can use against me.

In Belgrade, I buy good cheeses and salami. Sometimes I buy Coca-Cola. I find clothes for my children. I'm not the only woman who does this. Romanian women with passports do it all the time. Together we get off at the station in Belgrade and cross the road to a big shopping complex. They do their shopping and wheel their trolleys back to the station before returning to Romania.

For them it's just a shopping trip. For me it's far more important. I must renew my visa. This time I decide I will try to get a tourist visa to Italy since I've heard that their immigration authorities are kinder than others. Once in Italy I will go to a police station. 'I don't want to go back to Romania,' I'll tell them. 'I want political asylum.'

Back in Bucharest I don't apply for a tourist visa to Italy. I'm not sure why. Something about this plan feels wrong.

'I want to see a psychic,' I tell Cornelia.

My sister doesn't believe in such things. 'Don't be stupid,' she says. 'People like that can't solve your problems or tell you what to do.'

'I know. But I need some hope.' I remind her that most of the monk's predictions have come true.

Through a friend, Cornelia finds me a psychic who lives in Bucharest. Her name is Josefina and her reputation is good. She says she is Romanian but most people believe her to be a gypsy. I need to find out from her the name of the faraway place of which the monk spoke.

Cornelia and I take a taxi to her house. My sister shakes her head at my foolishness.

'You didn't have to come,' I tell her.

'I want to be there,' she says. 'Then at least I'll know what craziness you're taking to heart.'

I shrug off her cynicism.

'I might even get my own fortune told,' says Cornelia. 'For a laugh.'

Josefina's house is made of thatched mud. It's old and rundown and the door is so low that when you enter you must stoop and bend your head.

'Are you sure this is the place?' I whisper to Cornelia. She shrugs.

Josefina greets us. She wears a long floral skirt and a top with green flowers on a cream background. Lost somewhere in the flounces of her blouse is a feeding baby. Her rust-coloured hair is tied back in a ponytail and a cigarette hangs from her mouth. She nods at us and I cannot imagine her serious face ever smiling.

We step inside and she sees me looking around her simple room. I notice she is embarrassed. Suddenly her demeanour changes. With the baby still clamped to her breast and the cigarette still dangling, she becomes an efficient businesswoman, indicating seats at a small wooden table covered by a cloth.

She sits down facing us and for a while looks silently into my eyes. Then she rises and boils some water in a pot on an old kerosene stove. Cornelia and I look at one another. Barely a word has been spoken.

Josefina takes the pot off the stove, adds sugar and boils it once more before adding coffee, which she leaves to brew. As she waits, a little boy with no pants on appears at her side. His nose is snotty and he holds something that presumably was once a toy.

'Mama?' he says.

'Get out of here!' Josefina screams at him. He runs away.

She returns to the table and pours coffee. 'Who first? You?' she asks me. I nod and she passes me the cup. When I've finished, I hand it back to her. She swirls what is left in the bottom and pours the excess into a saucer.

While she thinks, I examine her closely. Her hair is dry, dehydrated. Her face is square and her cheeks so swollen that it affects her speech.

The silence is broken by noises coming from the next room. The little boy is throwing things against a wall and his brother and sister are laughing.

'Be quiet! Don't you know I'm busy?' yells Josefina. She stares into my cup.

I continue to stare at her. For a reason I can't explain, I find my confidence in Josefina is growing. Or perhaps I'm just desperate.

Eventually she lifts her head and looks again into my eyes. 'Your ex-husband—his name starts with V. You have three children, two girls and one boy. You were with another man whose name starts with A.'

I am taken aback. I have no idea how Josefina knows these things. She's never met me and as far as I know, Cornelia has passed on no information about my life.

'What about my future?' I ask her.

She stares into my cup. 'You will go to a country that is very far away. Its name starts with an A.'

Part of me is amused.

'They've already refused me a visa for America,' I tell her.

Her expression doesn't change. She just repeats what she said. 'You are going to a country which starts with an A.'

I turn to Cornelia who, as I might have predicted, is rolling her eyes.

Josefina, meanwhile, has taken out her tarot cards. I shuffle them and cut the pack into three. She turns over cards from each pile and sets them out. As she works, she nods. 'Yes. It's telling me again. You will go on a long journey to a country that begins with an A.'

I shiver. There are goosebumps up and down my arm.

When Josefina has finished with me, she reads Cornelia's cup too. The facts she mentions from my sister's past are just as accurate as mine were—and the future she predicts is the same. She, too, will travel to a faraway country beginning with an A.

When we leave, Cornelia is scathing. 'What rubbish,' she says. 'You're a fool to believe her. She predicted the same future for us! She hasn't even got a good imagination. I'm not going anywhere.'

But I know what I feel. I believe Josefina.

A few nights later I wake from a vivid dream. In it I have been on a plane, the seats stretching down two very long aisles. From the window I can see a sky I've never seen before. It's gold, bright red and black, as if in flame. As I step out of the plane I see it again. It's a dawn sky, but not an African dawn.

55

'Starting with an A'

A gold bracelet I brought Cornelia from Ghana, a delicate chain, is stolen from our house. My sister takes it off whenever she washes or does the housework. Someone must have sneaked in and snatched it.

'I'm so sorry, Hellen,' says Cornelia and bursts into tears.

She has treasured the bracelet since I gave it to her, something beautiful from far away, from a place she will never visit.

'Don't worry. I'll buy you another one,' I promise her. 'When I'm next in Belgrade I'll look for a bracelet that's just as beautiful.'

I ask Marieta to come with me. 'I need the help of a professional shopper, Cherie.'

'Well you've asked the right girl, Cherie!'

We catch the train at ten o'clock that night. It stops at the border and the passport controllers come on board. 'Where are you going?' they ask.

'My dears,' says Marieta. 'We are going to London to visit the Queen.' We can't help but giggle. Having Marieta with me gives me the confidence to joke with officials like this.

'Ah—it's you again!' one of them says, recognising me. It's my seventh trip. I hand him my passport.

'What does your husband think about your staying away from him for so long?' he asks, seeing Alex's name.

'Why are you asking her that? She's a married lady!' says Marieta.

I smile at him. 'I'm going back soon.'

'You women and your shopping,' he says, stamping my passport and returning it with a grin. They move on and we sit back in our seats.

At the station in Belgrade, Marieta claps her hands. 'Right, Cherie, the centre of town. We need a jeweller!'

We catch a taxi and I gaze out the window. I have never seen this part of the city before. It's hilly and quite beautiful and I'm happy to be here. I feel calm and optimistic.

And then something happens that changes my life forever. We pay the taxi driver and I climb out of the car. In front of us is a flag I don't recognise and a metal plaque. *Australian Embassy*, it reads.

Immediately, Josefina's words come back to me. A country that starts with an A. I begin to tingle with excitement. Australia!

'Come on, Cherie, let's go!' says Marieta, behind me.

'Cherie, look at that!' I am staring at the building and can't move.

She comes and stands beside me. 'Are you crazy or what? Don't you know where Australia is? At the other end of the world. Have you lost your mind?'

I turn to look at her. Her eyes are wide. 'I sort of know where it is,' I say. In my mind it is at the end of the world, just as the monk told me. 'I know it has a big bridge because I've seen it on a postcard somewhere. And it produces wool.'

Marieta bursts out laughing. 'Come on, Cherie, don't be silly. Let's go shopping!' she says, tugging at my hand.

'No. I'm going inside to ask for a visa.'

'You're *what*?'

'I'm going in,' I repeat. 'Are you coming with me?'

She follows me inside. It is like a bank, with a counter and a transparent screen. There is a Yugoslavian woman behind the desk, but she speaks English. She must be about forty, with frizzy hair and a square face with high cheekbones.

I approach and give her my passport. 'I would like a tourist visa to Australia, please.'

She examines my passport. 'So—you're Romanian?'

Her manner is cool. There is no love lost between Yugoslavians and Romanians. They are Slavic and we are Latin. I take care not to react. I smile back at her. I don't want anything to get in the way of my application for this visa.

The woman passes me a form to fill in and Marieta sits beside me on the bench while I complete it. She keeps whispering to me. 'What are you doing? Are you crazy?'

She's distracting me. Besides, it occurs to me that perhaps what we say can be heard. 'Please, Cherie,' I finally say, 'will you wait outside?'

She quietly leaves. When I have completed the form, I take it up to the counter and hand it to the woman, along with my passport.

'I'll give these to someone senior in the visa department. Please wait.'

I wait and wait. I think of the gold bracelet that I must buy for Cornelia. I think of Marieta outside and how irritated she must be. I go to the window and look out. She is tapping her foot and smoking a cigarette. I nod for her to come back in. 'But only if you say nothing, Cherie,' I whisper as she joins me. She nods and winks.

There are pictures of Australia on the wall but I don't dare look at them. I don't want to become attracted to a country I may never see.

I just sit quietly in my chair and wait.

It must be an hour before the officer opens the security door and steps towards me. 'Mr Harrison will see you now,' she says.

I look at Marieta and see that she is biting her lip. She now seems keen for me to succeed.

Inside a big, beautiful room, a man is sitting behind a desk, dwarfed by the scale of everything around him. He seems to be sinking into his chair. He is bald, his face is skinny and he peers at me over half-spectacles. Above the desk hangs a photograph of the famous bridge. I stare at it and can scarcely drag my eyes away.

'Hello, nice to meet you,' he says, rising. He looks me up and down, politely, not in an inappropriate way. I suppose it's part of the job of an official, someone with the power to grant visas, to ascertain what kind of person they are dealing with. Nevertheless, I'm pleased I'm wearing my red dress and that my hair is loose around my shoulders. I feel confident and lucky.

'It's nice to meet you too, Sir,' I tell him. We shake hands.

'So you want to visit Australia.'

'Yes.'

He nods and we take our seats. 'I notice you have a different name from your children.'

'I'm divorced.'

'And where are your children?'

'In Romania.'

'With whom?'

'With my parents.'

'And now you want to visit Australia?'

'Yes I do.'

He pauses and I wonder what he thinks of me, what kind of mother and wife he imagines me to be.

'It's very unusual to be by yourself in Romania for such a long period, with your children and without your husband. Where is he now?'

'In Ghana.'

'If you don't mind my asking, what kind of marriage do you have? Is it a happy one?'

'Very happy.'

He looks at me and smiles a gentle, kind smile. Perhaps he can see through me, the desperation I can't voice, my need to escape and find a safe place where my children and I can be happy and respected, where I don't need to pretend I still have a man at my side.

'So how long do you want to spend in Australia?'

'I don't know. Perhaps a month.'

He takes off his glasses and puts them on the desk. Now his smile is broad. At this moment, I know this man is on my side. 'Guess what?' he says lightly.

'What?'

'I don't believe you're going to Australia to visit. I think you want to go and stay.'

'What makes you say that? The fact that I have a Romanian passport?' I can't help smiling back at him.

'Leave it with me. Ring me in three days' time.' He passes me his card and rises to open the door.

I leave, amazed at what has happened. I am taken by his openness and surprised at my own confidence and directness when he questioned me.

As soon as Marieta sees me, she starts to laugh. 'Something happened, Cherie! What?'

'I don't know.'

Later we sit over a coffee and I describe our conversation. She looks dubious and shakes her head. 'I'm worried for you, Cherie. Don't count on getting this visa.'

'Josefina told me the country I will go to would start with an A.'

Marietta purses her lips. 'Ah, you and your Josefina!'

'We'll see,' I say, finishing my coffee. 'Now, didn't we come to buy a bracelet?'

56

The Australian Visa

Three days later I ring Mr Harrison at the Australian Embassy in Belgrade.

'I remember you,' he says. 'And yes, your visa is ready.'

So easy. Words can't express my gratitude. On 20 February 1984 I travel to Belgrade to collect the crucial document.

I ask the receptionist if I can see Mr Harrison. 'I'll see if he can spare you a moment,' she says, reappears almost at once and holds the door open for me.

He rises from his big chair and gives me that broad smile again. 'So—you're going to Sydney.'

'Yes. Thanks to you.' I hold my hand out to him, and when he takes it, I grip his warmly and strongly, to show how much I appreciate what he's done for me.

I will never see him again, but this one man's generosity will change my life.

My Australian visa is valid until 23 June 1984. I have four months to organise everything. My immediate concern is my children. From Daniela in Geneva I know the hardship a refugee can encounter. Refugee camps are crowded places of confusion, fear and tears. I don't want to expose my children to memories that could haunt them forever as my childhood memories still haunt me. I tell myself that, for the moment, my children are safe with my parents and my sister while I work towards a new life for us all in Australia. It is their right, and mine, to live a happy, free life.

I go to a neighbour's house and pore over their globe of the world. In the flickering lamplight I trace my finger all the way from Bucharest to Sydney. I hadn't realised just how far away it is. I will fly over so many seas to the ends of the earth.

I visit Josefina once more. It is a cold winter's day in late February, the weather windy and wild with snowstorms. Cornelia cannot believe I'm dragging her out there again but I'm determined to find out if Josefina will see in the coffee and the cards the same thing she saw on our first visit.

We haven't made an appointment and Josefina, rugged up in a heavy winter coat with a scarf over her head, is surprised to see us.

'I want you to read my coffee grounds and cards again,' I greet her.

'But I've already told you what they say.'

'I want to see if anything has changed.'

She ushers us in. We sit in our coats as the wind and snow blow in under the doors and around the unsealed windows. Josefina's children are wrapped up like little bundles. She makes us coffee in the same way, asks me what I want to know about my future and tells me to think deeply while I drink so that my thoughts infuse the grounds.

I try to do as she asks but in fact I drink too fast because I'm cold and anxious to know what she'll say.

Josefina swirls the grounds in the cup, tips it upside down onto a plate, and then waits a few moments before she looks into the cup.

'It's a capital A for you. A country that begins with an A.'

I look at Cornelia and we laugh out loud. I pull out my passport and show Josefina the visa for Australia. She claps her hands together and her children gather round to see what the fuss is about. 'Oh my God! I've heard about that country!' Josefina shouts.

I can see that the accuracy of her prediction bolsters her confidence. She becomes very excited.

'You'll make this long journey alone—but don't worry, your children will soon join you. You'll be free and your children will be happy! You'll make a lot of money. Don't forget me when you're rich. Send me a little of your money.'

She leans across the table and takes my arm and I kiss her cold, worn cheek.

Only Marieta and Cornelia know that I'm going to Australia. My parents have no idea of my plans. I will tell them just before I leave. I know that once I apply for political asylum, the Australian authorities will contact the secret intelligence of the Securitate to find out if I have a criminal record. When they are alerted to what I've done, police will come to my parents' house and ask questions about where I've gone. If my mother and father know I am about to defect, they will be duty-bound to inform the police. So I must keep them in the dark for now.

I decide that I don't want to leave for Australia until after my children have had their birthdays. Although I'm full of hope, I don't know when I'll see them again.

I sit with Elsie on my bed and hold her hand tight. 'I'm going away for a while. I'll come back soon to get you and William and Nancy.'

Elsie nods slowly. 'How long will you be away, Mama?'

'Not long.'

She nods again and doesn't ask any more questions.

My feeling of guilt is overwhelming. However, I know I would feel equally guilty if I were to stay here and do nothing about changing our lives. Not that this makes it any easier to bear. All I can do is tell myself that my children will be safe and loved here.

I have a struggle ahead of me that I can't begin to imagine.

I spend as much time with the children as possible. We go to the park or tell stories and play games at home. One day we travel into town to go to a matinee at the children's theatre. While we're waiting to change trams, a man approaches us. He spits on my children and calls them *black crows*.

'Slut!' he shouts.

Elsie gazes up at me as if to ask why this is happening. Now that she's eight, her understanding of such abuse is quite deep and I can feel the pain inside her. Soon it will happen to William too and then to Nancy. I know we have to leave as soon as possible.

I never reply to anyone who insults my children or me. I remember Victor's retaliation on the street all those years ago. Violence breeds violence. I simply give this ignorant man a long stare. I hope he sees that I'm strong enough to survive anything he can throw at me.

When he finally goes away, I hug the children and say, 'Don't worry, he doesn't know what he's talking about. He understands nothing.'

My heart has never warmed to Bucharest. It is the city of pain.

57

One-way Ticket

On the first day of June 1984 I travel to Belgrade and buy a one-way ticket to Australia. I plan to leave Bucharest by the night train on 19 June and board a flight to Sydney from Belgrade the following day.

I have told my parents that I am going to Italy for a short trip. They have no reason to suspect I have planned anything else. I always come back.

Before I go, I organise the most wonderful birthday party for William and Nancy on a beautiful day in early summer. We prepare a feast and invite friends. The children race around, squealing with glee. Even my mother's face beams with happiness.

I try to fix these images in my mind. I know I will need them to sustain me in the coming weeks and months.

A few days before my departure, I draw all my money out of the bank and leave it with Cornelia so that she can look after the children. I am taking only $US200.

My sister and I have been sharing a bed just as we did when we were young. Sometimes my children will climb in with us during the night. On the day of my departure, I wake feeling excitement and fear, joy and sadness.

Suddenly I panic. I have forgotten to renew my Romanian passport! It expires in four days, on 23 June, the same day my Australian tourist entry visa expires. I must have a valid Romanian passport to claim political asylum in Australia.

I lie in bed frozen with fear. What if they send me back?

I reach out to my sister. 'Cornelia, my passport is about to expire. What I am going to do? I need to go straight to the passport office. But what if they ask questions? What if they can't extend it today?'

In less than an hour she and Marieta are waiting with me in the queue at the passport office. I need my sister and my friend with me to give me strength. I feel scared and nauseated. My mouth is dry and my voice is cracked.

When we reach the head of the queue, Marieta takes over, explaining to the passport officer that I am sick and may faint at any moment.

'I am a doctor,' she says firmly. She tells them I need a chair to sit on and one is brought.

The officer takes my passport, checks my photo and tells me to sit and wait. Marieta takes me outside and asks Cornelia to look after me while she goes back to wait for the passport. Soon she's back, waving my passport. It has been extended for another year. She is also shaking her head, unable to believe I could have forgotten this essential link in my plan.

Back home they help me iron my summer clothes and pack my suitcase. I decide that I need to dress more warmly on the plane; I will put on my jeans. My sister prepares my children's favourite meal, beouf salad, giving me more time to spend with them. We try to underplay the importance of the day. Cornelia keeps checking on me. I assure her that I feel better and am now in control of my emotions, even if I have felt fragile lately.

My children—Elsie, William and Nancy. I watch them, playing, laughing and chasing one another. I've made the right decision, I tell myself. At this point my children need the safety of the family home, not more uncertainty.

I dress and place my suitcase outside. I go into the garden, call the children and hug them one by one, as tight as I can. These hugs will have to last me a long time. I can feel Elsie's disappointment. She desperately wants to come with me and I feel guilty not taking her.

I need to think what is best for her in the long term. For an eight-year-old she has been through so much and left so much behind. The stability Cornelia and my parents can give her is what she needs now.

'Mama, why are you crying?' William asks. 'You've told us you're coming back. Please don't cry.'

I hug my baby, Nancy, and kiss her chubby cheeks. All she wants to do is run to the kitchen for her favourite salad.

Cornelia knows how to divert the children's attention and stays behind with them.

I go back inside the house looking for my father to say my goodbyes. He is in bed. Just like me, I think, trying to sleep away his worries.

'Make sure you come back,' he says. I don't answer, I just give him a kiss and go to find my mother.

She's in the kitchen trying to keep busy, her way of coping with anxious feelings. The look in her eyes tells me that she knows there is more than I've told her.

Parents know. Words are not needed.

Cornelia is the one who needs comforting. I hug her and entrust my children to her care.

'Be careful,' are her last words.

Marieta comes to pick me up. We arrive at the station in

good time and look up at the departure board. There is no train listed for Belgrade.

Marieta looks at me and I look at Marieta. We are speechless. We hurry to the ticket office.

'Sorry,' says the person behind the counter. 'The Belgrade train has already left.'

'How? Why?' we both start screaming.

A calm voice answers, 'The trains are now on the summer timetable.'

'What can I do?' I ask Marieta. My mind is totally blank. For the very first time, I give up. I feel I have ruined my only opportunity to escape. My visa for Australia runs out in four days and I *have* to catch the plane tomorrow.

'Cherie, I don't understand!' exclaims Marieta. She seems as shocked as I am. Her eyes are fixed on the huge clock as if staring at it will somehow turn back time and produce my train.

There is a wise old saying in Romanian: *Your train stops at your station only once*. If you miss it, it's gone forever. I repeat this to Marieta. But she refuses to share my gloom. 'Come on, Cherie! Let's take action!' she says, and I feel her hand on my shoulder encouraging me back to life.

'What can we do?'

'You can get another train.'

'That was the only direct one to Belgrade. All the others stop before they reach the border—so they won't get me there in time.'

Marieta is thinking quickly. 'You can get a train to Timisoara and from there make your own way to Belgrade.' Timisoara is some sixty kilometres short of the border.

'Come on! Let's go and get a ticket,' Marieta urges.

It's my only option and so I follow her. If she hadn't

been with me, I think I might have stood in front of the clock for hours, paralysed with confusion and disappointment.

'But how am I going to get from Timisoara to Belgrade?' I call after her.

'You'll have to ask someone for help. Or pay for a lift.'

The ticket costs $40. The train leaves in an hour but I board early to make absolutely sure I won't miss this one.

'Cherie, I'm really scared,' I tell Marieta as she helps me board.

She settles me in my seat and presses my ticket into my top pocket so I don't lose it. It's as if I'm a child. Then she takes my hand and holds it tight.

'Don't be scared. Be strong. You're going to make it.'

She waits until the train starts to pull out before climbing off. We wave like mad.

I can't sleep. I hold tight to my suitcase, trying to imagine how I'm going to make the flight in time. It leaves at two o'clock in the afternoon. Once the train arrives in Timisoara, I'll have eight hours to get to Belgrade.

I look around the compartment at my fellow travellers. A young man is watching me and seems concerned at how nervous I appear.

'Where are you going?' he asks me.

I should be wary about talking to strangers but I also need advice. 'Do you know how I can get there from Timisoara to the border of Yugoslavia?'

'When you get out in front of the main entrance to Timisoara train station, there'll be people hanging around in private cars. All you need to do is ask them.'

I'm relieved. The black market, prohibited by the Communist regime, will save me and take me to the border.

58

The Kindness of Strangers

When we arrive in Timisoara early in the morning, I am the first one off the train, hauling my heavy suitcase. The huge station is a wonderful old building. The Orient Express passes through it as do trains which travel all over Europe. Dragging my suitcase, I pass a kiosk selling food but nerves grip my stomach and I don't feel hungry. I head straight for the exit.

Outside the train station, men are standing by their Romanian-made Dacia cars waiting for fares.

'Can you please tell me how much it will cost for you to take me to the Yugoslavian border?' I ask the first man I approach. He tells me his price and I offer him even more: $US100. 'How close to the border can you take me?'

'A few kilometres away,' he says. 'I'll take you as far as I can.'

During the drive, he asks about my plans, but I'm focused on reaching the plane and barely hear him. Occasionally I come out of my reverie to ask him questions. 'What's the countryside like near the border? Will it be hard to walk there with my case?'

'It's mostly wheat fields but there are observation towers everywhere. You need to have a passport to approach the border—and I can only take you so far.'

I understand. Now that he has my American dollars, he's in danger of being caught and imprisoned and of course he will lose the money. That's if he can't bribe someone.

We drive very fast for over an hour and then he drops me off where the wheat fields begin. 'They'll think you're mad,' he says. 'I bet they've never seen anyone crossing on foot before. Just tell them you've got to catch a plane. Beg them to find someone to give you a lift. You should be able to make it in two hours.'

I thank him and hand over the money I promised him.

Around me, the wheat is ripe and yellow. Although it's early, the sun already beats down. I take off my jacket and fold it into my case. I look at the road ahead, flat and sealed. Once in a while, a car whizzes by, sounding its horn, its occupants hanging out to jeer and laugh. Sometimes the number plates are Yugoslav, sometimes Romanian. Nobody stops or even slows.

To the left and right, observation towers are visible beyond the fields. They stand about 100 metres apart like giant storks. I imagine soldiers peering at me through binoculars and wondering who this crazy woman is. In the distance I can see a shed with gates, like a toll booth, and I presume this is the border post. I have never before crossed the border on foot.

The walk is long and hot. I have never seen so much wheat rolling to the horizon. I tie my hair back but I can still feel the sweat running down my neck. There's not a breath of wind. Around me, the wheat burns in the sun. I lug my heavy suitcase for as long as I can, then put it down, walk around it, and pick it up with the other hand. Somehow I don't feel tired. I'm completely focused. I have to make that plane. This is my last chance.

Half a dozen armed guards watch as I approach the border post. 'Where do you think you're going?' one of them asks. They are rough and arrogant, bullish in their dark blue uniforms. Their heads are shaved and the looks on their faces tell me they know I'm mad.

'I have to be in Belgrade by two o'clock to catch a flight to Australia,' I say. I reach into my bag and show them my passport. They flip through the pages, examining them closely and consulting with the others. I know they think it's a forgery. One of them goes off to phone the Bucharest passport office to confirm its authenticity.

I wait, twitchy and impatient, while the other guards stare.

'Please, I have a plane to catch,' I say after what seems a long time.

Finally the guard returns with my passport. 'It's all in order,' he says. 'But how are you going to get to Belgrade?'

'I need a lift,' I say, with hopeful desperation in my voice.

'Just wait here.'

I have the rest of my American dollars. If I use them for a lift, I will arrive in Australia without a cent. But I have no choice. I have to get to my flight.

As cars and trucks pass through the border, passengers get out to have their passports checked and to be searched. They also wait while their vehicles are inspected. I watch as the guard who checked my passport approaches a car and speaks to the driver. The man looks across at me and shakes his head. The guard asks a few more travellers, but the response is always the same.

Then we see a truck approaching from the Timisoara road. It is carrying a load of new tyres, labouring slowly along. When it pulls in, the guard goes over to it and speaks to the driver.

Not this truck, I think to myself. It's so slow! I'll never get there in time.

'That woman over there needs to get to Belgrade in a hurry,' I hear the guard say.

The driver looks towards me. He is in his fifties, an average-sized man with a paunch. He is wearing the typical truck driver's uniform, a singlet and shorts. Grey chest hairs curl up around the neck of the ancient singlet. He has a round, happy face with deep-set eyes.

'Come on then. We'd better get a move on,' he calls out. I have no choice. I grab my case and hurry towards him.

It's unusual to find happy Romanians but this man is different. I tell him about needing to catch my flight. 'It's going to be a rough ride. You OK with that?'

I tell him I am, and he puts his foot down and we roar away from the border post. 'So what's the story?' he asks me. 'What are you up to?'

'I'm going to Australia for a holiday.'

He drives barefoot but there are battered sandals on the seat beside him. 'Sorry about those,' he tells me, tossing them onto the floor at my feet to join his short-sleeved shirt. The smell of sweaty shorts and old sandals wafts up my nose. He wipes the sweat from his face with a greasy towel.

But none of this matters to me. This man is my angel carrying me through the air on his battered wings.

He is astounded that I live in Africa and wants to know all about it. 'So are there monkeys in the streets? Do the men really have more than one wife?'

I answer as well as I can.

'And you married a black man?' he finally asks. The honesty of his curiosity is strangely refreshing.

'I did!' I laugh. He whistles.

'You sure must have beautiful children,' he says.

After all the insults we have suffered in Romania, all the bad memories, this kind, compassionate and understanding man is restoring my faith in humankind.

We reach Belgrade at twelve-fifteen.

'Want me to take you right to the airport?' he asks me. Since I have no idea how to get there, I feel tremendously grateful. I offer him all the money I have left.

'You keep it,' he says. 'Who knows when you'll need it?'

I bless him for his generosity with all my heart and wish him well.

59

The New Country

At the airport I check in and at last board the plane.
As we take off I feel freedom, pure and deep. I'm
the most alive I've ever felt. Although I'm exhausted,
in the air I'm happy. As I unfasten my seatbelt, a vision comes
to me of Josefina telling me I will travel far away to a country
beginning with an A.

'You were completely right, Josefina,' I tell myself.

Fear of the unknown descends with the darkness of night.
It's my habit to see only the immediate, to only deal with what
is in front of me. Now that seems daunting. What will my
reception be in the new country? Do I hand myself over to the
police or go to the immigration department?

On the plane are different people from our region,
Romanians and Yugoslavians, and some Australian residents
who have been visiting family in Europe. There are also
asylum seekers from the refugee camp in Belgrade. I talk to
no one but the air hostesses.

The flight seems interminable. I lose track of the time and
how many hours we have travelled. I wonder when we will
finally reach Bangkok.

In the Bangkok terminal, I stretch my legs and wander

about. I hear people speaking English in a strange way, with mouths closed around the sounds and no space between their words. This must be Australian. These people seem casual and easy-going and smile the same smile as the man in the Australian embassy in Belgrade. As I watch them, I find that I'm smiling too.

We board a Qantas flight. Strangely I feel as if someone is holding my hand and walking with me. I stop and stand in the aisle, gasping for air. A queue builds up behind me.

'Are you all right?' asks the hostess. I tell her I'm fine and start looking for my seat. I find it on the aisle beside only one other, which no one takes. I touch the fabric of the empty seat beside me over and over, tears in my eyes.

When the plane takes off, I find I cannot sleep. I feel feverish. I have no medication with me, not even an aspirin. The passengers behind me are drunk and loud. They are Romanians and make rude comments about the hostess and me in our language. I'm ashamed to be Romanian around these crude men from Moldova. I speak only English on the plane.

I reach for my earphones. When I put them on I hear a cheerful song I've never heard before, *Down Under*. I love its bouncy rhythms and keep waiting for it to recur on the music loop. What does *Down Under* really mean, I wonder. And I have no idea what a Vegemite sandwich is.

As the cabin lights dim for landing, beyond my window, a gold and red blaze rises above the blackness of the earth. My heart leaps. This is the sky I saw in the dream I had after my visit to Josefina.

We touch down at Sydney International Airport on a cold winter's morning. As I emerge from the plane I glance over my shoulder, seeking reassurance from the flaming dawn. My entry visa expires tomorrow. I have a one-way ticket, $US49 in my purse, and I know no one. Now I have to convince the immigration officials that I am here for a holiday.

'How long are you planning to stay in Australia?' The officer at the immigration check point is in his early forties. His face is calm.

'A month.'

'Do you have any friends or relatives here?'

'No.'

'Where are you going to sleep tonight?'

I clutch the edge of the counter. 'In a hotel.'

His stamp thumps on my passport. 'Enjoy your holiday.'

Why didn't he ask to see my return ticket? I smile back at him, a man completely different from the suspicious guards I left behind in Romania.

I haul my suitcase from the carousel and push through the crowds to the nearest foreign exchange window. Memories of Romania float in the air. I toss my head to shake off my last ties to that country.

I change my money, find a little coffee shop and buy a long black coffee. I am hungry and tired. Adrenaline kept me awake on the plane. I need to focus and decide whom to approach to ask for asylum. I smoke ten cigarettes, one after another, as I sip my coffee. I have two choices: I can hand myself in as a political refugee to the airport police or to the city immigration office.

I make the coffee last for two hours, the longest hours of my life. A very long black! I can't afford a second.

Tears blur my eyes. Already I miss my children. Two policemen saunter past my table, chins jutting below peaked caps. They look as though they would be only too happy to bundle me onto the next plane back to Europe.

I'm so tired I feel sick. The ten cigarettes haven't helped. I make a decision, pull out a mirror and touch up my lipstick. My hands shake. As I bend over to pick up my suitcase a stab of intense and familiar fear shoots through me. I am a child again in Cluj. The leaves are dying and falling. My father has parked his truck and is here to take me back to Bucharest, away from the safety and comfort of my grandmother's house. Walls of fear close around me. I cling to Mama Draga with wet cheeks and a shrinking heart. I feel the familiar sense of loss. How will I survive the nine months until I see her again?

Now my legs tremble. Then I sense her presence. Her hand grips my arm and her voice echoes in my head, 'Have courage, Lenuta.' Her warmth and strength carry me out of the airport building and over to the taxi rank.

'Please take me to the immigration department.'

'Chifley Square?'

'I don't know,' I say with a shrug.

It dawns on me that I know very little about this new country.

60

Lost Soul

It's a sunny Sydney morning, a chilly wind blows into my face. I didn't realise that here in Australia June is a winter month and I've packed only summer clothes. The only winter outfit I have is the jeans, the salmon coloured turtleneck and the light denim jacket that I am wearing. Fortunately it's warm inside the taxi as the sun shines through the window.

The road from the airport is smooth. In the distance I see tall buildings that must be the city centre and wonder which is the immigration office. As we leave one long road and turn into a busier one, I see the big windows of a luxurious car showroom filled with gleaming Porsches. The traffic is heavy and I constantly watch the taxi's meter, praying that I'll have enough money to pay when I reach my destination. To my relief, the taxi soon stops in front of an impressively large building that reminds me of the United Nations in Geneva—not the architecture but what it represents: a place where lost souls search for a better life.

I hand the driver his $12 fare and he helps me lift my heavy suitcase from the boot.

I wonder if he knows why I'm here.

I carry my suitcase through the glass door and look around

310

for the information desk. I put my case near the window, out of the way, then search for my passport at the bottom of my handbag. Then I join the long queue.

Everyone seems foreign and nervous. I wonder what all these people are waiting for. Do they seek political asylum too? The closer I move to the window, the more doubtful I feel. They're not asking questions like mine. I wonder if I should have handed myself over to the police patrolling the airport.

Too late now!

I finally reach the window. 'Can I help you?' asks a friendly voice.

I take a deep breath. 'I'm here to ask for political asylum.'

'To ask for what?' The officer is clearly surprised and her tone is stern.

For a moment I think that she must not have understood my thick accent, so I repeat, 'I'm here to ask for political asylum.'

'Sorry—we don't deal with those applications here. You have to apply from a refugee camp somewhere in Europe.' She gazes at me. 'Can I see your passport, please?'

I hand the passport to her. Carefully she looks through it while the queue builds up behind me. I hear people sighing in frustration.

'If you have a Romanian passport, the nearest refugee camp is in Yugoslavia,' she tells me. 'I see you came through Belgrade. You should have stopped right there.'

And then I hear the dreaded words, 'I'm sorry—but you'll have to go back.'

'But I can't. I only have a one-way ticket.'

She frowns. 'What do you mean?'

'My ticket is one-way.'

'But you must have a return ticket to get a tourist visa. Let me see your ticket.'

'I don't have a return ticket. I am here to ask for political asylum.'

I closely watch the officer's face as she tries to find a way to deal with all this. She looks confused and it's clear to me that she has never dealt with anything similar.

'I'm sorry,' she says. 'We have never had anyone coming to Australia on a tourist visa with a one-way ticket to ask for political asylum. I need to ring someone to help you. Please take a seat. Someone will attend to you soon.'

I thank her and go back to where I've left my case. I sit for hours and hours. I'm thirsty and I'm hungry, but I don't move because surely someone will help me eventually.

At long last a young well-dressed man approaches me and addresses me by my married name, Alex's name. He shakes my hand firmly and says that it's nice to meet me. I expected migration officials to be cold, but there's a warmth about him. He asks me to follow him upstairs where a senior officer is waiting to speak with me.

When we get out of the lift, a woman dressed in a business suit is waiting in front of an open door. She looks cold and arrogant and my throat constricts in fear. She extends her hand towards me.

'I'm Mrs Stephens,' she says in a stern voice. 'Come in.' She makes it sound like an order.

I place my suitcase next to my chair as she sits across from me at her desk making notes on a pad.

She puts down her pen. 'Show me your passport and your ticket.'

I place both documents on the desk. She studies my passport closely. She doesn't understand why I have so many entries to, and exits from Yugoslavia. I explain that I needed to renew my visa every three months to enable me to stay in Romania, the country of my birth.

'How long ago did you leave Ghana?'

'Early last year, after my second divorce.'

'Your second divorce?' she asks sharply. 'Where is the father of your children?'

'In Ghana. I divorced him in March 1981.'

She is looking crosser and crosser. 'What about your children? Where are they?'

'I left them with my family in Romania until I settle in Australia. For now, they need stability. I need to go through this asylum process on my own.'

'What kind of mother are you? You left your children in Romania and now you're roaming round the world? You should be ashamed of yourself!'

Her face looks really angry. I look at her and feel humiliated, just like the time I knelt, heavily pregnant, to remove the red soup stains from the upholstered chairs. I kept quiet then because of my children and I keep my mouth shut now. I know I'm doing this for my children. Argument will merely hinder my case. I begin to cry. Pride has no place at this moment.

'What is your profession?' she asks.

'Beauty therapist.'

'In our country we don't need beauty therapists. We need nurses and engineers.' I have my head down now and feel that I am at the mercy of this woman. I have never begged before but this time I might have to. Somehow I know that no matter what I say, it won't help my case. This official has made up her mind.

She repeatedly mentions *our country*. Not mine. I am well

aware that I don't belong here, but pointing it out so often makes me feel even more of a lost soul.

'Do you have any other documents with you?'

'Yes, all of them.' I open my case and search for the folder which I then place on her desk. She carefully examines every single document, takes notes and returns my papers to me.

Then she turns to me and announces, 'We do not process refugee applications here in our country. You need to go back to Europe. I understand you don't have a return ticket so I'll organise for the Australian government to pay for one. Do you understand what I'm saying?'

'Of course—but please, please don't deport me. The Romanian authorities will put me in prison. Who will look after my children then?'

'But you left them. You're not a good mother.'

'Yes I am!' I cry. 'I'm just trying to find a place where my children are not spat on and called *black crows*.'

She is unmoved. 'I'll make sure you can be deported soon. Now where are you going to sleep tonight?'

I look through the window and see that it's already dark. I haven't been aware that time has passed.

'I don't know. I know no one here in Sydney and I have no money for a hotel.'

I see more anger in her face. I am holding her up at the end of her working day and now I've created yet another problem for her. But I can see that she will help me. Somewhere inside her tough heart there must be a little kindness. Or does she just want to make sure I don't disappear? Perhaps both!

She makes a few phone calls, then tells me I must wait on the ground floor until someone comes to pick me up and drive me to a migrant hostel. I will stay there until she completes my deportation papers.

She stands up and leads me outside to the lift. When I reach the ground floor only the security guard is left. He approaches me and in a soft and caring voice says that I can lie on the metal bench to rest. I thank him.

I button up my jacket and try to find a comfortable position on the hard bench, resting my head on my handbag. I'm exhausted. I cry silently because I'm scared.

I awake to the noise of a vacuum cleaner. I've dozed off and now the cleaners are in the building. I drift back to sleep.

61

Two Angels

Someone is trying to wake me by gently tapping my shoulder. I open my eyes and look up at a tall older gentleman. His eyes shine with compassion. He speaks softly and calmly and I feel he has come to save me.

'I'm John from the St Vincent de Paul Society. I've been asked to drive you to the migrant hostel. Is that OK?'

I don't know what the St Vincent de Paul Society is, but I feel I can trust this man. I stand up, pat my hair and straighten my jacket, ready for the next part of my journey.

'The hostel that they've arranged is too rough for you,' says John. 'You're such a lovely lady. Let me see if there's a spare bed somewhere nicer.'

He leaves me waiting for a few minutes while he goes off to make a phone call. He is soon back with a smile on his face. 'I've found a bed for you in the Endeavour Hostel. I hope you don't mind sharing a room with another lady. She's from South America.'

I tell him I'm happy to share a room. This lovely man then offers to carry my suitcase to his car. 'It must be very heavy for you.'

I am only too pleased to let him. As we leave the office I can see that it is late, past ten. John's car is parked on the street nearby. I start shivering. It's cold and very, very tired.

John asks if I would like to take out some warmer clothes from my case. Of course I have nothing warmer, so I tell him that I'm fine.

As we drive, the air in the car warms me. Sydney looks beautiful at night. The streets are wide, well-lit and clean. After driving for about twenty minutes we reach the hostel set on a hill. We drive through two big iron gates and I see several blocks within the big compound. John says it used to be a navy base.

At the entrance of one of the blocks a man is waiting for us. He shows me around and indicates how I can find the dining room. On the way to my block he shows me the main office. The buildings are surrounded by attractive gardens full of plants I have never seen. They must be native to Australia.

We reach my room and knock at the door. A beautiful woman greets us in Spanish. The small room is divided by a half-wall made of red brick. There is a small wardrobe with a mirror fixed to it, and a single bed.

I am so grateful to have a bed in which to sleep. I thank John for rescuing me from the hard bench and for finding me a good place to stay where I feel safe. He wishes me luck and says goodbye.

I take a long hot shower and then lie down and try to sleep. I know this will revive me. When faced with challenges that seem too hard, I simply sleep and sleep.

I am woken up by the sound of a woman's voice. 'I'm Mrs Urlich and I'm in charge of the hostel,' she says. 'I've been worried about you. You've been asleep for two whole days. We've been coming to check on you. I could see how exhausted you were but now it's time for you to get up.

Have a shower and then I'll take you to the dining room for breakfast. Come and meet me in the office. Are you fine with that?'

I can't believe I've been asleep for such a long time. I do as she says and go to her office. She greets me with a kind smile that warms my heart. I feel she is another angel who, like John, has come to help me.

'Let's go and have breakfast together and then we can come back to my office for a chat,' she says.

As we enter the dining room in the main building we find a very long queue in which people are waiting to serve themselves. Mrs Urlich joins me in the queue despite the fact that she could have breakfast in the staffroom.

There is a lot of food of many different kinds set out on a long table. I'm impressed. This hostel seems a long way from the struggles and difficulties of a refugee camp. It's more like a good hotel where everyone can eat their fill. In the queue people talk happily to one another. It's all very different from what Daniela told me. Now I understand why she advised me not to apply for refugee status in Europe.

After we've eaten breakfast, Mrs Urlich invites me into her office for a cup of coffee.

'I had a look at your report from the immigration office. It says you're going to be deported.'

'Yes—and I'm scared. I know I'll be imprisoned once I get back to Romania.'

'You can't let this happen,' says Mrs Urlich firmly. 'Here we live freely and are entitled to legal advice to help us.'

'Mrs Urlich, I have no money. I can't afford legal advice.'

'You can get it for nothing. It's called Legal Aid and you'll find their office down the road in Kingsford. Do that. Seek legal aid.'

A seed is planted in my mind. I feel grateful. When John brought me to this hostel, he gave me a gift: Mrs Urlich. That evening I go into the dining room and sit on my own. I need time to make plans. Tears fall on to my plate and already I miss my children. But I know this will pass. I have been shown the way.

The next morning I go to see Mrs Urlich and ask for the address and phone number of the Legal Aid office. I then walk out of the hostel and down the road towards Kingsford Legal Centre. There, I may have to fight another battle. If I must, I will. I am determined not to be deported.

I make an appointment with a lawyer for the next day. I am told to bring in all my documents.

62

Cristina

The next morning at the Legal Centre, I am greeted by Cristina, a young lawyer in her twenties with a slim figure and short blonde hair. She tells me that she has extensive knowledge of refugee laws in European Communist countries and the United Nations.

I think that I am the most fortunate person on earth. Here in this friendly country of which I am not yet a citizen, I'm being offered help by a knowledgeable, specialised lawyer. Cristina and I speak for hours. She works hard on my case. She makes an application to delay my deportation until the case is reviewed.

Over the next few months I attend hours and hours of interviews conducted by immigration officials. The questions are always the same and so are my answers: nothing but the truth. Cristina is always with me and all her questions and my answers are recorded. I feel that this is a fair process needed to assess one's eligibility.

Most of the time I am in tears, scared of being deported, but Cristina always make me feel protected and reassures me that she will do her best to obtain my permanent resident visa on humanitarian and compassionate grounds.

She gives me strength. Each time I leave her office I feel more confident than when I arrived.

I walk all the way back to the hostel. From a distance I can see the hostel on top of the hill with its big gates wide open. It looks like two open arms ready to welcome me. Despite the difficulties I'm facing, the hostel feels like home.

I pray hard that Australians will accept me and my children.

It is winter, windy and cold. My light clothes don't keep me warm in the chill of the evening as I stand in the phone booth on the hostel grounds. I hear my mother say, 'Lenuta, why are you shivering? Where are you?'

'In Geneva, Mama.'

'It's summer.'

I quickly search for a response. 'I'm not well, Mama—that's why I'm shivering!'

I wonder if she believes me. As I speak with Elsie, Nancy and William, my body is still shivering but my heart is warmed by their voices. They sound happy.

I ring them every week, but we can never talk for long. Overseas calls are expensive.

I continue to tell my parents that I'm in Geneva. When they ask me when I'll be coming back, I try to avoid answering directly. Clearly the Securitate have not yet approached my family and no one knows I've defected except my sister and Marieta. I feel it's still best to keep what I'm doing hidden from my parents, just in case they're interrogated.

Every day I dress in the same jeans with my light jacket. I try not to show that I'm cold but sometimes I can't help shivering. One of the other migrants at the hostel notices and asks why I don't put on more clothes.

'I only have summer clothes. I thought it was warm here, like June in Europe.'

She smiles and the next day she takes me shopping. We walk to the St Vincent de Paul shop in Maroubra. For $5 she buys me a selection of winter clothes—even a woollen hat! I am never cold again.

During the next phone call, I hear my mother crying. 'Why did you go to the ends of the earth? Why? Why Australia?' I realise that finally the Securitate has told my parents I've defected and am in Australia.

'I've found freedom, Mama. I'll bring you here with the children soon!'

My promise fails to console her. I cannot ask what happened when she was questioned by the Securitate because our calls will be monitored. I'm now worried about my children's freedom to travel. Will they still be eligible for new Romanian passports?

Disturbing thoughts rush through my mind. Without passports they won't be able to leave Romania—and if I return I'll be thrown into prison. Will the Securitate show my children compassion? I remember one of our wise old sayings: *It's not the child's fault but the parents'*. I don't really trust the Romanian authorities.

Where can I turn? What can I do? I feel lost again.

I turn to Cristina for advice. She tells me that once I'm granted permanent Australian residency, I'll be able to seek assistance in bringing my children to join me. She tells me not to worry. There are ways of obtaining passports and getting them out of Romania.

I have faith in her experience and expertise.

I'm not to know that it will take Cristina a whole year to convince the Australian authorities to grant me permanent residency. Each time we're rebuffed she calls on her knowledge of the law and works even harder. I don't have enough words to express my gratitude to her for saving me from deportation.

The anniversary of my arrival in Australia is celebrated with a precious gift: not just permanent residency for me but also an application for my children to enter the country. I'm told that this could take another year. With Cristina's help, permission is granted within a few weeks and the Romanian office, at my sister's persistence, issues their passports.

Next time we talk on the phone, I tell the children my good news. Only Elsie fully understands what I'm saying. She is so excited! I hear her loudly telling William and Nancy that soon they will go with Mamaie on a big plane to Australia to live with me.

I am ecstatic. A heavy weight has been lifted from me. I have been given the opportunity not only to experience freedom, but also to create good lives and futures for my children.

Now at the age of almost thirty-two I feel I have reached the top of one mountain.

63

Thea

I answer many job advertisements. 'I'm sorry, Hellen, but you're too skilled at your profession,' Marie, a French beauty therapist tells me. She explains that my practical test was above the accepted professional standard and that she's worried her clients will prefer me to her.

Time after time I hear, 'Sorry—we need someone with experience in Australia.'

I know I can find the right job. I keep on reassuring myself and I keep on trying.

I remember Mrs Urlich's advice when I first met her at Endeavour Hostel.

'You know, Hellen, you could do well on the Lower North Shore. There are wealthy people there, women who can afford the luxury of beauty treatments.'

I decide to follow her advice and hope that it will again bring me luck. I search the ads in the Lower North Shore papers and find a job advertised in Crows Nest. This time I don't demonstrate the full range of my professional skills. Surprisingly, in spite of such little effort, I'm given the job.

'Where do you live?' Thea, a client, asks. She lives near the salon in Crows Nest.

'In east Sydney,' I tell her.

'How long does it take you to come to work in the morning?'

'A long time. I need to catch a bus and a train. Then I should take another bus, but instead I walk to save the fare.' Then I smile. 'But that's fine. I'm grateful to have a job and I'm used to walking long distances. When I had to do all the interviews with the immigration office, I walked from the hostel in Coogee all the way to Chifley Square in the centre of Sydney.'

'Hellen, I'm divorced and there's only me and my adopted son in a very big house. You can have the downstairs part of the house.'

I'm overwhelmed. 'Thank you, Thea. That's so kind of you. But I can't afford to live on the North Shore. I need to save money for my children's airfares.'

'I'll only charge you $50 a week rent.'

I can barely believe Thea's generosity. Another angel! So many people are kind to me in Australia. The following evening after work, Thea picks me up from the hostel. She helps me carry my two suitcases, my only assets.

Her house is big and modern and tastefully furnished. A breeze wafts from the nearby park. As I fall asleep that night I can smell trees and grass and flowers. I lie in a comfortable bed with a big smile on my face, once again feeling extremely lucky. Soon I fall asleep.

The next morning I open the windows and see that the park is actually a cemetery. I'm usually scared of graves, but this time I'm not.

Not long into my new job I get my first warning. I need to change my ways, to work faster. Everything doesn't have to be perfect all the time, I'm told.

Marie was right. My employer feels threatened by me. Most clients now prefer my work and ask for me by name when they make their appointments. I know I can't change the way I work. I tell my employer I'll leave but stay until she finds someone to replace me.

It's clear that from now on the only way I can practise properly as a beauty therapist is to have my own business. But I have no money. I need to find a way to earn some.

I know how to clean. The Sheraton is a big impressive hotel in Chifley Square which I often passed on the way to my immigration interviews. One morning I make a snap decision. I go in and ask for a housekeeper's job. I know I can do it and still continue with my other jobs too.

The day I walk into the Sheraton, I wear my bright red dress and my long hair is down. I look elegant enough to be a guest of this luxurious hotel. At the employment office, the young woman asks if she can help me. When I tell her I'm looking for a cleaning job, she looks me up and down. I try hard not to laugh. I'm hardly dressed for the part.

'Can you clean?' she asks doubtfully.

'Certainly—and I'm very good at it.'

She looks me over again while handing me an application form. Two days later, I'm hired. At 5.30am, I stand before a mirror looking at myself in the maid's uniform of the Sheraton Hotel.

For a moment I feel I have fallen a long way. I'm now a servant. Tears fill my eyes and images of the luxuries I enjoyed during my marriage to Alex float into my mind. I didn't choose that luxury so why am I feeling that I've failed myself by taking on a housekeeping job?

I now realise that I still hold deeply-rooted misconceived beliefs instilled in me by my Oltenian grandfather. He always reminded my mother that she was from the lower servant class and looked down on her. Now that I am a servant myself, those memories haunt me and cause me pain.

I feel Mama Draga's presence. She smiles at me as if to say, 'There are more lessons for you to learn. This is an important one. Don't let others judge you.'

I turn to begin work, concentrating on the wisdom behind her words.

64

My Children Arrive

All my time in Australia I've been missing my children and preparing for their arrival. I need to rent an apartment. I can't afford to spend much on furnishings or kitchenware.

One of my clients suggests I look in the St Vincent de Paul shop for quality goods at very reasonable prices. I remember that wonderful shop in Maroubra where a friend bought cheap winter clothes for me.

The shop in Crows Nest is much smaller than the one in Maroubra. All the pots and pans are piled up on top of one another on the cement floor. At the bottom of the pile I find a piece of what looks like wood covered with burgundy velvet material. I lift it up and turn it round.

I start reading the words inscribed on it which sound like a prayer. The Serenity Prayer touches my heart in a way I have never been touched before. I read it over and over again. I walk out of the shop carrying only this talisman which has cost me twenty cents. I keep it close and read it when I need help. It becomes one of my treasures:

LORD
grant me the
serenity to
accept
the things I
cannot change;
the courage to
change the
things I can;
and the
wisdom
to know
the difference.

On 28 August 1985, fourteen months after I landed in this new country, I watch my three children coming through the arrival doors at Sydney Airport. They are accompanied by an air hostess. I wanted my mother to bring them to Australia, but the Romanian authorities refused to issue her a passport in time.

The terminal is crowded and busy and I'm really nervous. I haven't seen my beautiful children for more than a year. They all wear outfits in the same style, William in blue and white and Elsie and Nancy in red and white. Unknown to me at the time, my sister sold her jewellery to buy these smart new clothes for them and they look beautiful.

I give each of them the biggest hug. I feel so much joy it's almost overwhelming. Finally my dream has come true. Here we are, together in a safe and beautiful country.

'Are you my mother?' Nancy asks while I hold her tight and kiss her. Elsie has no doubt I am her mother. She missed me terribly, she's overjoyed to see me again.

William is busy exploring the terminal. He's fascinated by the trolleys and keeps pushing empty ones around. Nancy continues to gaze up at me wondering if I'm her real mother.

When we reach our new home the children are excited. I've rented a two-bedroom apartment in Artarmon on Sydney's Lower North Shore. Before the children arrived, I painted it all, even their red and white bunk beds. I bought them cheerful red sheets and toys to play with and filled the fridge with their favourite foods including lots of strawberries.

After lunch I take them for a walk to show them around the area. As we approach the park we pass a couple who smile at us and say how beautiful my children are. I answer for them because they have forgotten their English. We chat, and when they move on, Elsie turns to me.

'Mama, why don't people here in Sydney spit on you and call us *black crows*?'

'Because Australians are kind,' I tell her. 'You'll like it here.' I give them another big hug and think to myself how lucky we are to be here.

That night after the children are in bed, I sit at our kitchen table reflecting on our lives and my journey. I still can't quite believe that we're all here together. I keep peeking into their bedroom to check if I'm dreaming.

I have finally fulfilled the monk's prediction. We are in Sydney, as far away as we can get from Romania. I thank him in silence. I also remember Josefina's predication of a country beginning with an A.

Silently, I thank her too.

I take a few days off work to help the children adjust to their new surroundings. Their first fun day out is spent at Luna Park. I can see the joy and happiness on my children's faces, they have never seen anything so big and exciting.

Their fun on the rides brings tears of happiness to my eyes. I don't want the day to end—nor do they.

65

Living Together

made a promise to myself when I had children that I would put their needs and happiness above everything else. This promise I now feel in my bones.

I sit down with them and explain the routines of our new life together. They need to understand the reality of our circumstances. I have to earn money to pay for our living expenses and for them to attend school. I point out that we have no family here to support us. My choice is either to apply for a single mother's benefit or to work at many different jobs. I tell them I have chosen to work and will provide for them as best I can.

I also tell them that there are many kind people who will help us from time to time. However, in the end we are responsible for ourselves.

I know that Elsie is mature and caring for a nine-year-old. I tell her how good she is at looking after her younger brother and sister, and that the air hostess who accompanied them from Belgrade to Sydney was amazed by how well behaved they all were. I tell Elsie the hostess said she was just like a little mother.

I attach a list to the fridge, setting out the daily routine which has to be followed. I believe in providing my children with equal amounts of love and discipline, along with meeting their material needs. In return they must do their best, behave well and study.

Being a single parent is a choice I made. I will have to be both mother and father to them. I believe a child is better off with one happy parent than with two unhappy ones, a lesson I learned from my own childhood.

I think hard about where my children should go to school. I've heard that the Catholic school in Chatswood is good but difficult to get into. I ring for an appointment with the principal and am told to wait while Sister Carmel is called to the phone.

The voice that comes on the line is warm and cheerful.

'Please come and see me tomorrow morning after 9am,' she says. She doesn't sound like a stern nun. The Romanian nuns I've met had a very cold side to them, perhaps because of the isolation and hardship they had to endure under the Communist dictatorship.

The next day I meet with Sister Carmel for more than an hour, outlining our story and telling her why I'd love my children to receive a Catholic education.

She asks me to bring the children to school by 8.30am the following day. I tell her I'll need to ask for time off from work to bring them in, so maybe it can be the day after.

'I can arrange with a mother whose children attend our school and who is a very good friend of mine to pick your children up at 8am tomorrow. Just give me your address and phone number.'

I panic. 'But what about uniforms? School bags? Shoes?'

'Don't worry,' she says, smiling. 'Those can wait a day or two.'

She makes it all so easy for us. I am so grateful.

The children are excited and nervous. They don't speak or understand English. Their little faces look worried when they hear that I need to work, and someone they have never met will be coming to pick them up. I assure them that the lady will be as kind to them as the couple we met the day they arrived, and that they will have fun in their new school. Slowly, they begin to smile.

That night I prepare their lunch boxes and iron their clothes. I explain to Elsie that around 8am a lady will arrive at our apartment and knock on the door. I will need to leave the house by 6am, but before that, I will prepare their breakfast.

I wake them up with hugs and kisses. They are excited about their adventure at a new school. I promise I will pick them up at school that afternoon just before 3pm.

I finish work around midday and go straight to the school hoping to see them during their lunch hour. I look for Sister Carmel but am told that she has taken the children to Chatswood Chase shopping centre. I head there and as I look across the road I cannot believe my eyes. There are the three of them all dressed up in school uniforms, with new shoes and bags. Sister Carmel is holding Nancy's hand and in the other hand my daughter holds a peeled banana.

I am speechless. Sister Carmel has bought them everything they need to start school. 'Hellen, this is a gift from me. Please don't even think about paying.'

The next day and the one after, I take time off work to show my children the way to the Artarmon train station and how to safely board the train to school. I tell them I'll come and pick them up every afternoon.

In September 1985, a few weeks after my children's arrival, I receive a phone call from my mother. Her passport has come through and she can come for one year to help me as soon as I send her the plane ticket. For a Romanian to buy a ticket to Sydney is out of the question and the Romanian airline, Tarom, only flies within Europe. In any case, the price of tickets puts them beyond most people's reach.

I'm delighted that she's coming. This will give me the chance to get another job to save more money and help pay off some of my debts. When my mother arrives, the children are overjoyed to see her. They have missed one another.

I immediately look for another job and find one as a kitchen hand on Saturdays and Sundays from 7am to 7pm. The job is in a nursing home near Bondi.

I'm now working seven days a week, trying to make the most of the time my mother is with us. I come home late every day, spend time with the children and fall asleep, often without even changing my clothes.

A few months after my mother's arrival, my sister rings. She wants to talk to our mother and I sense something bad has happened. I watch my mother's face become pale and her mouth fall open. I try to ask what the matter is but she pushes me away.

'I'll be home as soon as Lenuta changes the date of my ticket,' she says, putting down the phone. She starts pacing up and down the room, rubbing her hands together. 'How dare he do this!'

I've thought there may be another woman in my father's life, someone he sees while my mother is away, yet I never suspect what has actually happened. He has moved his girlfriend into our home and told the neighbours he's going to divorce my mother and marry the other woman.

I see how distressed my mother is. I wish she would muster the courage to leave him since he has humiliated her all the way through their marriage. When we were young I often heard her say that she stayed married for her children's sake. But now we're all grown up and she's still suffering.

'Mama—don't go back,' I say. 'I'll apply for you to stay here permanently. You know you'll be happy—and the children will be too. Leave him! He's always humiliated you with his affairs and his lack of respect for you. Enough is enough.'

She refuses. 'Tomorrow, change my ticket and I'll leave. It's my house. How dare he bring that woman into my house?'

Now her excuse is not the children but the house.

That night she doesn't sleep, just paces up and down. Next morning her suitcase is at the door, packed for her flight. As I prepare to go to work, she reminds me about the ticket. I nod and leave. I'll wait until tomorrow; she may change her mind.

I get back from work late in the evening and find her waiting up for me, sitting at the kitchen table.

'Is my ticket booked?'

'I'm sorry,' I tell her. 'I'll do it tomorrow.'

She stands up and starts crying and screaming. 'I have to get back! I need to be in my house!'

The children are woken by her distress. They are upset and start crying in sympathy with their grandmother. I manage to calm them and spend the night on the floor in their bedroom.

In the morning I ring work and ask for the day off to deal with a family crisis. I go to the airline office and change my mother's ticket. The following day my children and I take her to the airport.

The moment I see my mother pass through the departure door I feel relieved and at the same time sad and disappointed. She has let me down once again.

This is the last time, I promise myself.

66

Treats and Work

Difficulties strengthen the mind, as labor does the body.
Lucius Annaeus Seneca

We're all excited that Christmas is coming and that we can spend it together this year. William and Nancy don't understand how their Christmas gifts will be delivered by Santa, since there is no snow for his sleigh. In Romania Santa's story makes perfect sense. William questions me closely about this every day and is beginning to have doubts. My explanations don't satisfy him. Reason and logic are his strengths. Nancy still believes and Elsie knows the truth.

I take them to Chatswood Chase to have their photo taken with Santa. When we get home, we decorate our Christmas tree, a real one. Nancy is full of smiles and excited, while Elsie and William work hard at the decorating. I remember how happy I used to be when I woke up to find Santa's gifts under the tree. Watching my children enjoy these festive rituals reminds me of my fondest memory of Christmas, singing carols in Bucharest to collect treats from the neighbours.

At 2am on Christmas morning I'm woken by a police siren. I run into the lounge room and find William playing with the present I've bought him: a police car with a siren. This wakes up the girls too and marks the beginning our first Christmas Day in Australia. They are overwhelmed by the number of gifts they receive and rip them open at once. Every single wish of theirs has come true.

After Christmas we take our first family holiday in Australia. Sister Carmel offers us her family cabin at Culburra Beach on the New South Wales south coast. Her sister lends us her car since I doubt my old Holden Barina will last the distance. We spend a week having fun. It's a holiday we will always cherish.

Back in Sydney I decide it's time to open a small beauty salon. I already have a few clients and I'm sure that once I start working outside my home, business will increase. I'm ready to move on. I make an appointment with the bank in Crows Nest. I need to borrow $3000 to start a business.

A man in his early fifties interviews me. He goes through the normal questions and then he comes to, 'What assets do you have?'

'I have no assets.'

'What about savings?'

'Just a couple of hundred dollars.'

He looks me in the eye and says, 'Your place is in the social security queue. Apply for Single Parent Benefits.'

I thank him and leave. I need to sit down because my legs are trembling. I don't know if I should be angry with him or sad that I'm not trusted to repay a loan. On paper I can't make much of a case for a loan to be approved, but I do have a credit card which shows that every month I pay back my debt, in full and on time.

I walk home and his words 'Your place is in the social security queue' echo in my head. We single mothers are boxed and labelled. I'm grateful that I've learned through my experience at the Sheraton not to judge others and not to allow anyone to limit my potential.

I'm determined to make it in the business world. I will find a way. I work even harder at cleaning and waitressing to save sufficient money to open my own salon.

I find an advertisement offering an opportunity to establish a beauty salon in a hairdressing shop. It's far away in Pennant Hills in Sydney's north west, but it looks promising. The owner assures me that there is great potential for me, since he will introduce me to all his clients.

Excited, inexperienced and trusting, I've failed to take into consideration a few important factors—the loud music, the persistent noise of the hair dryers, the constant chattering. I need quiet and calm surroundings for my work. Facials must be relaxing. My clients follow me to the Pennant Hills salon, however, many find the noise irritating and stop coming to see me.

After a month, I've spent my meagre savings. I realise this arrangement will never work, so I leave and continue to work from home.

One day Thea tells me she's spoken to Delfina who works as a beauty therapist in a Crows Nest hairdressing salon. She also wants to open her own business. 'Maybe the two of you could go into partnership?' Thea suggests.

What a great opportunity! Delfina and I meet and decide to rent a small space on Alexander Street. She brings her clients and I bring mine. My income is still far too low for our living expenses so I continue to do cleaning jobs. I also take a waitressing job from 8pm to 1am, three nights a week, in the

Hollywood Café on the Pacific Highway. It's the only place that stays open late. I tell myself that this is only temporary, until our business builds up.

I draw strength from the love and smiles of the children, my pride and my joy. We struggle but we're happy managing with what we have. We always look forward to Sunday, our only day together, and make the most of every minute of it. We visit friends, have little picnics in the park, and when we can afford it, take ferry trips to Manly or travel to the Blue Mountains. We treat ourselves to lunch out, usually pizza or Chinese food.

Money is always tight. We can't afford to buy much fruit at our expensive greengrocer in Artarmon. Elsie suggests they go by themselves to Flemington Markets. They know the markets, I have taken them shopping in the past, but I'm worried about them travelling on their own. Elsie is only ten years old, I trust her. She promises that they will be fine.

Every Saturday becomes a fun day for them as they take our two-wheeled trolley on the train to the Markets. William loves pushing the trolley. In the late afternoon when I come home from work I find them separating the fruit and vegetables and stacking the shelves of our fridge.

I am so proud of my children. I can't be sure what life has in store for them but I do know that each of them is a survivor in a special way.

Despite our financial struggles, it's important that my children don't miss out on having a special birthday. I always make sure that each year their birthdays are celebrated and that each of them has a new outfit for the party. Elsie has her birthday with friends, going to the movies or on the rides at Luna Park, while we have a combined birthday party for William and Nancy, since they share the same day.

We can't afford to buy cakes and I'm not a gifted cook. Sometimes I'll have to bake several cakes before one is good enough. I try to be creative with the decorations and most times I succeed. My children's friends are excited at how beautiful the cakes look—like no one else's!

67

Family Reunion

In Romania in 1989, the paranoia of the Ceausescu regime is at its height.

My sister has been promoted to a head waitressing position in one of the finest restaurants in Bucharest. This is a reward for her talent and hard work, and she has even been offered six months of further training in France. She is overjoyed: only twenty-eight years old and almost at the top of her professional ladder. Then she receives a phone call and is asked to see the director of the restaurant chain.

'Tell me about your family,' he says.

'Comrade David, I live with my parents. My father is a truck driver and my mother is a housewife.'

'What about your brother?' he asks. She tells him that Gheorghe is a truck driver too, and that he lives in Colentina with his wife and children.

Then comes the question she has been expecting, the question that will end her job. 'What about your sister? Where does she live?'

Cornelia's legs start trembling under the table. However, she always faces difficult situations with confidence. Very little fazes her.

'My sister lives in Australia, Comrade David,' she says. Her voice is clear and strong and she pauses between each word.

'You're done with us,' says the director.

As punishment for being the sister of an 'enemy of Romania', as I am now considered, Cornelia is sentenced to work in the beer garden of a pub. It smells of stale beer and she is run off her feet. Waiters and waitresses have to carry large trays with several heavy jugs of beer on them. It is hard work, especially for such a tiny young woman. Her back starts to ache.

She resolves to follow me to Australia. An intricate escape is organised by a Romanian emigrant living in Austria. In March 1989, she and her friends, George and Ana, escape by crossing the Danube River into Yugoslavia in the dark in an inflatable raft. After deflating the raft they must find the cemetery on the main road and wait in an empty grave to be rescued.

So far, the daring plan works. An Austrian contact picks them up and hands each of them a map and some cash, in case the Yugoslav police stop them and they need to run for their lives. If they are caught travelling illegally in Yugoslavia, they will be returned to Romania.

After a four-hour drive they are dropped close to the Austrian border. Now they have to reach their Romanian contact on the other side, in Austrian territory. The border is a ditch.

As they approach on foot, two heads pop up: Yugoslav armed guards. The guards shoot into the air and demand that Cornelia, Ana and George halt. But they don't. They run. My sister and Ana jump across onto Austrian soil. Behind them, one of the guards has caught George just on the Yugoslavian edge of the ditch. George wrestles with the guard, then jumps the ditch into Austria while the other guards open fire.

My sister runs for her life, zig-zagging to avoid the bullets.

They continue running until they are picked up by their Romanian contact. The three of them are driven to a police station near Vienna where they ask for political asylum.

Afterwards, the Yugoslavian guards will have to count the number of bullets they fired to prove to their superiors that they actually tried to prevent the escape. For each returned defector, the Romanian government rewards Yugoslavia with a free cart of salt.

From Austria, Cornelia files her application to migrate to Australia. She arrives in Sydney in February 1990.

The following year, after the recent fall of the Ceausescus and, incredibly, of Communism itself in Romania, my parents come to Australia for a year-long visit. I am surprised at my mother's determination over this issue: her insistence that my father accompany her.

My children are happy to have their grandparents around. Elsie is pleased that her responsibilities are over and that my mother now looks after the younger children and does all the chores around the house.

I'm now working twelve hours a day establishing my business and still waitressing at night.

While on their tourist visa my parents apply for migration on the basis of a family reunion. Their permanent resident visa is granted. My mother is overjoyed, but my father is of two minds. He will always long for his birthplace. His ties to Oltenia are incredibly strong. Only when he is with his own people in his own village, does he feel complete. None of us will ever fill that part of his heart.

I am now surrounded by a supportive, extended family, the kind of family I longed for as a child. More adults mean more help and more love for my children as they grow.

Every struggle we face strengthens my relationship with my children. As they become teenagers, they realise how fortunate they are to be offered the opportunities Australia gives us. They study hard and make the most of every chance that comes their way. I encourage them to participate in sports: tennis, gymnastics, rugby, volleyball, basketball and swimming. They learn to compete to win—but also how to cope with losing.

Elsie is growing into a fine young lady. She is defined by her determination and lack of fear. She's a doer, someone who doesn't procrastinate but goes after what she wants. She studies Economics with a double major in Marketing at Macquarie University. I see how she could become a successful businesswoman, but she constantly tells me that all she wants is to be a stay-at-home mum, something I was never able to give her.

Nancy has a beautiful nature, caring, considerate and loving. She is aware of other people's needs and places them before her own. She is also creative. Her dream is to become a fashion stylist and my dream is for her to have a university degree. Nancy is also accepted into Macquarie University, but only stays a year. Instead she goes to London to study fashion at Istituto Marangoni. She completes her fashion course before returning to Sydney.

When William is only sixteen he decides he'd like to experience more of the outside world. He applies for a student exchange program and receives a placement near Michigan in the US. He is full of life, sociable, ambitious, hard-working and determined to succeed. His big heart and sense of humour keep us all entertained. He impersonates me very well. He will always argue his point of view, trying to persuade me to change my mind. Resisting him is hard.

Trying not to laugh is even harder, but I have a line which always saves me. 'William, I'm your mother and you will do what I tell you to do.'

Our journey together has made the four of us very close and has bonded us forever. I am so proud of them.

Mother's Day is always special at home and so is Father's Day. I am honoured on both. I receive flowers and notes from my children. The year William was away in America he wrote me this poem:

There is a lady I know
a lady so great
a lady whose love
isn't up for debate.
This lady I know
means the world to me
because without her
I could not be.
When I was young
she held me tight
she always made dark times seem bright.
Even when
I'm miles away
I think of her nearly every day.
She will always remain
in my heart and mind
because a lady like her
is hard to find.
She knows me well,
knows me like no other,
that's why I love her
that's why I call her MOTHER.

68

Farewell Victor

To forgive is to set a prisoner free and to
discover that the prisoner was you.
Lewis B. Smedes

It is William's and Nancy's birthday, a cold winter's day in
June 2003. I am woken early by a bad dream while it's still
dark outside. My dream was about Victor, someone has
drawn black crosses on his back.

I try to dismiss the dream. I need to go for my run before
the children wake up for our birthday ritual. The cakes with
candles burning will arrive at the bedroom doors accompanied
by the singing of Happy Birthday. Every 11 June we have two
cakes.

I put on my shoes and I start my run. This usually makes
me feel free and at peace, but not this morning. Questions run
through my mind: will Victor remember what today is? Does
he ever think of his children in Australia?

Since we left Ghana, there has only ever been one birthday
card from him—to Elsie. There has never been one for William
or Nancy.

I feel guilty all over again. I chose the wrong father for my children and this thought often overwhelms me.

Back in the kitchen I decorate both cakes with candles and Elsie and I carry them to William's and Nancy's bedrooms. After our ritual we have breakfast. I usually talk a lot in the mornings, never running out of words. This morning I'm quiet. Something is wrong. Perhaps I should ring Victor.

I get up and go over to the phone. I make myself pick it up and dial our old number in Ghana. I ask to speak to Victor.

'Daddy died a couple of hours ago,' I hear a voice cry.

At that moment it's as if a piece of my heart broke away. I find myself weeping uncontrollably.

My dream must have coincided with his passing.

Victor's brother Michael is now the head of the family. He asks us to the funeral, an important event in Ghana. I discover that Papani has also died just a few weeks before Victor.

William has just returned to Sydney after working as a pilot in Ghana for two years. After gaining his degree in aviation from the University of Western Sydney, he decided to build up his flying hours in Africa.

Elsie is desperately anxious to say goodbye to her father, but she has just had an operation and I am worried for her welfare. Nancy doesn't want to go.

I would like to attend Papani's and Victor's funerals but I have a choice to make. Attending Victor's funeral will mean observing all the Ghanaian traditions, including sitting with his second wife in a vigil with the body.

I did not accept his second wife during his life nor will I now that he's dead.

I ask William to accompany Elsie to Ghana.

Victor's family respects my decision not to attend. I'm

asked to write a eulogy to be delivered at the funeral. I have no idea what to say. Two days before Elsie and William are due to leave, I haven't yet started to write.

I wake at two o'clock in the morning, switch on the lights and look for a pen and paper. I remember the night in Papani's house when I needed a pen and paper to write to my family in Romania and found Naomi's letter in Victor's briefcase. That was the beginning of the end.

This is what I write:

Despite our separation, the news of your passing has touched me deeply. On hearing the news, I felt that a part of me had gone which later in the day was replaced by your smiling face. That made me feel better: that wherever you are, you are happy.

I thank you and am grateful for our children. Throughout my life they have been my strength and comfort and have given meaning to my life.

I have always admired your strength and determination in giving yourself totally and unconditionally to the sick. Your compassion towards those in need had no limitations regardless of whether they were rich or poor, black or white, educated or not.

In Romania you will always be remembered as being one of the kindest doctors, working day and night to save lives and giving hope to those in need and in pain.

I am sure that people in Accra feel the same way and that your memory will stay with them for a long time to come.

I am sorry that our marriage did not sustain us as we vowed, but I strongly believe that we both had lessons to learn on our separate paths.

Finally I would like to thank you for our beautiful children and the experiences we shared together. Your beautiful smile and joyous laughter sustained me in our times together.

I pray you find peace
With love
Hellen

At the funeral, before a huge gathering of over 1000 people from Ghana and overseas, William reads the eulogy on my behalf. The mourners include many women whose lives were saved or whose sufferings were eased by Victor. His final moments were spent in his hospital, where he collapsed. He gave everything to his patients. All his compassion, affection and kindness were dedicated to the world beyond his family, the outside world, the source of his emotional nourishment.

69

Return to Ghana

Our life is what our thoughts make it.
Marcus Aurelius

Africa still calls to me after twenty-one years away. I plan a six-week holiday, a mix of south, east and west. This time I take my sister with me. I want her to experience the unique sights, scents and sounds of the Africa I love.

We spend three days in Zambia at the Zambesi Inn built on the edge of the majestic Victoria Falls, one of the Seven Natural Wonders of the World. Nearby, Livingstone Town's bustle and colourful crowded markets, the enticing smells and unique tastes of food cooked on the side of the road all remind me of Ghana. We also experience tribal village life when we are invited to a traditional wedding.

Our next stop is Johannesburg for one night on our way to Accra to visit my old friends. We'll see William too as he is living there now, building up his flying hours.

As I'm repacking our luggage, I suddenly feel dizzy. I'm dripping with sweat. I run to the bathroom and am violently sick. I feel as if I'm dying. My sister helps me back to bed. I fall asleep, a dreamless night.

I wake up physically weak but mentally ready to face Accra. My sister believes that my nausea is related to the anxiety of revisiting my past. She suggests that we cancel our flight to Ghana. I refuse and we head towards the airport.

Our South African flight is full. As soon as we settle in our seats I notice the man on the other side of the aisle watching me intently. Puzzled, I start a conversation to find out if we've ever met. We haven't, but are both Romanian. His face is hard and somehow reminds me of my troubled past. He tells me that he and his family have been living in Johannesburg for many years among the *black crows* and now he is on a business trip to Ghana.

I am shocked into silence. *Black crows*. I haven't heard these hurtful words since I left Romania, all those years ago. They used to cut through me but now, looking at this stranger, I sense his anger. He is the one suffering with hatred.

I remain calm. I tell him that twenty-one years ago I left Accra and that now I'm back on a visit. I avoid further conversation.

As we fasten our seat belts for landing, I wonder if William will be able to meet us. I spoke to him by phone last night just before I fell ill. He rang us from Lagos, Nigeria. His flight back to Accra had an estimated landing time close to ours.

As we walk down the steps from the plane I see William in his pilot's uniform waiting for us on the runway. He gives us the biggest hugs. Behind us, silent, stands the Romanian stranger. I give him a smile, a smile of forgiveness.

I'm so happy to see William again that I've forgotten about my sister. She's right behind us. Her face is sad and her blue eyes seem troubled. Later that evening she tells me, 'I felt as if we were stepping into a closet full of skeletons.'

My friend Grace is waiting for us outside the terminal. She is as beautiful as ever. We drive to her elegant new house with its fragrant tropical garden and large swimming pool. One of Grace's elderly servants who helped me when we were neighbours greets me enthusiastically. 'Madam, you haven't changed. You are still beautiful.'

'Yes I have. Look at my grey hair,' I say.

We sit up until late that night sharing our stories. It feels as if we've never been apart. Our friendship remained strong despite the twenty-one years of separation.

We have ten days in Accra, before heading back to Johannesburg and then to Kenya and Zanzibar. Grace lends us her car and driver for our stay and on the first day, we visit Victor's grave. I stand beside his light coloured gravestone. My mind is blank. I feel the same absence of thought and feeling that enveloped me that night in September 1973—the night I lost my virginity along with the future I had planned. I don't cry.

We drive towards the house where Victor and I had lived. It is up the hill, near the cemetery. I burst into uncontrollable sobbing. I feel pain radiating from the very core of my body. We've reached the place where I encountered Victor driving his car on that day of torrential rain, twenty-four years ago, when I was heavily pregnant. The memories overwhelm me: the thunder and lighting, my fear of the car as I heard the screech of its brakes, and Victor's sarcastic smile as he drove away.

By the time we reach the house I have no more tears to shed. The street looks run-down and neglected, with tall grass on both sides of the road. We stop in front of Victor's house. The gates are secured with a thick metal chain, the ground is bare, the house is empty and the white paint is peeling and yellowed with age.

I planned to go inside the house and compound. The solid, thick chain stands as a barricade between my past and the present. I feel forbidden to re-enter my past.

It is only a year since Victor's death. I look over at Cornelia and know what she's thinking: 'a closet full of skeletons'.

As we stare through the locked gates, I hear a voice, 'Madam, do you remember me?' A man is standing near us, smiling. He does not look familiar. He continues, 'I remember you from the time you lived in this house. I'm still working for my master down the road. You were so kind.'

He remembers me! I look into his eyes. I'm amazed that people can touch one another's hearts without even being aware of it. The warmth and respect he gives me as a white woman is what connects me to Africa and to the Ghanaian people. It's as if I have never left. I think how easily I could have lived here for the rest of my life.

I left a message for Amartse. Soon William's phone is ringing and Amartse tells me he is nearby.

I run out of William's house and see my friend approaching, arms outstretched. We embrace.

'You know, Hellen, you're still the first and only European woman to divorce a Ghanaian man through the courts,' he says.

I laugh. It all seems so long ago.

The next day, William and I take Cornelia to Labadi Beach where I found solace when I was at my lowest. The last memory I have of the beach is of vast white sands with powerful blue waves and the shady coconut tree sanctuary, the place where I always felt safe and at peace. Now it is different for me, even the water doesn't seem as blue.

The day before we leave for Johannesburg, I decide to join William on a flight to the inland city of Kumasi. Nearly all on board are Ghanians. I hear my son's voice welcoming us, he is at the controls. We ascend smoothly.

Not long after, William asks us to fasten our seat belts as we are approaching an unexpected storm. He assures us that we are safe and explains that such sudden changes in weather conditions are common along the Equator on Africa's west coast. During the rainy season, storms develop without warning.

'The cabin lights will need to be switched off,' he announces. The lightning is so powerful, it illuminates the inside of the aircraft. The passengers are terrified, including me. William comes back on the microphone, reassuring us that we are safe and soon will be landing. We feel comforted.

The storm passes. We touch down smoothly and immediately the singing and clapping break out, as the Ghanaians celebrate a smooth landing and show their gratitude to the pilots.

By the time the last passenger has left, it's late. As we walk towards the Kumasi International terminal, William starts undoing his tie and removing his epaulets. Surprised, I ask him why.

'Mum, I don't like the "pilot's walk",' he says. 'The only difference between me and the young man who'll clean the aircraft is that I had opportunities he never had.'

I fall silent.

Twenty-five years ago when my son was born, I wondered what kind of a man he would become. Now I see that he is similar to the doctor who delivered him: gentle, humble, responsible, trustworthy and respectful.

I am proud of him.

70

Believing

My actions are my only true belongings.
I cannot escape the consequences of my actions.
My actions are the ground upon which I stand.

Thich Nhat Hanh

Since I was young, spirituality has been central to my life. I have always searched for answers beyond the everyday, beyond what we see and perceive. I was intrigued by what we call coincidences: why we are sometimes either at the right place and the right time or at the wrong place and the wrong time?

Born and baptised a Roman Catholic, then brought up with Orthodox beliefs, I fail to find comfort from either faiths in times of need.

2005 is a difficult year for me. Revisiting Ghana has been unsettling. I feel that the pain of my past is still lingering within my heart and my mind keeps running from one thought to another like a wild horse. I need to find inner peace but I don't know where to start.

One of my very good friends suggests that I take a weekend

off and book myself into the Nan Tien Buddhist Temple in Wollongong. I arrive on a sunny Saturday morning, without realising that this is the day Buddha's birthday is celebrated. I am surrounded by colourful decorations, fresh flowers and sweet music. The powerful scent of incense pervades the air.

I move towards the main temple and feel something change deep within me. I feel as if I've finally arrived home, lighter after discarding heavy garments that have been weighing me down.

This is another life-changing moment.

I search for a meditation practice. I want to find practical tools to help me deal with my life and learn at a higher level.

Back in Sydney my intuition leads to a wonderful teacher and a place to meditate not far from my home. Through reflecting on Buddhist teachings about cause and effect and through practising meditation, I come to understand my inner self much better. Through Buddhist mindfulness, I learn to control my anger and resentment.

I have come to understand that coincidences are very meaningful and I now accept them as such with a sense of gratitude, deep respect and wonder.

71

Mama's Good Friday

In October 2009, Mama is rushed to Royal North Shore Hospital in Sydney with severe bleeding. She is diagnosed with advanced cancer of the bladder and she undergoes a ten-hour operation. The post-operative results are grim. 'Six months to live,' the surgeon tells us.

Cornelia and Nancy tell Mama the results without mentioning how long she is expected to live.

I call my mother. 'I need to say something to you,' she says in a trembling voice. 'I want to thank you for all you've given me and done for me despite the fact that I was not a good mother to you.'

I assure her that she has done the best she could do. My hands shake, I feel a lump in my throat and I cannot breathe. I struggle to contain my tears. 'Mama, I need to go. Soon I have a client. I'll ring you later.'

I put the phone down and sob.

Confused thoughts come and go through my mind: memories of my childhood, questions. All along, I thought she didn't know! But now her confession tells me she does. When did Mama realise she was not the mother I needed?

I'm confused. What am I to believe? I feel resentment

welling up. Suddenly a memory comes to me. I am thirty-six years old and we're in Sydney, in my mother's apartment. Mama holds my hand, looks deep into my eyes and says, 'Lenuta. I love you.'

I cannot believe what I am hearing! I laugh nervously. The words sounded strange then, unnatural, but now I understand how important that moment was to my mother. Now it is important to me also. I hold onto that memory.

The hospital staff strongly advises us that Mama will need around-the-clock care and only a nursing home will be able to provide for her needs. In Romanian culture, a nursing home is seen as neglect on the family's part and Mama found it hard to accept the notion of being cared for by strangers. On 24 January 2010 she finally agrees to move into a nursing home in Lane Cove.

My father is impressed by what he can, by now, barely see and joins my mother a week later. Of course Mama is overjoyed. Finally her wish has come true: my father is paying attention to her emotional needs. She has him all to herself, just the two of them sharing one small room, each in their own bed.

Despite the fact that they're together, Mama still feels alone. One day in early March, I see a stunned, sad look on her face as she is lying back on her pillows. My father is asleep on his bed.

'What's happened?' I ask.

In a very low, heartbroken voice she says, 'I've wasted my life with him. I caused so much pain to the people around me, especially to my mother.'

I look at her, hardly believing what I've just heard.

'Don't call him "Father" ever again,' she says. 'He doesn't deserve it.'

Then comes the real shock. 'Please bring me divorce papers. I want to divorce him.'

I am struck dumb. Finally my mother is speaking the truth, rather than pretending not to see what her life was, and still is, ever since she met my father. He has always put himself first. Their worlds have remained apart.

In my head I hear my father's voice, his mantra, 'I married you because of Lenuta.'

I promise my mother that I will bring her divorce papers but I delay it. Is this what I should be doing? Every time I visit she asks for the papers.

Over the next few weeks, Mama's lips and mouth become dry, full of sores, as she lies in bed. The rash caused by increased morphine is spreading across her emaciated body. I know that her death is closing in. Death, real and brutal. On the Thursday before Easter, Cornelia and I visit her. Her body is breaking down and she is becoming weaker.

She leans back on her pillows. The divorce papers are on my mind. I have promised to fulfil Mama's last wish yet something is still holding me back. I am torn between my promise and my fear, the fear of being blamed. I decide to keep my promise.

I ask, 'Mama, do you still want the divorce papers?'

'No, I've taken him out of my heart,' she says.

I am overwhelmed. She has found strength in herself at the end. Taking someone out of your heart is far more courageous than simply signing papers. They are only a formality. She has truly abandoned my father. I realise then that my mother has an inner strength that I have never seen. It has been overshadowed by depression and, above all, pride.

I sense that she is restless. Even though we've said nothing, she knows death is upon her. And like Mama Draga, she fears it, the crossing of the unknown bridge.

I know my mother now needs her own mother to comfort her. My grandmother's indomitable presence will give Mama the strength she needs to cross over. I believe only a mother can give true courage and comfort to her daughter.

Since Mama Draga's death, I have often heard Mama say, 'I miss my mother.'

I always told her, 'Look for her. Speak to her. She's always around.'

Today I encourage Mama again to reach for her own mother. 'Mama, please look for Mama Draga. Look for our rock.'

She nods.

I moisten her cracked and bloody lips. Nothing can help her now. Only death will release her. Meanwhile, I know she needs to feel she is being supported, loved.

The next morning, Good Friday, my sister and I arrive early at the nursing home. I see by her pale face that Mama is fading away. Her mouth is so dry she can barely speak. I kiss her damp forehead.

'How are you, Mama? Have you found Mama Draga?'

My mother nods her head and very faintly answers, 'Yes, and she asked me how old you are.' She is finished with talk and now she lapses into semi-consciousness.

At that moment shivers pass through my body and I feel my grandmother's presence, solid and dependable. She *does* want to know how old I am. 'I'm fifty-seven,' I tell Mama Draga over my mother's head.

On this Good Friday, 2010, Mama Draga is here with my mother and me. The three of us sit together: my mother, the loyal and committed Orthodox believer; Mama Draga, the faithful Roman Catholic who presides, and me. Three generations of women, each of whom has lived hard-fought lives.

My sister, children and niece spend the whole Saturday with Mama as she moves in and out of her unconscious state as if she is in two worlds. They witness her fight against death and her struggle to stay alive.

We know she will lose. We will all lose this battle.

By the end of the day her breathing shows she is giving up and setting out on the last stage of her life journey.

Annie, a client, sends me a gift for Mama, a nightgown of fine white cotton printed with little pink flowers. Mama would have chosen that, I tell myself. I finish work late that Easter Saturday. Cornelia comes to pick me up. We drive to the nursing home and when we arrive, we sit together in the car while I show my sister the nightgown.

Memories flood my mind. Mama always bought us new clothes to wear on Easter morning. I remember the shiny black patent leather shoes with the strap and the buckle. Now I hold the last present I will ever give her.

As we walk into her room we hear the sound of her hard and loud breathing. She is sweating profusely. I hold her head while I massage her forehead. My sister rubs her feet. Sometimes Mama will open her eyes and look at us. Our presence comforts her. She always loves us to fuss over her, especially my sister.

I hang the nightgown on the wardrobe door and ask the nurse to see that tomorrow morning, Easter Sunday, my mother is dressed in her new Easter gown. I sense immediately that tomorrow will be too late. My sister agrees and we now ask the nurses to dress Mama in her new nightgown after her body is washed tonight.

We leave the nurses to attend to her.

When we return, she looks so peaceful. 'Mama, do you like your new nightgown?' I ask. She simply touches the top and strokes the material with her fingers. She always loved the soft feel of cotton. Then she smiles, opens her eyes and nods.

This is the last smile we will ever see.

'We'll come back early tomorrow,' Cornelia says. Mama opens her eyes and fear and worry spread across her face. She becomes agitated and starts moving her head left, then right, then left again, as if begging us not to leave.

'I think Mama wants me to stay,' I say to my sister. I tell Mama that I will spend the night with her. She looks relieved.

At the end of the afternoon shift, the nurses come one by one to Mama's room to say what I know will be their farewells. 'We'll miss you,' says one. 'You're one of the few patients who always thank us for caring for you.'

I am proud of Mama. She has not been a burden to the nursing staff. I have always heard her being polite in her limited English, kissing their magic hands. She feels humiliated by her sickness. Cancer is the final cross she has to carry as she climbs the last mountain to meet her own mother.

The nurses tell me that death usually arrives between three and five in the morning. The sign to look for is when the feet become cold.

This is new to me. I slip out of my shoes and climb into my mother's little bed. I wrap my body around hers and hold her. It is becoming harder and harder for her to breathe. Her head is on my chest, my dress wet from her saliva. I feel love in the warmth of our intertwined bodies. I feel a deep connection with my Mama, something I have never experienced before. I want to keep her like this so that her feet will never go cold.

It's a windy autumn night. Outside in the dark, the trees

are bending and the windows are rattling as they fight against the storm. Inside, Mama is fighting her own battle. She is trying to summon the courage to die.

The television is on. On the screen is the Orthodox Easter Eve service broadcast from Romania, something my mother loves watching. Easter always marked new beginnings, a day of hope for new change, a day with no fights and no arguments and the one day of the year when my mother seemed happy.

Tonight is different. She moves in and out of consciousness and her body is still hot.

I doze off but am wakened by her deep sigh. The priest on TV is singing, 'I have come to take away all your pain and sorrow,' one of her favourite Easter anthems which has a special place in her heart. I am confused by her sigh. Is it a sign of the sorrow in Mama's heart or of the soul leaving the body?

I start crying, I am scared.

The deep sigh reminds me of the sorrow Mama lived with, the heavy cross she had to carry all her life because of the choice she made in marrying my father.

On the other side of the room my father is sleeping. For him tonight is like any other night. I think of all the sacrifices Mama made for him, while he made none for her.

Another shiver suddenly passes through my body. I jump out of bed and grab the candle my sister has prepared for me. Romanians believe that a lighted candle helps the soul leave the body and move towards the light of eternal life. I light it. As I do, I remember how we lit the candle in the monk's hut, my father and I.

I get back into bed but keep my eyes on the burning flame. I've prepared the light for Mama's journey.

In the background, the Easter Eve service continues. The

flame flickers. Suddenly I feel Mama Draga's presence. The clock shows 3am Easter morning. I'm frightened. Mama is still breathing and her feet are still warm.

A soft-spoken Indian nurse enters the room. There is something calming about her, something wise and deep. She calls the night nurse to check Mama's pulse. He tells me that medically she is just a few hours away from dying, but his gut feeling tells him it will be around midday. I trust his instincts.

The candle is burning down. The Indian nurse returns and offers to make me tea. While I wait in the kitchen, she tells me that in the six years she has worked here, she has never seen what she saw tonight.

'I've seen many people die, but their relatives usually just sit beside the bed. Since I left India I haven't seen a daughter lying in bed with her mother, comforting her in the face of death.' She smiles gently at me. 'Your mother is so lucky.'

I thank her.

I am the lucky one, I tell myself. She doesn't know my story. Tears are streaming down my face. On this final night, the physical and emotional warmth I receive from my mother is a gift I will always treasure.

I return to Mama's bed. It is early morning and there is an eerie silence. I wipe the last sweat from her brow as I feel the warmth leaving her body. I feel her toes. They are becoming cold. It is five o'clock Easter morning. I call my sister and children as they want to be here to comfort and support Mama.

Once they are in the room, and I let go of my strength, I am overwhelmed with nausea. I walk outside for some fresh air.

When I return, I hold my mother for the last time. With my eyes full of tears, I kiss her forehead, say goodbye and thank her for her gifts to me. She gave me all she could: life, and on her last night, warmth.

I then drive home on my own. It is seven o'clock on Easter morning. Everything around me feels and looks different. The air is clean, cleared by last night's storm.

The streets are quiet and seem lonely.

I feel lost. I have entered an unknown space.

Not long after I get home, my sister calls to say she has sent Tata to her house for a few days.

'Every time he speaks he upsets Mama. She needs to die in peace,' Cornelia tells me.

She also encourages the children to go home for something to eat. She wants to spare them from what she feels is coming, their grandmother's final battle.

My sister fulfils her promise to our mother, 'Cornelia, please stay with me when I die. Don't leave me.'

Cornelia sits alone with Mama as she dies on Easter Sunday. She does not go peacefully. She fights death until her last breath.

The look of horror on Mama's face still haunts my sister.

72

Blame

The morning after my mother died, my father wakes from a dream, shaking. We are all in my sister's kitchen making arrangements for my mother's funeral. He approaches us, agitated.

'Your mother came to me in the night,' he says. Then he shakes even more before adding, 'She told me she has taken me out of her heart.'

We all stare at my father.

I then say, 'Mama used those very words just days ago.'

The week before Mama died, the nursing home asked me to make the funeral arrangements. I rang the funeral directors to organise for her body to be taken away when the time came. The funeral director insisted that I choose a burial plot. To me, it felt as if I were burying my mother alive.

I was given the phone numbers of three cemeteries. I just wrote down their telephone numbers and not their names.

When offices open on Tuesday, I ring one of the numbers, the one in the middle.

'Rookwood Catholic Cemetery,' a voice answers.

I am taken aback.

My grandmother's wish is now fulfilled.

We, the family, honoured Mama's loyalty to the Orthodox Church by having her funeral service in the church she loved but her body would return to her beginnings. She was born a Catholic and she is buried in the Catholic cemetery.

After Mama's burial, we are given two choices by our father. Either we look after him at home, or he returns to Romania where our brother will take care of him. His wish is to be buried in Oltenia. His medical condition requires round-the-clock care. He is heavily overweight, legally blind, often experiences diabetic fits and has no control over his bladder. Before he joined Mama in the nursing home, we often found him collapsed on the floor in their apartment.

We cannot look after him and I insist he stay in the nursing home. He says, just as strongly, that he wants to leave.

*

A few weeks after my mother's burial, my father decides to return to his roots. Elsie, his favourite granddaughter, does as he wishes and accompanies him back to Bucharest where he will live with my brother and his family.

They look after him and care for him well. His illness takes over his body. He is confined to bed for many months. Then he decides he wants to return to Australia, to the nursing home.

'It is the only place I want to be,' he tells me over the phone.

I encourage him to get better so he can fly back to Australia accompanied by my brother.

His medical condition worsens daily. I doubt if he will ever be able to make the journey back to Australia. I wish he had listened to me! It's too late now.

I think of him constantly. I decide to ring.

'Get me out of this living Hell!' His anger bursts through his faint voice.

'Tata, I tried to stop you going back to Romania—but you insisted.'

He repeats over and over again, 'Get me out of this living Hell,' and continues with more accusations, 'You gave me no choice. It's all your fault.'

He refuses to acknowledge my responses.

I take a moment to process my father's words. My relationship with him is ending the way it began: in blame. I was and still am the source of his suffering. My first memory of my father was of his angry words directed at my mother, 'I married you because of Lenuta.' And now his angry words are directed to me, 'It's all your fault.'

For the first time, guilt does not touch my heart. I do not accept his blame any more. I am at peace.

73

Life's Blessings

Have a heart that never hardens, a temper that never tires,
a touch that never hurts.
Charles Dickens

It is 21 September 2013 and my friends and family are all around me to celebrate my sixtieth birthday. It is a beautiful day. As I walk down the stairs towards my guests, I am suddenly transported back to the arrivals door at Sydney Airport, twenty-nine years ago, the day I entered Australia. Now 150 guests are here to honour me on my birthday. I feel as if I'm being carried on the wings of another angel, somewhere between the earth and the sky.

The house where we celebrate my birthday overlooks the sweep of light sand and rolling blue waves at Whale Beach, a northern suburb of Sydney. Above us stretches the brilliant blue sky of a perfect spring day. I see in each ocean wave the process of our existence: emerging, continuing, transforming and vanishing.

As I look back on my life's journey, I feel no regrets, only gratitude.

When I was young, I dreamed and planned my future carefully. Then came the day when all my dreams shattered. I now know that this was only a new beginning, showing me a different path, one beyond my dreams.

My path was to learn life's lessons by living life. I chose life over despair. From an early age, I learned that however unpromising things might seem, overcoming hardship can foster resilience, the strength we need to face the winds of fate. I had to learn to live one day at a time, do the best I could each day. Now, the older I get, the more intense is my search for life's meaning.

For a long time I carried the residue of my fears at an unconscious level. I experienced nightmares in which I struggled to find my way out of situations that confined me. But I awoke from my nightmares and realised that I am here in Australia. I feel gratitude that we have been granted freedom and opportunities beyond our dreams. My children and I are blessed with a wonderful life.

At a young age I experienced prejudice. Watching the gypsies cope helped me later when my children and I experienced hurt and abuse. I learned to deal with racist abuse without feeling pain. I feel proud that my children can also rise above prejudice and are able to transform negative experiences in a positive way. William is now a lawyer and he dedicates his free time to helping others fight prejudice.

The greatest gift life has given me is the irreplaceable bond between children and their mother. My children gave me purpose to live. I was determined to overcome my circumstances to create better lives for them. Their love sustained me.

As young women, Elsie and Nancy demonstrate the strength and courage to embrace life with a vitality that welcomes new beginnings. Their confidence draws people to them.

With the birth of my first granddaughter, Amira, I felt a deep nurturing bond with strong heartfelt roots, a reminder of the connection I had with my own grandmother. Now I have another beautiful granddaughter, Leila. Love is passed from one generation to another, from one grandmother to the next.

I have many precious memories of my children and my granddaughters stored in my heart and many others hang on the walls of our home: photos, paintings and beautiful handwritten letters. Among them, at the entrance of our home, is a birthday gift received from my three children, an African painting, a mother carrying her child.

A privilege for which I'm deeply grateful is the help and friendship I have received from so many people I met on my journey. As the monk predicted, I travelled over many seas and lived my life on three continents. The kindness, support, encouragement and loyalty I receive from those around me continue to carry me through life.

We are all one Universe
an eternal wholeness
We complete
each other's existence
'Alone' is never an option.
Anita Krizzan

Acknowledgements

In February 2009, on a hot Sydney summer night, my friend Nell persuaded me to begin. Supported by my family I began to write my story, parts of which they'd never heard. Developing the book has been a collective effort relying on the dedication of many professional people. Thank you for opening doors that I never knew existed and for showing me that I was the only person who could truly tell my story. Dangar Island, where I wrote many of these pages, was the source of deep inspiration. To my friends and my clients, those who are part of my journey, those who have listened, those who have contributed, I thank you.